Research and Inequality

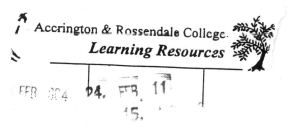

It has been noted by researchers from a variety of backgrounds that the dominant research paradigms of social research have frequently failed to represent the viewpoints of many marginalised groups. The authors of this collection confront this imbalance by looking at how issues such as ethnicity, sexual orientation and identity, disability, gender and ethnicity and health and old age might be addressed in research conducted among groups of people who may often be the objects of research but seldom have any control over what is said about them.

Written by people from a wide range of backgrounds, cultures and nationalities, the chapters explore ways in which issues of social diversity and division within the research process might be addressed. While considering whether they might be addressed through an emancipatory research paradigm, the book also examines the philosophical tenets and methodological implications of such an approach.

Carole Truman is Lecturer in Applied Social Science at Lancaster University.

Donna M. Mertens is Professor of Educational Foundations and Research at Gallaudet University.

Beth Humphries is Principal Lecturer at the Department of Applied Community Studies at Manchester Metropolitan University.

Research and Inequality

Edited by Carole Truman, Donna M. Mertens and Beth Humphries

First published 2000 in the UK and the USA
by UCL Press
11 New Fetter Lane, London EC4P 4EE

The name of University College London (UCL) is a registered trade mark
used by UCL Press with the consent of the owner.

UCL Press is an imprint of the Taylor & Francis Group

© 2000 Carole Truman, Donna M. Mertens, Beth Humphries selection
and editorial matter; individual chapters, the contributors

Typeset in Goudy by Taylor & Francis Books Ltd
Printed and bound in Great Britain by Biddles Ltd, Guildford and King's
Lynn

British Library Cataloguing in Publication Data
A catalogue record for this book is available from the British Library

Library of Congress Cataloging in Publication Data
A catalog record for this book has been requested

ISBN 1–857–28963–3 (hbk)
ISBN 1–857–28962–5 (pbk)

Contents

Contributors

Kalwant Bhopal is a Research Officer at the Thomas Coram Research Institute, Institute of Education, University of London. Her research interests include gender/feminisms, 'race'/ethnicity and the use of different research methodologies. Her book *Gender, 'Race' and Patriarchy: A study of South Asian Women* was recently published by Ashgate.

Joanie B. Cohen-Mitchell has been working in the fields of adult education and community development in Latin America, the Caribbean and the US for 13 years. She has been involved in programmes and research concerned with adult education, early childhood education, adult literacy, women and development, participatory and action research and alternative evaluation. She is currently finishing her EdD at the Centre for International Education at the University of Amherst, Amherst, US.

Grindl Dockery has been working as a freelance community research and training consultant for the last 6 years, based in Liverpool. She worked in Papua New Guinea for 10 years co-ordinating a district health service before coming to the UK. Her main interests are in developing participatory frameworks which facilitate individual or collective education and empowerment through her community research and post-graduate teaching activities. Much of her work in recent years has been training local people to plan and conduct their own research.

Beth Humphries is currently Director of Postgraduate Studies in the Department of Applied Community Studies at Manchester Metropolitan University. She is joint editor of *Rethinking Social Research* with Carole Truman, and of *Welfare, Exclusion and Political Agency*, with Janet Batsleer.

Julie Kent is a Senior Lecturer in Sociology at the University of West of England. She has written one other book, *Social Perspectives on Pregnancy and Childbirth* (OUP), and is co-editor (with Hatt and Britton) of *Women, Research and Careers* (Macmillan). She teaches postgraduate research methods and the sociology of health and illness. Her current research is looking at issues around the regulation of human implant technologies.

Marion Martin is a lecturer and researcher in community health and higher education at Manchester University and has published on participatory research and adult learning in health and professional education. She has worked in the UK, rural South India and Tanzania. Marion is Director of the MEd in Education for Primary Health Care and is co-editor with Korrie de Koning of *Participatory Research in Health: Issues and experiences*, published by Zed Books.

Donna M. Mertens is a Professor in the Department of Educational Foundations and Research at Gallaudet University, in Washington, D.C. She teaches research methods, programme evaluation, statistics and educational psychology to deaf and hearing students at BA, MA and PhD levels. She has conducted research and evaluation studies on topics such as improvement of special education services in international settings, enhancing the education experiences of students with disabilities and preventing sexual abuse in residential schools for deaf students. She recently completed a three-year project with the American Judicature Society on improving court access for deaf and hard of hearing people.

Dr Mertens is Past-President of the American Evaluation Association. Her publications are numerous, including: editor of *Creative Ideas for Teaching Evaluation* (1989); co-author (with John McLaughlin) of *Research Methods in Special Education* (1995); and author of *Research Methods in Education and Psychology: Integrating Diversity with Quantitative and Qualitative Approaches* (1998). In her work, she integrates the viewpoints of people with disabilities, ethnic/racial minorities and feminists in order to be inclusive of groups traditionally not represented in the research and evaluation process.

Jim Mienczakowski is Dean of the Faculty of Education at Central Queensland University and of Creative Arts at The Central Queensland Conservatorium of Music. After training and working in the performing arts, Jim moved into secondary education and has taught in England, the West Indies and Australia. His postgraduate studies involved performing research findings gathered consensually in health settings. Since 1991 this research work has involved creating and developing new research understandings around the emancipatory potential of ethnodrama. Current work has involved Jim and the ethnographic performance research unit in developing better understanding of possible trajectories of recovery from sexual assault and of harm minimisation in health research performances.

Constantinos N. Phellas has completed his studies in England at the universities of Essex, Warwick and City. His doctoral thesis examined the construction of sexual and ethnic identities of Anglo-Cypriot men resident in London who have sex with men. His research interests are broad and include the use of qualitative and quantitative research methods in researching ethnic minority groups, qualitative evaluation research and its

...aviour and sexual identities

...t extensively at undergraduate

...ecturer at City University. He has

...counselling over the past 8 years.

...n sociology and M.Ps. He is Full Professor in the ...Department at the University of Quebec (UQAM), Canada, and Director of the Joint PhD Program in Communication (UQAM) at the University of Concordia and the University of Montreal. He is a member of the Quebec Psychological Professional Association and also a member of the International Sociological Association and of l'Association internationale des sociologues de Langue française (AISLF). His research interests include qualitative and clinical sociology (methodology), social theory and social practice, mental health issues in the workplace, and social problems.

Shirley Roy has a PhD in sociology and is Full Professor in the Department of Sociology at the University of Quebec. She is a member of the International Sociological Association and of l'Association internationale des sociologues de Langue française (AISLF). Her research interests include quantitative and qualitative methodology and social problems (homeless people and community development).

Anne Ryen is Associate Professor of Sociology at the Department of Social Science, Agder College, Norway. She has published articles and reports on the welfare state, on occupational welfare or fringe benefits and on methodology. Her work includes projects on access to public benefits, the de-institutionalisation of the mentally retarded, dilemmas in project work to solve welfare sector problems, several projects on fringe benefits, such as non-monetary remuneration in private business, and qualitative methodology. She has held several scholarships. She is involved in research collaboration between Norway and Tanzania, where she has publications on fringe benefits and on methodology. Other current projects are within cross-cultural interviews and remuneration in private business.

Carole Truman is Lecturer in Applied Social Science and a member of the Institute for Women's Studies at Lancaster University (UK) where she teaches on research methodology and on gender. She has served as Chair of the Women's Studies Network (UK) Association. Carole Truman has a long-standing interest in the relationship between social research and marginalised groups. She has conducted a wide range of policy and applied research and addressed issues of citizenship, participation and user-evaluation. *Re-thinking Social Research* (co-edited with Beth Humphries) was published by Avebury in 1994. In addition to her work on research methodology, she has published on the areas of women and the labour market and on sexuality, violence and citizenship.

Stanley L. Witkin is a Pr
University of Vermont in th
the editor-in-chief of *Social W*
Social Workers, and the most widely
world. The author of numerous articles in
uted collections, Dr Witkin is currently editing a bo
social work.

Clare Woodward completed her PhD on representations of self and identity in childhood sexual abuse at Lancaster University. With Corinne Wattam, she co-authored the report ' "And Do I Abuse My Children? No!" Learning about prevention from people who have experienced child abuse', for the National Commission of Inquiry into the Prevention of Child Abuse. Dr Woodward is currently a psychologist in clinical training at the Universities of Coventry and Warwick.

Editors' Acknowledgements

In 1996, the organisers of the International Sociological Association's Fourth International Social Science Methodology Conference took the brave step of agreeing to include a conference panel under the somewhat vague title of 'Anti-discriminatory/Emancipatory Research'. We (Carole Truman, Donna Mertens and Beth Humphries) were the proposers of that panel, and at the time we suggested the theme, we had little idea of what (if any) papers we might attract. The panel was included in the conference call for papers, and subsequently attracted enough contributions for three conference sessions. These sessions provided an initial forum for exploring why and how, social research may operate where issues of social inequality and social marginalisation are at the heart of the research process. Subsequently, we were able to explore the similarities and differences in issues raised during the confrerence. We then attempted to bring these issues together within a coherent framework. This book represents the fruition of that exercise – the success of our endeavours is for our readers to judge.

We are grateful to Jackie Batstone for collating and typing the first draft of the book and for her patience and diligence on subsequent drafts (and every time we promised it was the last draft). Special thanks to Robyn Ertwine who indexed the book with great care and attention to detail. Her work is appreciated by the editors, and will, we trust, be of great benefit to the readers, as well. Above all, we would like to thank our contributors, whose patience and belief in this project have helped to produce what we hope will be received as an interesting and thought-provoking volume.

This book represents an example of collaboration which spans across disciplinary boundaries and across continents. As editors, we have exploited national postal services, international courier services and every form of electronic communication. After months of commitment, encouragement and cajoling, we can report that we remain good friends and colleagues. It therefore seems fitting that our final acknowledgement should be to each other. Thanks.

Part 1

The researcher—participant relationship

Chapter I

Arguments for an 'emancipatory' research paradigm

Beth Humphries, Donna M. Mertens and Carole Truman

In recent years there has been increasing interest in and controversy around politically motivated research – research which questions the meaning of 'objectivity' and 'elimination of bias', but which has an explicit concern with ending inequality and with taking the side of oppressed and marginalised groups. Cameron *et al.* (1992) characterise research as 'ethical research' – research on   'advocacy research' – research on and for – and 'empowering research' – research on, for and with. The additional 'with' implies the use of interactive or dialogic methods, as opposed to the distancing and objectifying strategies positivists are constrained to use. This volume has brought together a range of approaches in order to examine the issues raised and to reflect on their potential to 'empower'.

The notion and aims of emancipatory research are not a recent development (indeed, the emergence of the age of Enlightenment was seen as a radical and potentially emancipatory break with the past). In the development of modern social theory, marxism, structuralism, critical hermeneutics, humanistic psychology, feminisms, Black perspectives and poststructuralism have all claimed to have emancipatory aims. Their various influences emerge in particular attempts to develop emancipatory social research.

As a result of the variety of critiques of positivist-influenced approaches to research, particularly with respect to the implications for power, a more recent movement has grown which has as a central aim the empowerment of research participants, which may include the sharing of decisions about the aims, methods, conclusions – indeed all aspects – of any study (although de Koning and Martin (1996) warn against adopting a purist attitude). To suggest a 'movement' is somewhat misleading, since the epistemological bases of different claims to emancipatory research are wide-ranging and often contradictory. In this chapter we examine the main approaches and attempt to uncover the knowledge assumptions which underpin them. We go on to outline our guidelines for the contributors to the book, in terms of the kinds of questions they might address in their chapters. Finally, we offer a summary of the contents of each of the chapters themselves.

The language used to describe 'emancipatory' research includes 'participatory' research, 'empowerment' research, 'collaborative inquiry' and 'participatory rural appraisal'. Furthermore, emancipatory research methodology has not a single but a range of knowledge bases. Tandon (1996) identifies six theoretical influences in his discussion of contemporary tendencies. The result is a complex picture in which the elements all make claims to be 'emancipatory'. In this discussion the approaches are categorised under headings which indicate the primary knowledge assumptions which inform them, although, as we shall see, they also draw on other traditions. We shall look at the major theoretical influences: humanistic psychology, critical/Freirean ideas, feminist theories and poststructuralism. We shall take each of these in turn.

Approaches based on humanistic psychology

The validation of experiential knowledge is at the heart of approaches informed by humanistic psychology. Their Enlightenment roots can be traced through the classical liberal tradition which underpins them. The subject is conceived as an autonomous and self-directing agent. Through co-operation, collaboration and dialogue, she/he is able, by reflection on her/his experiences, to come to a consciousness of her/his need for emancipation, and to enter into co-operative research with others in order to achieve this end. The best-known collections based on these ideas are to be found in Reason and Rowan (1981) and Reason (1988). A contributor to both of these collections, John Heron, in setting out the philosophical basis for what has become known as 'new paradigm' or 'participatory' research, does not reject the empiricist concept of the application to social research of causal laws in nature, but he posits a thesis of 'relative determinism', in that 'there are creative acts of self-directing agents within that order' (Heron 1981: 21). He suggests that the basic explanatory model for research behaviour (in both researcher and researched) is that of intelligent self-direction – commitment to purposes in the light of principles – combined with relative determinism. Subjects become co-researchers, since if they are not privy to the research thinking, they will not be functioning as intelligent agents. A central idea here is the notion of intentionality – in any action, people are conscious of their purpose in doing what they are doing, their meaning in acting. In collaborative research such intentions are available mutually to the researcher and research participants. The general explanation of human behaviour which is drawn from this is that human beings are 'symbolising beings, who find meaning in and give meaning to their world through symbolising their experience in a variety of constructs and actions' (*ibid.* 23). To fully understand this, one has to participate in it through overt dialogue and communication with those who are engaging in it.

These are ideas taken from phenomenology, but a model of participatory research takes this further in research practice in the attempt to share power and to aim for equality at every stage of the research process.

Within this scheme, language is viewed as the original archetypal form of human inquiry which enables people to state propositions about their particular experiences in terms of general concepts. In other words, agreement about the meaning of language is what gives it its peculiar symbolising power. So long as the rules governing a language are generally accepted, language is a channel for direct and clear communication.

A final assumption is that empirical research on persons 'involves a subtle, developing interdependence between propositional knowledge, practical knowledge and experiential knowledge' (Heron 1981: 31). The researcher's experiential knowledge of the participants is most adequate when researcher and subject are fully present to each other in a relationship of reciprocal and open inquiry, and when each is open to construe how the other manifests as a presence in space and time.

In terms of the 'truths' which emerge from this process, it is accepted that the hope of effective research is to generate true propositions. The truth value of a proposition is partly a function of its correspondence with extra-propositional dimensions of the world as encountered. Where 'truth' purports to be about persons other than the researcher, it has indeterminate validity, no secure status as truth, until she/he knows whether those other persons assent to and regard as their own the norms and values of the researcher:

> For an authentic science of persons, true statements about persons rest on a value system explicitly shared by researchers and subjects, and on proce-dural research norms explicitly agreed by researchers and subjects on the basis of that value system. Here again, the model of co-operative inquiry.
> (Heron 1981: 33)

The assumptions described above raise a number of questions about, for example: the feasibility of power sharing and a goal of equality in the research process; the feasibility of dialogue (and implicitly consensus), the failure to acknowledge a wider social and political context; and about commitment to the ideal of participation (see Martin (1994) and Kent, this volume, for further discussion). Some of these problems have been tackled by theorists drawing into the idea of 'emancipatory' research other knowledge bases to inform and expand its potential. The main contributions have come from critical and feminist theories.

The influence of critical theory

Critical social research draws on marxist assumptions about social relations (though Harvey (1990) argues that it is not bounded by any single grand theoretical perspective). At its heart is the idea that knowledge is structured by existing sets of social relations, and it aims to challenge prevailing, oppressive social structures. As Bauman says, 'Emancipatory reason does not struggle with common sense but with the social reality that underlies it' (Bauman 1976: 75). It assumes that all social structures are oppressive, that they are maintained through the influence of political and economic power, and legitimated through ideology. These structures have their relevance in historically specific processes which provide a context for an examination of class (or gender or 'race') exploitation. Through a systematic questioning of how ideology or history conceal processes of control, it aims to reveal the nature of the exploitative relationships within concepts such as, for example, 'work'. As a result of this process, knowledge is produced which gives insight into such oppressive structures. Such knowledge facilitates strategic planning towards the emancipation of oppressed groups. Traditionally these groups were perceived as class-based, but critical approaches have expanded to accommodate gender or 'race' as the primary oppressive mechanisms (see Harvey 1990).

Fundamental to the epistemological basis of this approach is the belief that knowledge has no (literal) objective status, but attention must be paid to the production of knowledge – the *processural* nature of knowledge. At the same time, however, critical approaches claim that critically informed knowledge is more 'true' or more objective than prevailing knowledge systems because they uncover the hidden aspects of reality around which other kinds of knowledge collude in order to conceal it. For critical methodologists, knowledge is a process of moving towards an understanding of the world and of the knowledge which structures our understanding of that world (Harvey 1990: 4). The methods used by critical researchers may not in themselves be any different from those used in other research approaches. The difference is that critical approaches begin with structured relationships and then pursue empirical inquiry in order to allow structural analysis (Willis 1977). Harvey describes the role of the critical ethnographer, for example, as

> to keep alert to the structural factors while probing meanings: to explore, where possible, the inconsistencies between action and word in terms of structural factors; to see to what extent group processes are externally mediated; to investigate how the subjects see group norms and practices constrained by external social factors; to see how prevailing ideologies are addressed; to analyse the extent to which subversive or resistant practices transcend prevailing ideological forms.
>
> (Harvey 1990: 13)

In addition, the emancipatory notion of praxis, what Harvey calls 'practical reflective activity' (*ibid.* 22), is engaged in critical social research. Knowledge is not only about finding out about the world, but about changing it. Therefore, not only are the participants of any inquiry analysed in terms of their potential for developing group action, but critical researchers themselves engage oppressive social structures, and their own inquiries thus embody praxiological concerns. According to Harvey, knowledge exists in our everyday lives; it is dynamic, changing as a result of praxis and of fundamental reconceptualisation of the world. The activity of engagement is at the root of further development and transformation of knowledge.

The general approach of critical research described above is taken further in some versions of participatory research. The work of Paolo Freire (1972) has been particularly significant in moving ideas of participatory research away from individualistic models to take account of the political context which directly affects people's lives, whilst also bringing marxist ideas into participatory research. The volume edited by de Koning and Martin (1996) contains a number of contributions developed from the ideas of Freire. This emphasis has led to a stressing of the importance of education and social action as two important pillars in some versions of emancipatory research. Freire's notion of critical pedagogy identifies ways in which traditional education has been 'domesticated' by the dominant order and does not address inequalities. It asserts that marginalised and oppressed groups need 'education for liberation'; that is, an opportunity to develop a dynamic understanding informed by critical thought and action towards the goal of 'critical consciousness', where the person is empowered to 'think and act on the conditions around her or him, and relates these conditions to the larger contexts of power in society' (Shor 1993: 32).

In other words, people begin to recognise the ideologies – the myths, values, language – which serve to mislead and cloak reality, and which reinforce the status quo, where some social groups have power over others.

Although a Freirean model sees traditional research methodologies as problematic, it accepts fundamental Enlightenment assumptions about the rational individual, an essence of Being and a reality external to the person. Through a process of critical education, through reflection on her/his situation, the individual or group can move towards 'conscientization' and action for transformation. It is thus compatible with and has expanded ideas from humanistic psychology, and has increasingly informed the work of a number of researchers (for example, Fernandes and Tandon 1981; Tandon 1988). It also adopts a binary view of oppression, in that it assumes the 'oppressed' and the 'oppressor' are clearly identifiable groups.

On the other hand, as with critical approaches more generally, it manifestly rejects any notion of value freedom and neutrality, and locates itself in an emancipatory research tradition. It is ambivalent about 'objective truth' in that although it argues that all knowledge is socially and historically produced, it wants to 'show what is really going on' at a societal level.

Feminisms and emancipatory research

The range of feminist research approaches claim *per se* to be emancipatory – to create knowledge which improves the position of women in societies. The writings of Bowles and Duelli Klein (1983), Fonow and Cook (1991), Harding (1987), Mertens (1998), Mies (1982), Oakley (1981), Reinharz (1992), Roberts (1981) and Stanley and Wise (1983) have all developed differing versions of feminist research, but all premised on the knowledge of women's oppression and the vision of her liberation through research activity as one of a range of strategies. A unique contribution of feminist research has been the exposing of the centrality of male power in the social construction of knowledge. Some versions of feminist research are exploring the contribution of poststructuralism to the development of theory. We discuss these in the next section.

Feminist research has challenged some fundamental binaries of traditional approaches, such as objectivity and 'distance' from the participants, hierarchies amongst knowers, both within research teams and between research and researcher, and universality and uniqueness. It also exposes androcentrism in research language which excludes women, which separates researchers from the people they are investigating and which facilitates elite male control. It has raised questions about how language is used in the subordination of women, though not all versions of feminism challenge the Enlightenment assumption of the potential of language to convey transparent meanings.

Although feminism has claimed to challenge, for example, the universalist assumptions which sustain traditional research, it becomes clear that White feminisms have themselves frequently adopted universalist and imperialist assumptions. Critiques from Black and Third-World women (for example, Bhavnani 1991; Mohanty 1991), and from lesbian and disabled feminists, expose the Eurocentric, heterosexual and oppressive underpinnings which marginalise other 'Others' and raise questions as to whether such research can be claimed as 'emancipatory' and, if so, for whom. Black feminists such as Lorde (1984), Hill Collins (1990) and hooks (1984, 1989) have insisted on the interconnectedness of gender, 'race', class and sexuality for understanding and researching women's oppression. Hill Collins (1990) has attempted to describe an Afrocentric feminist epistemology, emphasising the 'ongoing interplay between Black women's oppression and Black women's activism' (*ibid.* 237). hooks offers a global vision:

> Feminism as liberation struggle, must exist apart from and as a part of the larger struggle to eradicate domination in all its forms. We must understand that patriarchal domination shares an ideological foundation with racism and other forms of group oppression, and there is no hope that it can be eradicated while those systems remain intact. This knowledge should consistently inform the direction of feminist theory and practice.
>
> (hooks 1984: 22)

In the development field there is now a promotion of feminist perspectives on sustainable development in both the economic/global South and the North, part of which is a re-examination of research approaches which emphasise women's participation in, for example, needs identification and the planning process of development at community level (see Sen 1994).

Within feminist constructions of knowledge, a number of other influences may be traced. For example, Freire's vision of social justice and transformation has attracted the interest of many feminists (including hooks (1984), quoted above), some of whom have attempted to develop feminist research by building on his ideas. Both Freirean and feminist pedagogy rest on visions of transformation; they share common assumptions concerning oppression, consciousness and historical change. Both 'assert the existence of oppression in people's material conditions of existence and as a part of consciousness ... (which contains within it a critical capacity) ... and both see human beings as participants and actors in history' (Weiler 1991: 450). Nevertheless, feminists have been critical of the abstract quality of Freire's use of terms such as 'humanisation', ignoring particular meanings imbued by women and men, and Black and White people, for example. He leaves unaddressed the forms of oppression experienced by different actors, by his use of universal categories, without considering the varying experiences and definitions of different groups. Freire's insistence that all people are participants and knowers of the world and that their political literacy will emerge from their reading of the world – that is from their experience – leading to collective knowledge and action, does not question whether that experience might be divided, leading to the discovery of different truths. The nature of their perception of the world and their oppression is assumed to be uniform for all the oppressed. There is no possibility of a contradictory experience of oppression. Furthermore, his binary division of the oppressor and the oppressed elides contradictions in the experiences of oppression, for example, where the man oppressed by his boss may at the same time oppress his wife. The tensions and complexities of oppression across and within race, gender and sexuality are not taken into account.

At the same time, feminists (and in his later work Freire himself) have been able to adapt Freire to take account of gender. For example, Martin (1988) describes the influence of Freire's notion of critical pedagogy on women's education in Britain, particularly in non-formal education. Her research on a women's health group was constructed by building a feminist participatory methodology on Freire's theories of oppression and liberation, and his ideas about 'conscientization', the concepts of 'banking education' and the 'culture of silence'. Dominant in the research approach were methods using dialogue, the idea of the thematic universe, problem solving and holistic education.

Patricia Maguire's (1987) research with women survivors of domestic violence also acknowledges the influence of Freire, and is clearly based on a notion of critical inquiry towards the emancipation of research participants. Her review of participatory research reports reveals similar problems of what she calls 'male monopoly' (ibid. 48) as those in more general research reports. Women are often invisible, submerged or hidden in case-study reports, and there is little evidence of their empowerment. She says:

Having established that people are frequently exploited by traditional social science research, participatory researchers are attempting to develop research that has the potential and intention to empower people and transform social systems. But we must ask, exactly which people are empowered and which social structures are challenged?

(Maguire 1987: 50)

The androcentric problems she identifies within such research include: male-centred language; women's unequal access to project participation; inadequate attention to obstacles to women's participation in projects; women's unequal access to project benefits; unsubstantiated generalisation of the benefits from primarily male projects to women; absence of feminism from theoretical debates on participatory research; and exclusion of gender issues from participatory research issues agendas. She concludes that participatory research is not pushing men to uncover, analyse and transform their patriarchal attitudes and practices.

In these various ways, feminist researchers, for whom a basic assumption is inevitably the goal of women's liberation, have tried to work through the issues of power and participation which are raised in practice.

Poststructuralism and social research

Poststructuralist approaches to knowledge rest on assumptions which are dismissive of the Enlightenment 'truths' which are central to the approaches we have thus far discussed (though it should be said that feminisms are generally ambivalent to Enlightenment assumptions). In contrast to the notion of an irreducible humanist essence of subjectivity, i.e. not of social participants but of a subject that is abstract and atomistic, general and universal, divorced from the contingencies of historicity as it is from the particularities of social and political relations and identities, poststructuralism proposes a subject that is precarious, contradictory and in process (Goldberg 1993). By abandoning the belief in essential subjectivity – decentring the subject – subjectivity is opened up to change, the individual becomes both the site for a range of possible forms of subjectivity and at any particular moment of thought or speech, a subject, subjected to the regime of meaning of a particular discourse and enabled to act accordingly.

Language, far from reflecting an already given social reality, constitutes social reality for us (Weedon 1987: 22). Neither social reality nor the 'natural' world has fixed intrinsic meanings which language reflects or expresses. Meaning is constituted within language and is not guaranteed by the subject which speaks it. Language is viewed as a system always existing in *historically specific discourses*. If language is understood in terms of competing discourses, competing ways of giving meaning to the world, which imply differences in the organisation of social power, then language itself becomes an important site of political struggle. Language, organised into discourses has, according to Burman and Parker (1993) an immense power to shape the way that people experience and behave in the world. It therefore becomes a focus for research in order to uncover discourses of social regulation and classification which are maintained by means of normalising practices within state systems. Foucault's notion of a discursive field was part of an attempt to understand the relationship between language, social institutions, subjectivity and power (Foucault 1979). Discursive fields consist of competing ways of giving meaning to the world and of organising social institutions and processes. Within them, not all discourses will carry equal weight or power. Some will account for and justify the appropriateness of the status quo. Others will give rise to challenge to existing practices, and are likely to be dismissed by the hegemonic system of meanings or practices as irrelevant or bad. Research focused on these processes opens up spaces for the oppositional agency of people subjected to normalising practices.

Feminists have made use of poststructuralist insights, using its theories of language, subjectivity, social processes and institutions to understand existing power relations and to identify areas and strategies for change. Weedon comments:

> (the theory) is able to offer an explanation of where our experience comes from, why it is contradictory or incoherent and why and how it can change. It offers a way of understanding the importance of subjective motivation and the illusion of full subjectivity necessary for individuals to act in the world. It can also account for the political limitations of change at the level of subjective consciousness stressing the importance of the material relations and practices which constitute individuals as embodied subjects with particular but not inevitable forms of conscious and unconscious motivation and desires which are themselves the effect of the social institutions and processes which structure society. It is for these reasons that ... poststructuralism is a productive theory for feminism.
>
> (Weedon 1987: 41)

Feminist poststructuralism insists that the individual is always the site of conflicting forms of subjectivity, of political struggle waged mainly through language (discourses about the family is an example). Through an examination of discourses, feminist poststructuralism is able, in detailed, historically specific analysis, to explain the working of power on behalf of specific interests and to analyse the opportunities for resistance to it.

It needs to be said that the majority of theorists developing poststructuralist theories are men, and feminists are aware of the 'riskiness' of adopting some of the effects of male privilege and androcentrism in their work. For example, Sawicki makes the point that Foucault's emphasis on the dangers of identity formation can all too easily become the basis for repudiating women's struggles to attain a sense of identity not defined by patriarchal interests (Sawicki 1991: 105).

Another problem for feminism is poststructuralism's rejection of generalised metanarratives and its emphasis on the local and the specific. This questions any notion of 'emancipatory' research, which depends on an acceptance of the transcendent goal of liberation as a starting point for research. It is argued there are no such universal values, but instead limited, local and strategic values. McNay (1992) observed the dichotomy within feminism. On the one hand, some feminists are concerned that an over-monolithic model of sexual difference leads to a failure to consider other fundamental differences, such as 'race' and class, which structure the experience of women. On the other hand, it is recognised that an extreme theoretical particularism may deprive feminists of the tools with which to examine how differences – especially sexual differences – are inevitably articulated into hierarchies of inequality. McNay disputes the falsely polarised terms of this debate, which results in misleading oppositions between difference and legitimation, theory and practice, the individual and the collective, and the particular and the general. She sees a way forward in exploring the extent to which theory is compatible with the local. For a debate on some of these issues, see Humphries (1998 and this volume), Hammersley (1995) and Cealey Harrison and Hood-Williams (1998). At the end of the day, one can only judge the usefulness of poststructuralist theory for feminist research in the practical implications for empowerment that adopting such insights and methods may bring.

Towards a framework for anti-exclusionary research

In the preceding discussion, we have described some of the major theoretical approaches, together with some of the tensions and contradictions which underpin or influence a broad emancipatory paradigm of social research. How as social researchers can we make sense of it all when undertaking research? How can we use these theoretical influences to shape a framework which will allow us to engage in research practice? What does research practice need to embrace when it has at its heart the potential to empower and to contribute to end the exclusion of relatively powerless groups of people? It is at this juncture that we turn our attention to the implications for the practice and interrogation of social research. The range of theoretical influences we have discussed point to the way that all knowledge is socially produced and, as such can be disputed and contested. If knowledge, which forms the outcomes of empirical social research is thus contested, how can empirical researchers deal with the contradictions contained within the social research process?

These questions form the key strands within this book. The chapters within the book each in their own way address emancipatory or anti-discriminatory issues within the research process. The chapters originate from a sub-theme of the Fourth International Conference on Social Science Methodology. We invited researchers who identified their work to be dealing with emancipatory or anti-discriminatory issues to present papers within a conference theme at Essex '96.[1] The task presented to our contributors was for them not only to identify ways in which they were dealing with emancipatory or anti-discriminatory concerns in their work, but, moreover, how these concerns affected their research practice. Thus, our contributors have been able to bring a broad range of insights from a diverse arena of research areas to illustrate the emancipatory potential and emancipatory constraints within research practice. As editors, we set ourselves the task of developing synthesis across and between issues by exploring emancipatory and anti-discriminatory issues in differing research situations. In this way we have been able to identify ways in which insights in one area of research may also provide insights for other researchers. We have thus been able to devise a framework in which our contributors have been able to further interrogate their research. This strategy was used as a means to prompt our contributors to go beyond their original insights into the research process. We are grateful to those who stuck with us and whose contributions have been included in this volume.

We now go on to present and illustrate the framework which has evolved. We use the word 'evolved' advisedly since an important learning process for each of us has been the way in which the task of developing a framework has been characterised by process as much as by outcome. The framework which follows is not intended to offer a fixed maxim for research practice, but more of an evolutionary framework within which social research may be viewed for its emancipatory and anti-discriminatory potential. We present our framework as interdisciplinary. Many of the elements within the framework will be found in other disciplines and research paradigms; for example, in feminist research, participatory research and disability research. However, we are also conscious of a lack of cross-fertilisation between disciplines and research paradigms. By adopting an interdisciplinary approach, our aim has been to facilitate this process of cross-fertilisation. The elements of the framework used in this book are:

(a) Locating the 'self' in the research process in terms of personal, social and institutional influences on research and analysis.
(b) Exploring the political/power dimensions of empowerment.
(c) Being explicit about the tensions that arise in research, and relating as much about how the tensions remain as about how they were resolved.
(d) Linking research to wider questions of social inequality/social justice.

In each chapter, we asked contributors to provide a balance between theoretical and methodological approaches in their discussions and accounts of research. In working towards this balance, we hope to achieve two objectives: first, to avoid accounts of research being at the level of theoretical abstraction on the one hand, or simply relativist in relation to aspects of process on the other; and second, that the balance between theory and method in accounts of research addresses our aim for readers to think about the ways in which concerns of each chapter may be transferred to other research situations. We now go on to explore how our contributors have related to the editorial framework.

Locating the 'self' in research

As Truman outlines in Chapter 2, location of oneself in research is a common component of feminist research and disability research. In terms of research practice, we asked our contributors how they identified themselves within the research project and how their experiences, analyses and power position informed both their research approach and research outcomes. In Chapter 13, Witkin locates himself as an academic social worker and also as someone with personal experience of trying to organise care for his disabled son. He then goes on to identify how this locates him within the concerns addressed in his chapter. Thus, for Witkin there are strong parallels between his personal experience and the perspective he brings to research practice: this provides the basis for empathy with those who are commonly disempowered.

For Woodward (Chapter 3) there are parallels with Witkin's empathetic location. In her discussion of research using the written accounts of survivors of sexual abuse, Woodward identifies herself as a survivor. This location of self can be a means to achieve an empathy with research participants, and a means of avoiding objectification through the research gaze. However, Woodward extends this location of herself and consciously seeks to explore ways of 'giving a voice' to survivors of abuse whose situations and experiences are very different from her own. Woodward recognises a power relationship between herself and her research participants and identifies that her position of power is one which she should use with a sense of responsibility.

Although in very different contexts, for both Phellas (Chapter 4) and Bhopal (Chapter 5) location of the self in research was a source of empathy but also tension as important differences between researcher and research participants emerged. For Phellas's study of gay male Cypriots, and Bhopal's study of South Asian women, commonality with research participants sat uneasily alongside differences in expectations of research participants. In the case of Phellas, there were tensions in the research process where his research participants saw the research process as potentially providing an opportunity to meet a new partner. Bhopal describes how her identity as an Asian woman rested uneasily alongside her task as a researcher.

Location of self in research can also position researchers in the wider social relations of the research process – both in relation to the researched, and also to research audiences. This can then be a means of avoiding essentialism. As Truman (Chapter 2) discusses, experience should not be conflated with simplistic and essentialist notions of experience or identity, since identities are complex, multiple and subject to change. Equally, the subjectivities of identity are also counterbalanced by the possibility for others to position individuals.

Exploring the political and power dimensions of empowerment

The social relations contained within the research process are central to Martin's chapter (Chapter 12) on critical education for participatory research. By transferring 'location of self' into a wider framework, Martin identifies a series of questions which learners in the field of participatory research need to ask. This provides the basis for researchers to identify what it means to be a human being living within the social relations of present-day society. In using a questioning approach, Martin enables learners to see the influence of power in their daily lives and thus develop the basis for researchers to become co-investigators of knowledge in the process of dialogue. Dockery continues this theme and uses alliances between researcher and those who are marginalised as a means of avoiding practices which exacerbate inequality. Thus research becomes *for* research participants, rather than *on* research participants.

The fluidity between researcher and researched is not always attainable. In contrast to Martin (Chapter 12) and Dockery (Chapter 7), Ryen (in Chapter 14) identifies how in research conducted in a Tanzanian–Norwegian collaboration an underestimation of the cross-cultural dimensions of research might lead to research participants becoming 'victims of methodological discrimination'. Here, the historical relationships of coloniser versus colonised provide a forceful impediment to the types of knowing which can be achieved. We re-visit this theme later, where we identify any research study as being part of a wider set of power relations. However, the main point made by Ryen is that unless the absolute detail of dominant assumptions in the research process is unpacked, the potential for emancipatory research is limited.

A number of our contributors consciously disrupt or invert the traditional social relations in which knowledge is usually traded. In describing ethnographic research with a health consumer community, Mienczakowski (Chapter 9) shows how the medium of theatre can be used to create a 'nascent' moment through which individuals comprehend their self-conscious location within the circumstances of oppression. By using drama as an alternative to a written report, audiences become emotionally engaged with research narratives based upon real lives. This emotional engagement on the part of a powerful research audience can be used to provoke change when they subsequently plan and provide health services. The political and power dimensions of empowerment impact upon every stage of the research process. In the next section we examine ways in which accounts of research can reflect tensions within the 'truths' that are created at every point in the research process.

Tensions within the research process

The tensions between knowledge and power are key concepts in Kent's chapter (Chapter 6). Kent describes a study which uses group inquiry based on active participation and dialogue to explore knowledge and power in midwifery education. Kent's chapter thus takes up many of the concerns addressed in our previous theme. She notes that participation ideally involves principles of equality, but that differences in power or status deriving from organisational settings or social position make this problematic. This raises important questions about how diversity is represented in a group and whether at a micro-level this can lead to silencing. Kent explores the different types of investment in the research process. Participants were excluded by the group if they did not agree to follow the rules of engagement; at another level, the students who remained could be vulnerable in terms of employment prospects if their names were associated with any critical outcome from the inquiry. Ultimately, Kent questions whether an ostensibly participatory process provided the basis for empowerment, or if it was simply a means for co-option through a mechanism that enabled participants to speak, but whose voices would have little chance of bringing about change. This identifies a tension in research where an emancipatory or participatory process does not necessarily lead to an emancipatory outcome.

Part of the job of a professional researcher is to produce a 'polished account' of research and, at best, declare how tensions were resolved, but tensions remain in many research projects. Another exemplar of this is the chapter by Rheume and Roy (Chapter 15). Here they elucidate the consequences of using certain conceptual categories in defining street youth in major Canadian cities. The research was centred around the provision of community-based housing for homeless youth belonging to diverse ethnic communities. Tensions arose because there was no agreement between housing centres on what actually counted within the category of 'homeless youth' or within definitions of cultural or ethnic identity. The formulation of categories could not take place in isolation from the consequences of using one category over another. The desire to distinguish one group from another also provided the basis of excluding people from that category. Thus, in naming, a basis for discrimination was created.

The tensions identified by Roy and Rheume in Chapter 15 also reflect the issues relating to the fourth aspect of our framework: namely, the way in which social research links to questions of social inequality and social justice because it leads to providing the basis on which groups of people get resources and which do not.

Wider questions of social inequality and social justice

Mertens' chapter (Chapter 8) deals with the wider questions of social inequality and social justice within the evaluation of a project intended to improve court access for deaf and hard of hearing people in the United States. To this end, she designed the study to allow the expression of the needs of deaf and hard of hearing people to drive the development of a training programme for judges, other court personnel, and deaf and hard of hearing advocates on how to improve access to the courts for this population. Several of the focus group participants were featured in a videotape entitled 'Silent Justice' that was used as part of the training. In addition, some were also invited to participate in the training as faculty and on planning teams for improving court access in their state court systems.

Cohen-Mitchell (Chapter 10) uses as her starting point wider questions of social inequality and exclusion experienced by disabled women in El Salvador. She asserts that the women with whom she worked had been framed by society within a fixed identity and hence limited possibilities. The societal label of disabled meant 'not able'. Through the research process, the women discussed the use of language and how their self-perceptions could change in a way which opened up new possibilities and autonomy.

In Chapter 13, Witkin locates his discussion not around the micro-political process or methodological issues within the research process but around research goals. For Witkin, the power of social research rests with its ability to create and control conceptual categories and generate new forms of under-standing, but knowledge should be generated in the service of action. The creation of knowledge within an integrative human rights framework provides a perspective which encompasses a vision of the kind of world we want for future generations.

We stressed earlier that our intention has been to provide a collection of work, each item of which in its own context has explored the nature of power, politics and social relations within research situations and the way in which this understanding of power impacts upon research outcomes. Because each chapter has been written within the same broad editorial framework, we hope that the end product is greater than the sum of its parts. Ultimately, we hope that this book will contribute to researchers being more open to the influences within research which can either empower or disempower those who experience social inequality and, furthermore, identify what research can do to facilitate progressive change.

The structure and content of the book

The issues that formed the framework of this book are represented in overlap-ping ways throughout the chapters, with most of the chapters addressing multiple themes. However, there also seems to be a greater emphasis within chapters on one or more aspects of emancipatory and anti-discriminatory research. Based on this degree of emphasis, we have organised the book into three major parts.

In Part I, we have included chapters that deal with the relationship between the researcher and the participants in the research process. Truman in Chapter 2 discusses her work on a health-needs assessment of men who have sex with men in the north-west of England. She determined that the client (Healthy Gay City/HGC) believed that potential funders of programmes related to

HIV/AIDS prevention would be responsive to a clear, objective and definable need for safe-sex materials, and that engaging Truman as principle researcher, with the weight and status of a professional research organisation associated with the university, would off-set the apparent structural inequality of HGC as an organisation with relatively low power as compared to the power position occupied by potential funders. Truman also arranged for the research funds to stay in the gay community by recruiting interviewers from the gay community. In this way, she attempted to avoid the exploitative nature of some academic research.

In Chapter 3, Woodward raises the issue of the emotional impact on the participants and the researcher of revealing their experiences of child sexual abuse. She starts her chapter with a poignant story of the suicide of a respondent, by the pseudo-name of 'Virginia', who had volunteered to complete a questionnaire on her child sexual-abuse experience. Woodward wonders if asking Virginia to write in depth about her life could have contributed in any way, however small, to her suicide. She explores the responsibilities one has towards research participants within the entire research process.

Studies involving two different cultural groups provide additional insights into the influence of the personal characteristics of the researcher in collecting data from in-depth interviews. Phellas in Chapter 4 explores the identity implications of doing research in the community of Cypriot men who have sex with men who are living in the Cypriot community in London.

The second major section of the book contains chapters that relate to ways to design research and interact with research participants in order to strengthen the relationship between research process and findings, and social action based on the research.

In Chapter 5, Kalwant Bhopal explores the relationship between her identity as a South Asian woman and her research participants. Kent in Chapter 6 reviews her study of the educational experiences of student midwives as part of a national evaluation project carried out using group inquiry in the context of feminist participatory research methods. She discusses tensions which arose because of the perceptions of some of the participants that the group inquiry process was powerless to change the programme, and the perceptions of others that they felt vulnerable if their names were associated with a process that resulted in a critique of the programme in which they were enrolled. Kent explores the implications of feminist theory in terms of providing a way to adopt value positions in order to judge the adequacy of accounts, and a procedure for enabling others to discern between these value positions.

Dockery's chapter (Chapter 7) contains a reflection on the meaning of participatory research within the context of two case studies where community groups, consisting predominantly of women, conducted research with the aim of bringing about changes in the delivery of local health services. One case study focuses on the struggle by community groups to keep a local community health centre open and the other case study looks at issues related to women's sexuality and sexual health services. Dockery recognises the danger in seeking the participation of people who do not normally have access to influencing service planning where, without a commitment to the political concept of empowerment by those facilitating the process, participation becomes merely a process of manipulation.

Mertens examines in Chapter 8 how she applied the emancipatory paradigm to the first stage of a training programme for judges and other court personnel to improve deaf and hard of hearing people's access to the court system in the United States. The study began with a needs assessment designed to 'listen to the voices' of the deaf and hard of hearing people in order to develop training for judges, other court personnel and deaf and hard of hearing people and their advocates that validly represented the experiences of those with least power in the court system. The processes used in the study to include diverse voices from the deaf and hard of hearing communities revealed both technical and cultural issues related to improving court access for this population.

Mienczakowski's chapter is entitled 'Ethnography in the form of theatre with emancipatory intentions'. In his work, Mienczakowski used the experiences of the health consumer community representing schizophrenic psychosis and institutionalised detoxification processes as a way of communicating to groups of health and student communities. He terms the medium 'ethnographically derived theatre' because the meanings and explanations of the performances are negotiated with audiences in forum discussion at the close of each performance. Thus, the potential is created to share insights and negotiate explanations with an eye to provoking change amongst those who play an active part in the construction of health services.

Cohen-Mitchell's chapter (Chapter 10) is entitled 'Disabled women in El Salvador reframing themselves: a case study of an economic development programme for women'. The women in the study had been framed by society; i.e., they had been assigned a fixed identity and with that identity their possibilities in the world were determined. Society had defined them as 'not able'. However, Cohen-Mitchell constructed her research in a way that facilitated the women in changing their self-perceptions. Her case study examines the way that poor disabled women in El Salvador could participate in a collaborative process that would alter and/or create development programmes in their immediate environment in ways that would potentially impact on their lives. Cohen-Mitchell draws on the tenets of participatory and feminist research in order to design research that can be tied to the emancipation of people from oppressive structures.

In Part III of the book, the authors explore the underlying premises and principles of anti-discriminatory/emancipatory research. Humphries, in 'From critical thought to emancipatory action: contradictory research goals?' (Chapter 11), critiques Hammersley's (1995) concerns about the feminist postmodern vision of research and other explicitly political research as being based largely on stereotypical, selective debates which do not do justice to the controversies to be found in alternative research approaches. She explores the possibility that both the positivist and the emancipatory researcher are implicated in power relationships that can perpetuate the relations of dominance in that emancipation cannot be conferred on one group by another. While avoiding a simplistic solution to the dilemma, she suggests a commitment to self-reflexivity in order to maintain a grounding in the struggle for survival of the most disadvantaged, and not in the privileging of the researcher.

Martin's 'Critical education for participatory research' (Chapter 12) contains an explanation of the basic principles of conducting training in participatory research. She addresses three questions: (1) What constitutes critical education for participatory research? (2) Why is this approach to learning crucial? And (3) What form can it take? She sets her explanations within the context of a course in education for primary health care that is taught on a postgraduate level for development professionals who include health professionals such as nurses, medical assistants, health visitors and medical doctors, as well as teachers from all levels of education, community development workers and social workers. She provides a brief history of participatory research as a way of raising questions about the power relationships between researchers and research participants.

Witkin, in 'An integrative human rights approach to social research' (Chapter 13), makes the argument that human rights is an appropriate organising concept for our inquiry because human rights offers a useful alternative to the more typical practices in the sense that it opens up the opportunity for us to create the kind of world we want for future generations. He bases his argument on the premise that a focus on human rights would result in an emphasis on research goals, not methods – that rather than having a value-neutral process that discovers ahistorical, acultural truth, human rights-based research would be value-driven and openly ideological. He does explore the additional challenges associated with this approach in terms of obtaining funds from organisations that might favour more conventional views of research.

In 'Colonial methodology' (Chapter 14), Ryen explores methodological challenges in cross-cultural research in a Tanzanian–Norwegian collaboration in which structured interviews were used in short-term projects. Different uses of language and norms of politeness can lead to misunderstandings. Use of structured interviewing without observation and participatory research could be viewed as colonial methodology that objectifies the Africans if the interpretation is made through the researcher's cultural eyes.

In the final chapter, 'Defining without discriminating? Ethnicity and social problems' (Chapter 15), Rhéaume and Roy report the challenges they faced in a study to define the ever-changing population of street youth in major urban centres in Canada. In their study, street youth referred to homeless, 12- to 18-year-old children of both genders from a variety of cultural backgrounds: French Canadians, English Canadians and various cultural minorities. The researchers discuss their efforts to avoid the use of negative labels such as juvenile delinquents or abandoned children for their population, because such labels might reinforce the basis for discriminating against these children. They consciously changed the language used in their study from street kids to troubled youth who had sought community support voluntarily in an effort to emphasise the need for continuing social services for this group.

As one volume, these chapters bring together an international and diverse collection of experiences and perspectives which, though they may not be agreed on what constitutes 'emancipatory' research, are united in their commitment to a need for continuing struggle towards change in an increasingly unequal world. We hope the book will form a constructive contribution to that struggle.

Note

1   Essex '96 was the International Sociological Association's Fourth International Social Science Methodology Conference held 1–5 July 1996, at the University of Essex, Institute for Social Sciences, Colchester, UK.

References

Bauman, Z. (1976) *Towards a Critical Sociology: an essay on commonness and emancipation*, London: Routledge and Kegan Paul.

Bhavnani, K.-K. (1991) 'What's power got to do with it? Empowerment and social research', in I. Parker and J. Shotter (eds) *Deconstructing Social Psychology*, London: Routledge.

Bowles, G. and Duelli Klein, R. (eds) (1983) *Theories of Women's Studies*, University of California, Berkeley: Women's Studies.

Burman, E. and Parker, R. (eds) (1993) *Discursive Analytic Research*, London and New York: Routledge.

Cameron, D., Frazer, E., Harvey, P., Rampton, M.B.H. and Richardson, K. (1992) *Researching Language: issues of power and method*, London and New York: Routledge.

Cealey Harrison, W. and Hood-Williams, J. (1998) 'More varieties than Heinz: social categories and sociality', in 'Humphries, Hammersley and Beyond', *Sociological Research Online*, vol. 3, no. 1, http://www.socresonline.org.uk/socresonline/3/1/XXXX.html.

de Koning, K. and Martin, M. (1996) 'Participatory research in health: setting the context', in K. de Koning and M. Martin (eds) *Participatory Research in Health: issues and experiences*, London and Johannesburg: Zed Books.

Fernandes, W. and Tandon, R. (1981) *Participatory Research and Evaluation: experiments in research as a process of liberation*, New Delhi: Indian Social Institute.

Fonow, M.M. and Cook, J.A. (eds) (1991) *Beyond Methodology: feminist scholarship as lived research*, Bloomington and Indiana: Indiana University Press.

Foucault, M. (1979) *Discipline and Punish*, Harmondsworth: Penguin.

Freire, P. (1972) *Pedagogy of the Oppressed*, Harmondsworth: Penguin.

Goldberg, D.T. (1993) *Racist Culture*, Cambridge, Mass: Blackwell.

Hammersley, M. (1995) *The Politics of Social Research*, London: Sage.

Harding, S. (ed.) (1987) *Feminism and Methodology*, Bloomington: Indiana University Press.

Harvey, L. (1990) *Critical Social Research*, London: Unwin Hyman Ltd.

Heron, J. (1981) 'Philosophical basis for a new paradigm', in P. Reason and J. Rowan (eds) *Human Inquiry: a sourcebook of new paradigm research*, Chichester: John Wiley and Sons.

Hill Collins, P. (1990) *Black Feminist Thought: knowledge, consciousness and the politics of empowerment*, New York, London: Routledge.

hooks, b. (1984) *From Margin to Centre*, Boston: South End Press.

—— (1989) *Talking Back: thinking feminist, thinking black*, Boston: South End Press.

Humphries, B. (1998) 'The baby and the bath water: Hammersley, Cealey Harrison and Hood-Williams and the emancipatory research debate', *Sociological Research Online*, vol. 3, no. 1, http://www/socresonline.org.uk/socresonline/3/1/9.html

Lorde, A. (1984) *Sister Outsider*, Trumansberg, NY: The Crossing Press.

McNay, L. (1992) *Foucault and Feminism*, Cambridge and Oxford: Polity Press.

Maguire, P. (1987) *Doing Participatory Research: a feminist approach*, Amherst, Mass: Center for International Education, University of Massachusetts.

Martin, M. (1988) 'The contribution of the well woman centre to women's health education', unpublished MPhil thesis, University of Newcastle upon Tyne.

—— (1994) 'Developing a feminist participative research framework: evaluating the process', in B. Humphries and C. Truman (eds) *Rethinking Social Research*, Aldershot: Avebury.

Mertens, D. (1998) *Research Methods in Education and Psychology: integrating diversity*, Thousand Oaks, CA: Sage.

Mies, M. (1982) *The Lace Makers of Narsapore*, London: Zed Press.

Mohanty, C.T. (1991) 'Cartographies of struggle: Third World women and the politics of feminism', in C.T. Mohanty, A. Russo and L. Torres (eds) *Third World Women and the Politics of Feminism*, Bloomington and Indianapolis: Indiana University Press.

Oakley, A. (1981) 'Interviewing women: a contradiction in terms?' in H. Roberts (ed.) *Doing Feminist Research*, London: Routledge and Kegan Paul.

Reason, J. (ed.) (1988) *Human Inquiry in Action: developments in new paradigm research*, London: Sage.

Reason, P. and Rowan, J. (eds) (1981) *Human Inquiry: a sourcebook of new paradigm research*, Chichester: John Wiley and Sons.

Reinharz, S. (1992) *Feminist Methods in Social Research*, New York and Oxford: Oxford University Press

Roberts, H. (ed.) (1981) *Doing Feminist Research*, London: Routledge and Kegan Paul.

Sawicki, J. (1991) *Disciplining Foucault: feminism, power and the body*, New York and London: Routledge.

Sen, G. (1994) 'Women, poverty and population: issues for the concerned environmentalist', in W. Harcourt (ed.) *Feminist Perspectives in Sustainable Development*, London and New Jersey: Zed Books.

Shor, I. (1993) 'Education is Politics', in P. McLaren and P. Leonard (eds) *Paolo Freire: a critique encounter*, London: Routledge.

Stanley, L. and Wise, S. (1983) *Breaking Out: feminist consciousness and feminist research*, London: Routledge and Kegan Paul.

Tandon, R. (1988) 'Social transformation and participatory research', *Convergence XXI*: 2–3.

—— (1996) 'The historical roots and contemporary tendencies in participatory research: implications for health care', in K. de Koning and M. Martin (eds) *Participatory Research in Health: issues and experiences*, London and Johannesburg: Zed Books.

Weedon, C. (1987) *Feminist Practice and Poststructuralist Theory*, Oxford: Basil Blackwell.

Weiler, K. (1991) 'Freire and a feminist pedagogy of difference', *Harvard Educational Review*, vol. 61, no. 4, November 1991.

Willis, P. (1977) *Learning to Labour*, Westmead: Saxon House.

Chapter 2

New social movements and social research

Carole Truman

There is considerable diversity amongst the contributions within this volume, but the essential characteristics which each contribution shares is that the subjects of the research described experience forms of social and or economic marginalisation. As we have discussed in our introductory chapter, anti-discriminatory/emancipatory research may be informed by a range of debates relating to the nature and conduct of social research. It is important to recognise that questions about the nature of social research have been raised not just within the arena of academic research, but also within a policy perspective. In the policy context, there have been important contributions from new social movements about ways in which research may be used to complement or advance the wider aims of pressure groups. Participatory approaches to emancipatory research recognise and are centred upon the transformative potential of the social research process. In many forms of participatory research, the transformative potential is most obviously achieved where research participants become the direct users of the research findings. Beyond this, there are also other ways in which social research may be used more directly by new social movements. One example is the way in which new social movements may use research to influence the thinking and to alter the knowledge bases of others — particularly those in powerful positions. In this chapter, I will explore the micro-politics contained in one such example of how new social movements may, by design, seek to exert influence on research users. The example I will use is based upon a sexual health-needs assessment of gay and bisexual men in the north-west of England. I will look at ways in which a gay men's health movement as 'outsiders' in the research process developed alliances with a university in order to develop a research study which would be acceptable to local policy makers.

Research from the margins

I begin this chapter by exploring debates about the nature of research which have emerged within and relate to social movements and marginalised groups. Specifically, I will look at ways in which discussion in feminist research and disability research have sought to transform the lives of women and disabled people respectively. In drawing from these discussions, I want to identify where similarities and differences may help us to develop a more sophisticated understanding of ways in which social research may be conducted where the interests of those at the margins of society are central to the research process. I will draw upon fragments within these debates for purposes of illustration and recognise that in doing this I can in no way do justice to the depth of discussion which has been generated in any individual area. Another limitation of my approach is that marginalised groups are not internally coherent or homogeneous: there is no universal woman; in the area of sexuality, lesbians and gay men may occupy some common areas of interest, but also occupy distinctly different power positions in different aspects of society. Likewise, debates within the disability movement have challenged essentialist notions of disabled people. In drawing upon research debates, I am not assuming commonality/homogeneity within the groups around whom those debates are centred. On the other hand, where these debates have provided particular insights into the research process and the social relations of research, I feel it important to acknowledge their influence. In this chapter, I want to explore ways in which social research may attempt to redress this imbalance and also to examine the potential and constraints of conducting research which attempts to centralise the experiences of a marginalised group. Although I do not want to condense sophisticated discussions about research into simplistic research 'models', I want to explore how themes within the debate reflect some of the concerns of differing new social movements in relation to strategies for change.

Methodology, epistemology and process

The relationship of marginalised groups to the research process has been reflected in a wide range of discussions about approaches to research. These discussions have taken place at differing levels and have embraced epistemology, methodology and process aspects of research.

At a methodological level, discussion relating to marginalised groups has addressed problems relating to non-inclusion, under-representation or alienation. For example, Graham has described how in major sources of health data in Britain, technical processes of data collection and data analysis have resulted in the exclusion of minority group experiences. Consequently, the social positions that new social movements have sought to make visible are misrepresented or masked in major 'official' sources of data (Graham 1995). The problems of methodological approaches leading to the alienation of research subjects has been addressed within feminist research in relation to survey methods (e.g. Oakley 1981), and within 'race' research where the creation and collection of 'race' statistics has been the subject of controversy (Ahmad and Sheldon 1993). In the field of disability research, Booth identifies how research informants are often valued only in terms of being a source of data for the narratives of sociologists, rather than regarded as people with their own stories to tell (Booth 1996: 238). Consequently, there has been an important discourse around the micro-politics of social research in relation to marginalised groups which focuses upon the power relationships between the researcher and the researched (Bhavnani 1993; Haraway 1988). In contemporary research studies, more and more researchers are engaging in methods to ensure that research participants 'feel good' about taking part in research. Thus in terms of methodology, the needs of research participants have been recognised as central to the research process. Similar concerns have been addressed at an epistemological level.

Numerous theorists have discussed the epistemological basis of feminist research (Cook and Fonow 1986; Harding 1987; Smith 1988; Stanley and Wise 1993). Contained within these discussions are fundamental questions about the nature of knowledge which is produced through empirical research processes. A major contribution of feminist epistemology in relation to social research has been to draw attention to the way in which any knowledge is situated and specific to the way in which it has been produced and the social location of those who produce it (Stanley and Wise 1993: 228). This theoretical perspective has stimulated concerns with the processes of empirical research production and has provided a framework for feminists to explore the means through which women's lives may be explored (Maynard and Purvis 1994; Roberts 1981). Thus, interests in epistemology have addressed questions which foreground simplistic notions of the utility of empirical research as a means of deploying a method to reach outcomes.

Both methodological and epistemological concerns have fed into explorations of research process in relation to marginalised groups. A number of researchers have opened the 'black box' of the research process to explore the ways in which empirical knowledge is generated and also the social processes contained within research (Kelly et al. 1994; Shakespeare et al. 1993). These have been important contributions to the field of social research and have helped to reshape the research process towards the perspective of research participants. However, as we outlined in our introduction to this volume, social research must also have some cognisance of the wider arena in which it takes place. Whilst recognising the importance of declaring the situation and specifics of any research project, the impact and wider resonance of research findings must not be ignored. Questions of audience and the wider socio-political relations in which the research process takes place are an important, but somewhat neglected aspect of the social research process. Knowledge is not simply produced, it is also received, interpreted and, in some cases, used. As Cook and Fonow state, research should not merely exist to describe the world but to change it (1986). Giving voice to the oppressed does not ensure social change (Gorelick 1996). Whilst feminist research has contributed important insights into the potential for research to precipitate change at an individual or local level (Finch 1984; Kelly et al. 1994; Oakley 1981; Stanley 1990), the links between feminist research and wider social change have been somewhat neglected.

A focus on epistemology and the internal creation of knowledge may provide the basis for exploring the 'black box' of research production, but it does not necessarily provide the basis for social change. This point has been argued most forcefully within discussions of the nature and purpose of disability research. Zarb (1992) relates how there is no shortage of research 'on' disabled people, but there is very little research that has helped to change the material conditions of disabled people's lives. Thus, questions of epistemology, process and visibility have, within the disability movement, led to discussion about the role and nature of social research. If research is to be undertaken, its legitimacy must be established within the context of its potential to contribute to change in the lives of disabled people. Oliver sets the following challenge:

> The key issue is not how to empower people, but once people have decided to empower themselves, precisely what research can do to facilitate this process ... the social relations of the research production have to be fundamentally changed; researchers have to learn how to put their knowledge and skills at the disposal of research subjects, for them to use in whatever ways they choose.
>
> (Oliver 1990: 13–14)

In the context of the social relations of disability research, Oliver pinpoints several important areas for any researchers who engage in social research related to new social movements and social change. Thus Oliver re-orientates the relationships between researchers, research subjects and the research process from one where researchers manage research situations to one where they allow themselves to be managed by the requirements of those who identify that research may be concomitant with some aspect of a move from disempowerment to empowerment. Empowerment is not achieved through research which simply leads to self-understanding, but through research which locates any self-understanding in the contexts which have produced situations of marginalisation in the first place. 'It is not disabled people who need to be examined, but able-bodied society' (Oliver 1992: 112). Thus, research with marginalised groups which is oriented to meeting the aims of new social movements needs to be located within an analysis of the wider social relations which exist in the wider political and policy environment.

The social relations of social research

In exploring the social relations of the research process, researchers need to interrogate their own relationship to the research context and to research participants. In part, this leads to questions about identity and the rights of researchers to be involved in certain areas of research. Barton (1996), in the context of disability research, requires researchers to ask a number of questions of themselves. The first of these is: 'What right have I to undertake this research?' This question is set as a challenge to researchers generating Maslow's 'spectator knowledge' which has characterised research conducted on 'research objects' rather than with research subjects. 'Spectator knowledge' also reinforces positions of privilege occupied by researchers. Beneath Barton's question lie issues relating to the identity of individual researchers in relation to the research area and participants of the study in which they are involved. In relation to his involvement in disability research, and in response to Barton, Hurst (1996: 125) writes: 'As a non-disabled person, I have grown increasingly aware of the issues surrounding my right to undertake the work I do.' Here, Hurst relates the issue of 'right to undertake research' with his identity and social position as a non-disabled person. Thus, Hurst recognises tensions between himself and disabled people. However, a focus on singular dimensions of identity may lead to the pitfall of essentialist constructions of those identities. An alternative construction and a potential way forward might be to adopt Maria Mies's notion of 'conscious partiality'. Conscious partiality is achieved through partial identification with the research participants and provides a way of becoming involved in a research process by going beyond essentialist notions of identity (Mies 1983). In relation to research with new social movements, researchers might identify their conscious partiality with the aims of a movement.

A second question raised by Barton in relation to disability research moves beyond individual and fixed identities to explore issues of structural position and social advantage or privilege. Thus, he requires researchers to ask: 'What responsibilities arise from the privileges I have as a result of my social position?' In his own work in the field of disability, Hurst states that 'as a senior member of a national charity and of a potentially influential national policy-orientated group I experience dilemmas about my responsibilities'. Hurst's response relates to his structural position as a non-disabled person and the structural advantages accrued by occupying positions of influence in the arena of disability politics. The precise nature of the dilemma faced by Hurst is unclear. It seems to relate to issues around whether he should 'make way' for a disabled person to occupy his position of privilege, or whether given that he has the potential to influence, he should use that position for the benefit of disabled people. However, the choice need not necessarily be dichotomous, and in some ways the prospect of a dichotomy may mask the complexities contained within the web of identity, social advantage and structural position. In the remainder of this chapter, I want to develop a critical evaluation of these issues as they relate to my involvement in a piece of research. I do this by drawing upon debates within feminist research – the location of my 'home' in social research. However, as I have argued elsewhere, femininst perspectives alone are insufficient to address the complexities and diversity of research situations (Truman 1994). Therefore, I also explore parallels with the research and discussion and discourse from disability research, where the links between social research and social transformation have been to the fore.

Exploring social relations within research

It is in the context of these debates that I want to explore ways in which some research in which I was involved exposes the complexities of social research as an instrument to advance the aims of new social movements. In 1993 I found myself being invited to enter a research partnership, not with disabled people, but by an activist group of gay men, called Healthy Gay City (HGC)[1], tackling safe sex and health issues amongst the gay community in Manchester, UK (Truman 1995; Truman et al. 1996). As a voluntary organisation, the survival of the group depended upon being able to raise funds to enable them to produce and distribute safe-sex materials. The main source of funding available to them was from health authorities who had money specifically earmarked for the prevention of HIV and AIDS. Demand on this funding is extremely competitive both at regional and national levels and from a range of statutory and voluntary groups working in the field of HIV/AIDS prevention. Whilst the primary work of HGC might be viewed as a new social movement with the primary aim of promoting healthy lifestyles amongst the gay community, the quest for funding was a central issue for HGC in the continuation of their work. The fight for resources thus became as central as the fight against AIDS in terms of the day-to-day workings of the organisation. One way of making a convincing case to attract funding was to establish an objective or proven case of health need in the local area. Thus HGC decided to undertake a health-needs assessment of men who had sex with men within the region. By establishing need, the research study would provide a means to help influence the decision-making processes of policy makers and fundholders in relation to local HIV/AIDS initiatives.

This needs assessment research provides direct links between social research and social activism. The group saw social research as being integral to their activism and campaigning work to secure resources in the fight against HIV/AIDS. The project we undertook was in the form of a large-scale health-needs assessment centred on the north-west of England. In the last ten years in Britain, this type of 'local' needs assessment has become a fairly common form of research activity for health professionals to undertake (Davies et al. 1993). Indeed, the study of the range of social aspects of HIV/AIDS has brought about what Boulton describes as 'interesting advances in research methods' (Boulton 1994: 1). However, it is more than simply the methodological aspects of the research process which need to be addressed when exploring the potential for social transformation and change. I want to locate the health-needs assessment, not just within HIV literature, but within debates around social change. This relates back to my earlier discussion of research not just being about describing the social world, but about transforming it. I will now go on to explore how HGC viewed the research in terms of its potential for transformation.

From my perspective, the opportunity to work to the agenda of a voluntary activist group was an exciting prospect – the opportunity to conduct research which might be directly useful to the group and the wider participants in the study. From the outset the research had the potential to be more than participatory, but actually emancipatory.[2] This was the starting point for the HGC study – the gay men wanted a research study – and in part, this was to create new knowledge. However, as activists knew, knowledge could not exist within a vacuum – the knowledge that was required needed to be linked with clear and definable change. Thus, the research needed to explore the health needs of gay and bisexual men and thus create new knowledge about the particular needs of gay and bisexual men in the north-west of England. In contrast with so-called 'national studies' of gay men – which are often heavily skewed towards populations in and around London – it was important to establish a local knowledge base as a means of providing an argument to securing resources locally.

The knowledge generated by the needs assessment also needed to be defined and presented in a way that could lead to positive changes in *addressing* the health needs which were to be identified. The activism of the group is centred on conveying safer sex messages to the local gay community through leaflets, peer education and publicity stunts at gay events and gay venues where safe-sex materials are distributed. As I have described, the acquisition of funding is essential for the ongoing continuation and success of the group's activities. One of the problems faced by the group was to convince potential funders that there was a clear, objective and definable need for safe-sex materials. As stated earlier, the group believed that a large-scale quantitative survey for gay and bisexual men would provide the 'factual evidence' for this need. Thus, a quasi-positivist framework for the conduct of the study was required to meet this criteria. The positivist construction of the research as 'scientific', or within the tradition of Enlightenment, was not based upon the values of the researcher, or of HGC, but on HGC's projection of the audience for the research where such research has achieved 'canonical' status (Stanley 1996).

The acquisition of 'factual evidence' alone was not enough. For a group with a highly developed and sophisticated understanding of the gay community and how to reach it, the task of undertaking a survey would have been relatively straightforward and this could have been achieved with minimal involvement on the part of a researcher. However, it was important that the study also had some credibility as a piece of 'respectable' research with policy makers and funders, who were the perceived audience for the study. In engaging me as research director, HGC were not just enlisting the technical skills of an experienced social researcher, but also 'buying' the credibility of the status that comes with my post as a university lecturer and the 'authority' of the university which employs me. The apparent structural inequality of HGC as an organisation relative to the power position occupied by potential funders was in some ways offset by HGC enlisting me as an academic employed by a university. Any research which we produced together would carry the institutional weight and status of a professional research organisation. The structural status of myself as principal researcher was thus as important to HGC's expectations within their research brief as any of the technical considerations required of the research. Indeed, the presentation of the final research report featured in early discussions about the remit of the research. HGC were clear that they wanted the university logo to appear on the final research report to give weight to its contents. Indeed, the report (Truman *et al.* 1996) appears as a university publication with its own ISBN number. The status of the research, the final report and the target audience for its findings were important factors in the design of the research process.

My structural position as an academic was not the only aspect of my identity that was important to the research process. A number of other issues emerge which have featured in debates about emancipatory research and the wider social relations of the research process. Although I am clearly not a gay man, my involvement with the HGC study was facilitated by a 'conscious partiality' (Mies, 1983) through my identity as a lesbian and therefore party to the broad arena of lesbian and gay politics. However, to reduce this aspect of the research process simply to aspects of identity masks important differences, tensions and inequalities between lesbians and gay men. It is inadequate to reduce the researcher's identity to a singular social position and unidimensional social relationship. Being a socially aware lesbian may have provided some basis for 'conscious partiality' with HGC, but did HGC share a conscious partiality with me? Whilst I was happy to support the furtherance of HGC's aims, I was always conscious that relative to my own communities, be it the lesbian community or the women's community, there were no gains within the social relations which developed through the research. Although the lesbian and gay community is often discussed as an homogeneous body, there are and always have been important differences and tensions between and within the social and political experiences of the two groups. There are no easy ways to reconcile these differences, yet they remain with me as unresolved tensions surrounding my involvement in the research.

The material base of social research is also a key factor and has political consequences for who benefits and how. For example, Barton's question and Hurst's response also draw attention to who has the 'right' to undertake research on disability. There is a material basis to research and where funding is made available for research, disabled people should have first call upon those resources. Conversely, if disabled people cannot attract funds to do disability research, under what justification can others? In the context of the HGC research, it is interesting to note that the funding for the research was given directly to them, rather than to an established researcher. In this way, being the grant holders, HGC had considerably more autonomy over the detail of how the grant should be disposed. Having secured adequate funding for their study, HGC had a commitment to ensure that research moneys be spent within the lesbian and gay community, rather than on employing 'outsiders' to do the research. Unlike much university research, where interviewers are recruited from within the university, we recruited our interviewers from within the gay community. Gay men were paid to undertake the face-to-face interviews. Apart from the direct benefits of receiving payment for their work, our interviewers received training and experience of research work, thus enhancing their skills. There was also a material basis to the strategy used by HGC to secure my involvement in the research. Of course, the conditions under which university staff can engage in collaborative research projects are carefully monitored and regulated. HGC's 'payment' for my involvement went to the university and then into the costs of data analysis and production of the final report. I was, nevertheless, the grant holder from the university's perspective. Interestingly, the research grant was identified by the university administration as a 'health' project rather than a 'gay' project. So, although the research benefited from the status of being done in collaboration, the university sought status through identifying the research as 'health' rather than as 'gay'.

I have discussed some of the social relationships surrounding the research, but what of the benefits to the research participants – namely those who completed the 972 valid questionnaires? Thinking about the research outcomes from this perspective brings into question other received wisdoms about emancipatory research. It has become a maxim within feminist research that research participants derive benefit from taking part in a research study. This is often conflated with empowerment of research participants. 'Empowerment' may take different forms. Empowerment may include the exchange of information between researcher and research participant, as in Oakley's study of new mothers. Empowerment may be thought of as the opportunity to exchange common experiences (Finch 1984). As Kelly et al. (1994) point out, researchers need to ask questions about what sort of empowerment is possible through social research of any kind. Social research is not politics and rarely transforms the conditions and lives of participants (Glucksman 1995). On one level the HGC study, using large-scale survey techniques and a face-to-face or self-complete questionnaire format, might be characterised as a research methodology of the most exploitative kind. However, from the perspective of the gay community, it was HGC who were seen to be conducting the research rather than me as an 'academic spectator'. Thus, a different set of social relationships were constructed in the research process because the research was seen to be a form of activism. Feedback from participants suggested that they were happy to participate in the study because they saw HGC as working for the gay community. From the gay community's perspective, it was involvement in the research that was important since involvement could contribute to the greater good. In other words, different criteria were used to establish credibility with the gay community than were required to establish credibility with policy makers. The findings seem of less direct importance to participants. Although summarised and published in the gay press, the charts, tables and statistics generated by the study are likely to be of little more than passing interest to the average gay individual out for a night on the town.

It follows from this discussion that the research had strategic aims which had been identified by HGC as an activist organisation. Although intended as a means to facilitate change for a broader gay constituency, the research was not intended to be for the benefit of individuals within the gay and bisexual community in a direct sense. The question of who benefits from research and how these benefits are accrued are again complex. With a few notable exceptions, wider notions of 'benefit' are obscured in much research of an emancipatory nature. Accounts of the research process all too often become focused on the relationships between researcher and research participants at a micro-political level. The wider influence of such research may be ignored. Similarly, Maguire (1987) observes that change at a local level may very often be limited and may become marginalised. In the HGC research, the local influence was not with the research participants, in terms of influence *for*. Instead, the research sought to have influence *on* local policy makers. There was also the potential for a certain level of national impact by drawing attention to a large gay population outside the environs of London.

Since publication of the final report, the HGC study remains one of the largest studies of men who have sex with men. It has been widely distributed and is well known amongst local policy makers. HGC as an organisation have continued to find resources to undertake their innovative approach to promoting safe sex within the gay and bisexual community. And lurking on the dusty shelves of the university library, is a copy of the research report itself: only, in the library, it is classified not as a 'health' publication, but as a 'gay' publication.

Conclusion

This chapter has drawn attention to a range of issues relating to the social relations surrounding research which is related to new social movements. I have drawn attention to the complex and in some ways contradictory elements of a research process which seeks to engage with research participants, but which also has a sense of wider strategic aims in terms of creating an impact on a research audience. Questions around structural privilege may be addressed at different political levels. In the HGC study, there was a clear and open agenda that the research should have the backing and hence authenticity which can be accrued by association with an institute of higher education. However, the credibility which provided this authenticity to potential users differed markedly from the authenticity required by research participants. From the research participants' perspective it was HGC, not the affiliation with the university, which authenticated the research. The social relations surrounding the study also embraced issues of identity. Thus, it was not only my sexuality which brought me into this research study, but also issues relating to my structural position as a permanent member of staff in a university. My position as researcher had a complex relationship to my identity as a lesbian as well as to my professional identity and status as a university lecturer and my 'right' to use the university logo on research reports. Referring back to Oliver's original quote, the relationship which was being forged could not simply be reduced to the 'researcher[s] ... learn[ing] how to put their knowledge and skills at the disposal of research subjects, for them to use in whatever ways they choose' (Oliver 1990: 14). It was more than skills and knowledge that HGC wanted to access. They had a clear understanding that the acquisition of technical expertise was only part of their investment in me, and that my institutional status was also integral to our relationship. From my perspective, I was happy to facilitate the use of university resources in this way and the university saw my involvement in the study as a legitimate part of my role as an academic. For HGC, the collaboration with me as an academic ensured the technical success of the study, but more broadly built into the project credibility for the final 'research product' which needed to appeal to and influence policy makers.

This chapter has attempted to bring together a range of issues that are raised when attempting to formulate and carry out research which addresses issues of social marginalisation from a participant's perspective but in a way that is also linked to social change. Building upon ways in which contributors to this book have described their attempts to work within an emancipatory/ anti-discriminatory research paradigm, I have tried to explore and address a range of continuing areas of concern relating to research which is attempting to use an emancipatory or anti-discriminatory approach within a strategic framework. In doing this, I have drawn upon some of the differing epistemological, methodological and socio-political arguments which may influence the basis for research and its claims to be anti-discriminatory and/or emancipatory. There are no easy guidelines, but I have identified a number of areas and questions which need to be asked in relation to research studies. Perhaps when knowledge claims are made, such dialogics should also be recorded as part of research reports. If this were to happen, the dialogue about legitimacy and truth claims would be as an important part of research as its methods and 'findings'.

Notes

1   For purposes of confidentiality, the name of the organisation has been changed.
2   For a discussion of the emergence of an emancipatory paradigm, and the role of researchers within emacipatory research, see Mertens 1998: 15–21.

References

Ahmad, W. and Sheldon, T. (1993) '"Race" and statistics', in M. Hammersley (ed.) *Social Research, Philosophy, Politics and Practice*, London: Sage.

Barton, L. (1996) 'Sociology and disability: some emerging issues', in L. Barton (ed.) *Disability and Society: emerging issues and insights*, London: Longman.

Bhavnani, K.-K. (1993) 'Tracing the contours: feminist research and feminist objectivity', *Women's Studies International Forum* 16 (2): 95–104.

Booth, T. (1996) 'Sounds of still voices: issues in the use of narrative methods with people who have learning difficulties', in L. Barton (ed.) *Disability and Society: emerging issues and insights*, London: Longman.

Boulton, M. (ed.) (1994) *Challenge and Innovation: methodological advances in social research on HIV/AIDS*, London: Taylor and Francis.

Cook, J. and Fonow, M. (1986) 'Knowledge and women's interests: issues in epistemology and methodology in feminist sociology', *Sociological Inquiry* 56 (Winter): 2–29.

Davies, P., Hickson, F., Weatherburn, P. and Hunt, A. (1993) *Sex, Gay Men and AIDS*, London: Taylor and Francis.

Finch, J. (1984) '"It's great to have someone to talk to": the ethics and politics of interviewing women', in C. Bell and H. Roberts (eds) *Social Researching: politics, problems'-practice*, London: Routledge and Kegan Paul.

Glucksmann, M. (1995) 'The work of knowledge and the knowledge of women's work', in M. Maynard and J. Purvis (eds) *Researching Women's Lives from a Feminist Perspective*, London: Taylor and Francis.

Gorelick, S. (1996) 'Contradictions of feminist methodology', in H. Gottfried (ed.) *Feminism and Social Change: bridging theory and practice*, Chicago: University of Illinois Press.

Graham, H. (1995) 'Diversity, inequality and official data: some problems of method and measurement in Britain', *Health and Social Care in the Community* 3: 9–18.

Haraway, D. (1988) 'Situated knowledges: the science question in feminism and the privilege of the partial perspective', *Feminist Studies* 14(3): 573–99.

Harding, S. (ed.) (1987) *Feminism and Methodology*, Milton Keynes: Open University Press.

Hurst, A. (1996) 'Reflecting on researching disability and higher education', in L. Barton (ed.) *Disability and Society: emerging issues and insights*, London: Longman.

Kelly, L., Burton, S. and Regan, L. (1994) 'Researching women's lives or studying women's oppression? Reflections on what constitutes feminist research', in M. Maynard and J. Purvis (eds) *Researching Women's Lives from a Feminist Perspective*, London: Taylor and Francis.

Maguire, P. (1987) *Doing Participatory Research: a feminist approach*, Amhurst: University of Massachusetts.

Maynard, M. and Purvis, J. (eds) (1994) *Researching Women's Lives from a Feminist Perspective*, London: Taylor and Francis.

Mertens, D. (1998) *Research Methods in Education and Psychology*, River Oaks: Sage.

Mies, M. (1983) 'Towards a methodology for feminist research', in G. Bowles and R. Duelli Klein (eds) *Theories of Women's Studies*, London: Routledge and Kegan Paul.

Oakley, A. (1981) 'Interviewing women: a contradiction in terms', in H. Roberts (ed.) *Doing Feminist Research*, London: Routledge and Kegan Paul.

Oliver, M. (1990) *The Politics of Disablement*, Basingstoke: Macmillan.

—— (1992) 'Changing the social relations of research production', *Disability, Handicap and Society* 7 (2): 101–14.

Roberts, H. (ed.) (1981) *Doing Feminist Research*, London: Routledge and Kegan Paul.

Shakespeare, P., Atkinson, D. and French, S. (eds) (1993) *Reflecting on Research Practice: issues in health and social welfare*, Milton Keynes: Open University Press.

Smith, D. (1988) *The Everyday World as Problematic: a feminist sociology*, Milton Keynes: Open University Press.

Stanley, L. (ed.) (1990) *Feminist Praxis: research, theory and epistemology in feminist sociology*, London: Routledge.

—— (1996) *Sex Surveyed*, London: Taylor and Francis.

Stanley, L. and Wise, S. (1993) *Breaking Out Again*, London: Routledge.

Truman, C. (1994) 'Feminist challenges to traditional research: have they gone far enough?' in B. Humphries and C. Truman (eds) *Re-thinking Social Research*, Aldershot: Avebury.

—— (1995) 'Feminist perspectives in research and evaluation: the challenge of "difference"', paper presented to the International Evaluation Conference, November, Vancouver.

Truman, C., Keenaghan, L. and Gudgion, G. (1996) *Men who have sex with Men in the North-West: a peer-led regional study*, Lancaster: Lancaster University.

Zarb, G. (1992) 'On the road to Damascus: first steps towards changing the relations of disability research production', *Disability, Handicap and Society* 7 (2): 125–38.

Chapter 3

Hearing voices?

Research issues when telling respondents' stories of childhood sexual abuse from a feminist perspective

Clare Woodward

> I am waiting for them to stop talking about the 'other', to stop even describing how important it is to be able to speak about difference. It is not just important what we speak about, but how and why we speak. Often this speech about the 'other' is also a mask, an oppressive talk hiding gaps, absences, that space where our words would be if we were speaking, if there were a silence, if we were there. This 'we' is that 'us' in the margins, that 'we' who inhabit marginal space that is not a site of domination but a place of resistance. Enter that space. Often this speech about the 'other' annihilates, erases: 'no need to hear your voice when I can talk about you better than you can speak about yourself. No need to hear your voice. Only tell me about your pain. I want to know your story. And then I will tell it back to you in a new way. Tell it back to you in such a way that it has become mine, my own. Re-writing you, I write myself anew. I am still author, authority. I am still the colonizer, the speak subject, and you are now at the centre of my talk. Stop.'
>
> (hooks 1990: 151–2)

This chapter is about some of the research issues and difficulties I faced in my PhD thesis, where a central concern was to how I represent respondents' stories of childhood sexual abuse (CSA) within my research. These stories were drawn from a sample of over a thousand letters written in a response to an appeal made by the National Commission of Inquiry into the Prevention of Child Abuse (NCIPCA).[1] When defining the contents of the letters I have used Plummer's view of 'a personal experience narrative … [which] overlaps with, but is not quite the same as a life story, a biography, a self story' (1995: 15). Plummer focuses on one sub-genre: stories of suffering, surviving and surpassing, and this best illustrates the stories told within the letters. For instance, some of the letters may only cover one aspect, such as describing the effects of the abuse on the writer's life, other letters tell how the writer is coping with having been abused, while other writers may talk of all three: their suffering, how they survived and how they surpassed CSA.

The research issues I will explore within this chapter are concerned with telling respondents' stories of CSA from a feminist perspective. First, I will outline what I mean by my feminist perspective and how this has influenced the research process and issues concerning representing respondents' stories of CSA. Second, I will illustrate why issues to do with representation are so salient within my thesis by exploring how adults who have experienced CSA have been represented within the research literature. And third, I will look at more practical research issues based around three questions: (1) Who am I representing? (2) How do I represent respondents' words? And (3) How do I represent respondents? However, before going into any of the above, and as an introduction to this chapter, I would like to tell two stories that influenced this writing and, perhaps for the very first time, really made me think about the research process and what impact this might have on the researched.

Virginia was one of my participants for a study looking at the long-term psychological effects of CSA (Woodward 1994). She had volunteered for the study but stated that she preferred not to be interviewed but would complete my questionnaire. As issues of confidentiality were of prime importance, all communication with Virginia went through a mutual friend. A few days after receiving back her questionnaire, I heard that she had gone missing. Several months later, and on the day that the project was due, I heard that Virginia's body had been found in the River Thames. I was much saddened by this news and while I never knew Virginia in person, not even knowing her real name, I felt I knew her through her writing. Virginia's final comments to me were:

> I admire you for your dedication and thoroughness, and wish you the very best of luck with what you are trying to achieve. I'd like to hear about the results please.

Obviously, I was not able to give feedback to Virginia about the results, and as a researcher I found myself wondering whether my research and the process of asking Virginia to write in depth about her life could have contributed in any way, however small, to her suicide. I console myself in several ways, one being that at the same time as receiving back Virginia's questionnaire I also received another questionnaire, where Mary wrote:

> If I had been asked these questions thirty years ago, life would have been very different. I disagree with those who say you cannot ask such questions; yes they are personal and one may not always be ready to answer, but when something has been pushed into the unconscious it needs a lot of help to bring it to the level of sharing. It has been helpful to think about these questions and I feel it has brought me a little closer to the truth and has given me the courage to share a little more with [my therapist], who is helping me to work through the many problems I have collected over forty years.
>
> (Woodward 1994: 67)

My second story does not in fact involve research respondents or even a research process, nonetheless, the issues raised are similar to those encountered when carrying out research. Several years ago, whilst reading the journal *Self and Society* I came upon an article written by my ex-therapist. As I read this case study, I instantly saw myself in the text. The names and a few details had been changed but, to me, I was instantly recognisable. I found myself to be quite upset by the fact that my story, which I had told in confidence, was now 'public'. It was not that I feared people would recognise me from this story but, because I did not know it was there, it came as a total shock and I felt angry and betrayed (Woodward 1995).

These two events, whilst very different, made me think about the responsibilities one has towards research participants within the whole research process. Recognition of the responsibilities I have as the researcher in wanting to ensure the well-being of my participants are further reinforced by at least two of my standpoints: (1) being a researcher trying to do feminist research; and (2) having my own story of CSA. First, in conducting feminist research I am very much aware of how power can be misused, and second, having my own story of CSA, I am also aware of the risks and benefits telling one's story of abuse can have in terms of how the storytellers see themselves and how in turn they are perceived by others. As I cannot cover the whole research process within this one chapter, my aim here is to explore the research issues that are involved in telling respondents' stories of CSA. First, I feel it is necessary to illustrate what I mean by conducting the research from a feminist perspective and how this has influenced the research process. In line with the central theme of the book – emancipatory research – one aspect of conducting feminist research is to see how (and where) issues of emancipation (i.e. to set free and liberate from constraint) and empowerment (i.e. to give power and authority) are possible within the research process.

My attempt at emancipatory research

In a previous attempt at trying to emancipate and empower participants, I used the feminist tool of conscientization (Mies 1983), which refers to the mutual sharing of knowledge so that participants themselves are able to detect sources of oppression in their lives and take appropriate action. While I feel that this process had perhaps been beneficial to some of my participants (as illustrated previously by Mary's words), I now feel that what was most beneficial to my participants was the fact that I wanted to know about their experiences; I believed them, and felt that they had something valuable and worthwhile to say. I had created a space where they could tell their story. The importance for respondents of being able to tell their stories of CSA in their own way (having full control over what they want to write about and include within the letter), as well as having their stories heard and their experiences validated, is now central both within my current PhD thesis and to my new attempt at trying to conduct emancipatory research. There are several reasons why this should be the case. To begin with, CSA has been one of society's 'best kept secrets' (Rush 1980), and even though it is gradually becoming more well known and accepted that children have been and are continuing to be sexually abused, the CSA taboo is far from broken. In itself it is the cause of many of the problems faced by those who have been sexually abused and who want to be able to talk about their experiences. This view is illustrated by Caroline Malone *et al.* who write:

> The silence, secrecy and shame that still besieges the whole area of child sexual abuse all too often results in the fact that we are afforded limited opportunities to hear each other's voices, to give and receive support, and to challenge much of the negativity that prevents us from talking about and living our lives in ways that are more complete.
>
> (Malone *et al.* 1996: x)

Not being able to talk about one's experiences of CSA is the reason I have chosen the phrase 'Hearing Voices?' as the title of this chapter. Hundreds of letters in my possession represent 'voices', which to a large extent have remained silent for a long time. In fact in 13 per cent of cases the respondent was telling for the very first time, having never told anyone including family or friends. The National Commission: did something new, on a national scale they gave people the 'space' to tell their story of childhood abuse and, moreover, to have their 'voice' heard.

The implications of being able to tell one's story of CSA on my attempts at emancipatory research is that I feel that for *some* respondents the process of writing down their experiences of CSA and its impact on their life did lead to them feeling more emancipated and empowered. For example, one respondent wrote 'at last I am now set free', while another respondent felt that writing down his experiences was the first step towards seeking help for himself. Where respondents did not make any comments regarding how they felt as a result of writing, my hope is that respondents, especially those who are telling for the very first time, did find some freedom, however small, through telling their story of CSA. What I feel was beneficial as well as being empowering was that by writing to the Commission, respondents were able to re-tell their negative experiences to be used in a positive way. So as well as helping themselves through a cathartic process, they were also able to help others.

Defining my feminist perspective

To further define what I see as my feminist perspective and how it has influenced my research, I refer to Liz Stanley and Sue Wise who regard the following areas where 'feminism' can be present in positive ways within the research process. These are: in the researcher–researched relationship; in emotion as a research experience; in the intellectual autobiography of researchers – therefore in how to manage the differing 'realities' and understanding of researchers and researched; and thus in the complex question of power in research and writing (Stanley and Wise 1990: 23). I will explore each of these areas in turn.

The researcher–researched relationship

Within the research there has been no direct contact between myself and the respondents, so the usual researcher–researched relationship does not apply, although issues of power differences between the two still exist. This is shown in respondents having the power and control over what they chose to write about, and with my having the control and power over how I interpret and represent their written words within my thesis. My preference would have been to have conducted participatory or action research, enabling me to have direct contact with respondents and for respondents to have the opportunity to say how their stories of CSA are to be represented. However, this was not possible due to issues of ethics and lack of resources that precluded contact with respondents. The issue of ethics may seem somewhat contrary to general beliefs about what is considered ethical (e.g. Yow 1994). Whilst I have always felt that it is best to get permission from respondents at every stage of the research process, this is unfortunately not always possible and in the case of the letters it is now several years since the letters were written. My supervisor and I felt that rather than sending them a letter now regarding their story (written some time ago), it would be more ethical *not* to contact respondents. Furthermore, the respondents are very likely to have 'moved on' from how they felt at the time of writing the letter and, having moved on, they may not want to go back to that time. I may, of course, be wrong about this but what is the most ethical thing to do? I have found not having any contact with respondents a difficult experience.[2] I have often, after reading a letter, wanted to make contact with its writer. One respondent wrote: 'this seems like a poor-me story and who ever reads it, I would appreciate someone giving me feedback. Have you heard me??' I remember saying to myself out loud that I had heard her and that I was very moved by what she had written. She had given so much information (ten sides of A4 paper written in small handwriting) detailing in depth how she felt about herself as a result of her experiences of sexual abuse, and it was a very valuable letter to me with regard to my research. I also wanted to say that I had read her letter to the end (she had written 'if you've read this far – thanks') and to say 'thank you'.

Emotion as a research experience

My understanding of emotion as a research experience in relation to my research is how my emotions as a result of reading so many letters about CSA affected me and the research process. This issue is particularly relevant when the subject of CSA is very emotive and where letters were often very sad and at times were very distressing to read. However, I would also like to stress that many letters were also very positive and a joy to read. Certainly my feelings following Virginia's suicide made me realise how emotions can be part of the research experience for me as the researcher, and how this has subsequently influenced other research I have conducted.

In terms of my current research, I have found myself with access to many stories – voices which, without the legitimate position of being a researcher, I probably would never have heard. I feel that I have benefited personally from this research experience, even though at times working with this material has not been easy. Reading the letters can bring up all kinds of emotions – contempt for the abuser, anger, disgust, sadness, guilt and happiness. I would often have tears in my eyes and feel my body shiver and go cold. Reading the letters also brought up issues relating to my own experiences of CSA, especially when I read a story where the experiences and feelings of the respondent were similar to my own. As I am studying a world of which I am part, issues of over-identifying with respondents could be a problem. However, I felt that I was never unable to hear other people's stories of CSA above my own, and that I was able to maintain the necessary distance between myself and my own experiences and those of respondents. This was achieved through what Mies (1983) refers to as a 'conscious subjectivity', which challenges the value-free objectivity of traditional research. Here, it is argued that conscious subjectivity or partiality is different from mere subjectivity or simple empathy, on the basis of having a limited identification with participants. While I recognise the many differences that exist between myself and the respondents, having the shared experience of CSA has been, in my view, a positive and significant factor in the research design and process. Respondents on the other hand wrote not knowing, in most cases, who was going to read their letters. However, several respondents did comment that they hoped that at least one person reading their letter did have first-hand experience of CSA. This was felt to be important if their letter was *really* to be understood. For those respondents who expressed that they would prefer to speak to someone in person, a telephone interview was arranged. For many others, it could have been that not being interviewed in person was the motivating factor that enabled so many people to write about their experiences: 'Liz Kelly, Shelia Burton and Linda Regan in their research into CSA, argued that using questionnaires produced more reliable information than interviewing because it allowed respondents anonymity in revealing distressing and sensitive experiences' (Maynard and Purvis 1994: 14).

The intellectual autobiography of researchers

Liz Stanley writes of 'intellectual autobiography':

by this rather clumsy phrase I mean making visible what is normally, usually, conventionally, hidden to readers: the shifts, changes, developments, downturns and upturns in the way that the biographer understands the subject with which she deals.

(Stanley 1986: 31)

An intellectual autobiography is used within my research as a piece of writing to show how interpretations and other decisions have been made within the research process, based on the data, theory and any beliefs and values that I hold. The aim of this is to make my readers aware of any biases I may have by showing how (relevant) past events in my life have shaped my research and continue to do so. Making myself and my decision process visible within this research is particularly salient for two reasons: (1) it would seem hypocritical for me not to do so given that the title of my thesis is 'Being visible: representations of self and identity within personal experience narratives of childhood sexual abuse'; and (2) because of my feminist perspective. The words of Karen Henwood best illustrates my approach to the feminist perspective, wherein

scientific research can never be wholly neutral, disinterested, or value-free because the process of knowing always begins in the concrete contexts and material conditions of people's lives, together with the standpoints, perspectives or understandings of the knower.

(Henwood 1993: 5)

And furthermore, as pointed out by Bennett Berger:

Autobiographical information may tell us literally where a writer is coming from and thereby supplying an added dimension which is seldom irrelevant to understanding of texts.

(Berger 1990: xvi)

In feminist research, situating *where one is coming from* has been regarded as essential. However, how far one is located within their research has been questioned. Carole Truman writes:

locating oneself in the research is not just about declaring marxist or radical influences, but at a more basic level declaring oneself as being white or black, able-bodied or disabled, young or old, inside or outside the academy, and so on. Often these influences are only located within feminist research when the researcher differs from the white, able-bodied, middle-class academic.

(Truman 1994: 26)

Therefore, as my PhD is entitled 'Being visible', I want to include as many standpoints as I can to show where I am coming from, so other influences or standpoints that I currently hold are a result of being a White, able-bodied, heterosexual, working-class, postgraduate, woman, who came into education as a mature student to do a psychology degree and who is not too far chronologically from reaching the big three-zero! Locating oneself within the research is particularly important when looking at issues of power in the research and writing.

The complex question of power in the research and writing

Central to the issue of power is the feminist critique of traditional research, where 'it is argued that not only does feminism challenge the basic assumptions of positivistic science, it has suggested real alternatives to it' (Wilkinson 1986: 16). Integral to feminist epistemology and methodology is 'reflexivity': the continual assessment of the contribution of one's knowledge to others, as well as the questions we have asked; the way we locate ourselves within our questions and the purpose of our work (Maynard and Purvis 1994). Several key concepts questioning the universal 'we' have emerged which have been addressed and debated by feminist epistemology. The central issue for me here is that of representation and acknowledging the responsibility to those I speak for, as well as the responsibility for where I speak from – questioning whether I should have the privilege to know other people's stories of CSA, whether I have authority to speak for my respondents and, most importantly, whether I can accurately represent and tell respondents' stories of CSA? While these are important issues to consider, I do not feel that it is always possible to adequately address them all. I have so far touched upon the responsibility of where I speak from. I also acknowledge the responsibility of those for whom I speak, having recognised the importance of difference between myself and my respondents. The question of responsibility of those for whom I speak will be explored later in the chapter. In addition, I feel that it has been a privilege to know other people's stories of CSA; however, whether or not I should have this privilege I cannot really answer. The answer to this no doubt lies in my thesis and how I have used the data and how I have represented respondents and their stories of CSA. Whether I have the authority to speak for the respondents is another difficult question to answer. Perhaps, being a survivor and a researcher I do have more authority than most, but once again I see the answer to this question being in how the thesis is perceived by other survivors. In terms of the idea behind my thesis, I have sought the views of friends who are also survivors. Furthermore, my aim is to allow wherever possible the respondents to speak for themselves. However, as the researcher, I still have power over the overall structure of where the words go and subsequently what the words ultimately say within the context of the thesis. So the question now is can I accurately represent respondents and tell respondents' stories of CSA? To explore this I will begin by illustrating why issues related to representation are so salient within my thesis.

There are three distinct layers in my research which all involve issues concerning representation: (1) how I represent myself within the thesis (which I have already explored within this chapter); (2) how I represent and tell respondents' stories of CSA (which is the main focus of this chapter); and (3) how respondents represent their sense of self and identity within their personal experience narratives of CSA (which is the main focus of the thesis). To explore whether it is possible to accurately represent respondents' stories I need to include here the outline to my thesis, which emerged, in part, as a result of the ways in which survivors have often been represented within much of the literature on adults who have experienced sexual abuse in childhood.

How respondents represent their sense of self and identity within their personal experience narratives of CSA

Central to my thesis are the following questions: (1) How do individuals who have experienced CSA make sense of their experiences? (That is, how do they see themselves in relation to their experiences of CSA? And what meanings do they attribute to such experiences?) (2) How do they construct and represent their sense of self and identity within personal experience narratives? And (3) What factors shape and influence those representations? In addition, I also aim to make visible the differences and diversity of people's identities, lives and experiences of CSA by providing an holistic view of what it means to have experienced sexual abuse in childhood. This perspective is in contrast to much of the existing research into CSA, where survivors have been represented as a homogeneous group and where the research focus has been predominately on the long-term negative effects of CSA, such as depression, self-mutilation, eating disorders, suicide attempts, alcohol and drug addiction, and sexual dysfunction (e.g. Apolinsky and Wilcoxen 1991; Bagley and King 1990; Cohen 1995; DiPalma 1994; Finkelhor and Browne 1986). Furthermore, survivors have been further stigmatised by still being portrayed as victims (implying a passive response to the events themselves and their aftermath), with the emphasis being on: (a) powerlessness and the inability to take control of one's life (e.g. Gold 1986); (b) the pathology and inevitability of problems which may be experienced by survivors; and (c) maladaptive rather than adaptive coping responses (Middelton-Moz 1992; Sanford 1991). This situating of victims within a pathogenic model, where the focus is on sickness and disease, often results in representations of victims as addictive, suicidal, abusive, violent (mad or bad) and in need of care or control. Moreover, within this framework the accounts of women who have experienced CSA are often dichotomised, disregarded or reinterpreted (Huntingdon 1995). Notable exceptions are the personal accounts of survivors (e.g. Spring 1987) and the mostly American self-help literature (e.g. Bass and Davies 1988) or treatment programmes (e.g. Jehu *et al.* 1988) where change is seen as possible. This negative image of people who have experienced CSA has begun to be challenged by survivors themselves. For example, Caroline Malone *et al.* write:

> As survivors we demand to be taken seriously for who and what we are, and not for what others assume us to be. For too long, survivors of child sexual abuse have been at the receiving end of knowledge. Much of this knowledge has been produced through the practices and beliefs of a number of 'experts' or 'professionals' who are not survivors themselves. We tend to be described by knowledge produced by these experts as being damaged and damaging citizens; citizens who are frequently seen as the flawed by-products of abusive relationships; damaged citizens who need to be described, examined, quantified, understood and ultimately controlled – for our own good.
>
> (Malone *et al.* 1996: x)

How do I represent and tell respondents' stories of CSA?

In my attempt at reconstructing what it means to have experienced CSA from a feminist perspective, issues of representation are of fundamental importance within the thesis. I now turn to three further issues: (1) Who am I representing?, (or acknowledging the responsibility of who I speak for)? (2) How do I represent respondents' words? And (3) How do I represent respondents?

Who am I representing?

Whose voices am I hearing? As the NCIPCA adverts were placed nationally, letters were received from all over the country. Of the letters, 88 per cent were written by females, while 12 per cent came from males. Telling one's story through letter writing is a medium that has allowed males in particular the opportunity to express themselves and tell their story. I wish to stress this point, as few studies into child abuse have included men in their sample (Draucker 1992). The respondents' ages ranged from 10 years to over 80 years of age. Of equal importance is the question of whose voices am I not hearing? It is likely that many people did not know that their stories of abuse were wanted, especially as the advertisements placed by the Commission appeared only once. Moreover, the advertisements were featured in the British tabloid newspapers, such as *The Sun* and the *Daily Mirror*, as well as in women's magazines such as *Bella*, *Chat* and *Woman's Own*. Consequently, the assertion that certain sections of the population were unrepresented in the sample seems eminently sensible. In addition, it is not possible to take on board population differences in terms of race, ethnicity, sexuality and disability as very few participants made explicit any of these standpoints. Additional 'missing voices' came from those who may have seen the advertisement but perhaps did not want to face their past or found it too difficult to do so. Finally, there are also those who unfortunately no longer have a voice to be heard. I found myself wanting to include everyone's story. In the end, my rationale for whose story I chose to use involved selecting letters in which respondents provided what can be termed as 'thick description' (Denzin 1989). This refers to the letters where respondents were able to be reflective and who included thoughts and feelings concerning their experiences of CSA and the impact this has had on their life.

How do I use respondents' words?

How do I best represent respondents' stories of CSA? I started out by not wanting to fragment respondents' stories. I felt that if I only select sections of the stories the letters could lose their uniqueness, as well as their meaning, through being represented out of context. My understanding of what was said in some instances may not necessarily be what the writer intended. However much insight or knowledge one may have in an area, it is still no substitute for the original words and contextual flavour of the writer's narrative. While I would prefer not to fragment respondents' stories, there are often factors which can take precedence, such as being able to protect the identities of respondents and their letters, as well as the restrictions on the word length available for including qualitative data. One way round this, for me, has been to have my interpretations on six whole letters, with all 'identifiers' which could identify the respondent removed, and which represent key features from all the letters. I have then used a wide selection of quotes from other letters to show differences and similarities between respondents and their experiences of CSA. My aim is to provide a balanced view of what it means to have experienced CSA. The last point here raises the question of whether or not I keep to the exact written words – including grammar and spelling. I must admit I have found it tempting to quote the most articulate respondents, as well as to turn to the letters which are either typed or are the more readable. For some of the letters, without editing it would be difficult to tell the respondents' stories due to the language used as well as protect their anonymity. Another point here is that some respondents, if they think their words are to be published, may want their letters to be edited.

How do I represent the respondents?

How does one describe and talk about people who have been sexually abused in childhood? The terminology now commonly used is that of survivor as opposed to victim. For example, one respondent wrote: '*by the way we are no longer called victims. We are survivors.*' This is an important issue as I want to look at how people who have been sexually abused construct their sense of self and the identities that they may use. For example, what does it mean to call oneself a survivor? There has been a recent shift by a small number of feminist researchers to reconceptualise how survivors have been represented by moving from a pathogenic model (which focuses on weakness and illness) to a salutogenic model (focusing on strengths and health). For instance, Kelly *et al.* (1993) highlight the victim/survivor dichotomy by outlining the connotations connected to both these labels (e.g. victim = powerless; survivor = powerful). I feel very strongly that in my research the power to name and define oneself and one's experiences must reside with respondents and not with myself just because I am the researcher. The letters provided an ideal medium whereby respondents were able to write what they were feeling at that moment in time. Some respondents who had *come to terms with* their abuse felt that they were indeed survivors, while some others stated that they still felt like victims, while others used neither label. There is a fine line between recognising people's strengths and the ways that they have coped, and acknowledging the pain that CSA can have on a person's life. In this, I agree with Kelly *et al.* (1993) who advocate that neither label (victim or survivor) is helpful as it posits individuals within two distinct camps with associated connotations rather than recognising that in fact they refer to different experiences which could exist throughout a person's lifetime. It is far too simple an idea that a person moves from being a victim to becoming a survivor, especially as the meaning of victim or survivor is likely to vary between different people. It may be, for example, that an individual wants to hang on to being a victim, along with whatever that means to her or him; or that the person might move between being a victim one day, then a survivor the next, followed perhaps by seeing themselves once again as a victim. There again, the survivor label may seem to be too limiting if the person feels that they do more than just survive but actually live or surpass their experiences of CSA. These are some of the issues which I am currently exploring within my thesis.

A further and very important issue which I have so far only touched upon concerns identifying respondents or their stories. In the research involving Virginia, I had originally assigned numbers next to participants. I think Virginia was number four. This I feel came from my training in psychology, where participants were referred to as subjects and where numbers were given instead of names. In fact, after I completed the research involving participant number four, I chose the pseudonym 'Virginia' after finding out that Virginia was a great fan of Virginia Woolf. Now, however, I feel numbers are too impersonal and that there are more suitable ways to protect identities – such as using pseudonyms, which I now prefer. When confidentiality is an important issue for respondents, it must mean more than making a promise not to use the person's name. It must mean taking the appropriate measures which will guarantee the promise of ensuring confidentiality. Ensuring total anonymity can also be problematic, especially in some research settings (see Yow 1994; Lee 1993).

Measures such as the use of pseudonyms and the changing or omission of specific details are often used to protect identification. But how effective is changing and omitting specific details as a measure of guaranteeing confidentiality and anonymity? As my story at the beginning of this chapter exemplified, my name and a few details had been changed but to me and maybe to others I was recognisable. While this example represents more the betrayal I felt, as my therapist had not informed me of the article, it also illustrates how difficult it is to tell a story without distorting too much of the original account. This issue is particularly relevant when looking at life histories and other research which draws very much on the personal. Nonetheless, with people who have already been exploited, I feel that this issue is particularly relevant and one that quite rightly does concern me, especially as I am not in the position of being able to go back to the respondents concerned. I have to accept that respondents wrote knowing that their experiences were likely to be used in the public domain. For many, it was not only important that their stories were heard but that they had the opportunity of being able to help others. My hope now is that by continuing to help others, my research can make further use of the contribution given by respondents as well as allowing respondents' stories of CSA to be *heard*.

Concluding remarks

The general aim of this chapter was to explore some of the research issues which I encountered when telling respondents' stories of CSA from a feminist perspective. In starting with the moving quote from bell hooks, followed by my own two stories, I wanted to highlight the responsibilities which researchers have to the researched, especially in wanting to hear people's stories and how those stories are then represented within the research. The research issues explored within this chapter are central to feminist research and include issues relating to the following questions: Who am I representing? How do I use respondents' words? And how do I represent respondents? Underlying these questions are many methodological, epistemological, ethical and practical issues which I have attempted to address in my efforts to conduct my research in a way which would most benefit respondents and the stories they told. How successful this effort has been is for others to judge. To conduct the research and hope that I have adequately represented respondents and their stories is perhaps the most realistic course available to me. I would have preferred to have had direct contact with respondents to check that I had indeed got it right. However, this is not always possible and all one can do is hope that being aware of issues such as power and inequality and how they can work within the research process will go some way towards ensuring that the best has been done. The process of being able to tell one's story of CSA and to have it heard and validated is an important first step towards greater emancipation and empowerment. On reflection, perhaps the person who has benefited most, in terms of liberation and power (through increased understanding and knowledge), is myself both as the researcher and as someone who has experienced CSA.

Notes

1   The NCIPCA was originally formed by the National Society for the Prevention of Cruelty to Children (NSPCC) but later became an independent body. The aims of the Commission were to review everything that is currently known about child abuse. Part of this work involved hearing from as many people as possible, which included over 450 submissions from organisations, academics and 'professional' individuals, covering most of the key agencies with an interest in child abuse. The Commission also felt it was important to hear from those people who have personal experience of childhood abuse, and subsequently advertised in the tabloids and women's magazines asking for people to write to them with their 'experiences' of 'abuse'. This appeal resulted in 1,121 letters ranging from one page to over twenty pages being received from people all over Britain and the Irish Republic. My involvement with the letters came as a result of providing an analysis of these letters, focusing on prevention issues, on behalf of the Commission (see Wattam and Woodward 1996).
2   Even though I have not had any contact with respondents, every respondent at the time of writing received a personal letter from the NCIPCA thanking them for their letter and providing a list of organisations offering help if requested. Furthermore, many respondents also received a reply from an Agony Aunt, as many advertisements were placed within Agony Aunt columns of women's magazines.

References

Apolinsky, S. and Wilcoxen, A. (1991) 'Adult survivors of childhood sexual victimisation: a group procedure for women', *Family Therapy* 18 (1): 37–45.

Bagley, C. and King, K. (1990) *Child Sexual Abuse: The search for healing*, London: Routledge.

Bass, E. and Davies, L. (1988) *The Courage to Heal: A guide for women survivors of child sexual abuse*, Great Britain: Cedar.

Berger, B.M. (1990) *Authors of Their Own Lives: Intellectual autobiographies by twenty American sociologists*, Berkeley and Los Angeles, California: University of California Press.

Cohen, T. (1995) 'Motherhood among incest survivors', *Child Abuse and Neglect* 19 (12): 1423–9.

Denzin, N. (1989) *Interpretative Biography*, a Sage University paper, Qualitative Research Methods Series 17.

DiPalma, L.M. (1994) 'Patterns of coping and characteristics of high-functioning incest survivors', *Archives of Psychiatric Nursing* 8 (2): 82–90.

Draucker, C.B. (1992) *Counselling Survivors of Childhood Sexual Abuse*, London: Sage Publications.

Finkelhor, D. and Browne, A. (1986) 'Initial and long-term effects: a conceptual framework', in D. Finkelhor (ed.) *A Sourcebook on Child Sexual Abuse*, Beverley Hills: Sage, pp. 180–98.

Gold, E.R. (1986) 'Long-term effects of sexual victimisation in childhood: an attributional approach', *Journal of Consulting and Clinical Psychology* 54: 471–5.

Henwood, K. (1993) 'Epistemology, methodology and feminist psychology', *The British Psychological Society*, Psychology of Women Section Newsletter, no. 11, Spring, pp. 3–11.

hooks, b. (1990) *Talking Back: Thinking feminist, thinking black*, Boston: South End.

Huntingdon, A. (1995) 'Intimate partners living with a survivor of sexual abuse: an exploratory study', unpublished MSc dissertation, University of Surrey.

Jehu, D., Gazan, M. and Klassen, C. (1988) *Beyond Sexual Abuse: Therapy with women who were childhood victims*, Chichester: John Wiley and Sons.

Kelly, L., Regan, L. and Burton, S. (1993) 'Beyond victim to survivor: the implications of knowledge about children's resistance and avoidance strategies', in R. Dallos and E. McLaughlin (eds) *Social Problems and the Family*, London: Sage Publications.

Lee, R.M. (1993) *Doing Research on Sensitive Topics*, London: Sage Publications.

Malone, C., Farthing, L. and Marce, L. (eds) (1996) *The Memory Bird: Survivors of sexual abuse*, London: Virago.

Maynard, M. and Purvis, J. (1994) *Researching Women's Lives*, London: Taylor and Francis.

Middelton-Moz, J. (1992) *Will to Survive – Affirming the Positive Power of the Human Spirit*, Deerfield Beach, Florida: Health Communications Inc.

Mies, M. (1983) 'Towards a methodology for feminist research', in G. Bowles and R. Duelli Klien (eds) *Theories of Women's Studies*, London: Routledge and Kegan Paul.

Plummer, K. (1995) *Telling Sexual Stories: Power, change and social worlds*, London and New York: Routledge.

Rush, F. (1980) *The Best Kept Secret*, New Jersey: Prentice Hall.

Sanford, L. (1991) *Strong at the Broken Places*, London: Virago Press.

Spring, J. (1987) *Cry Hard and Swim: The story of an incest survivor*, London: Virago Press.

Stanley, L. (1986) 'Some thoughts on editing the diaries of Hannah Cullwick', in L. Stanley (ed.) *Feminist Research Seminar – Feminist Research Process*, Studies in Sexual Politics, no. 16, Manchester: Sociology Department, University of Manchester.

Stanley, L. and Wise, S. (1990) 'Method, methodology and epistemology in feminist research processes', in L. Stanley (ed.) *Feminist Praxis: Research theory and epistemology in feminist sociology*, Routledge: London, pp. 20–60.

Truman, C. (1994) 'Feminist challenges to traditional research: have they gone far enough', in B. Humphries and C. Truman (eds) *Re-thinking Social Research*, Aldershot, Hants, UK: Avebury, pp. 21–36.

Wattam, C. and Woodward, C. (1996) ' "… And do I abuse my children? No!" Learning about prevention from people who have experienced child abuse', *Childhood Matters*, report of the National Commission of Inquiry into the Prevention of Child Abuse, vol. 2, background papers, London: HMSO.

Wilkinson, S. (1986) *Feminist Social Psychology: Developing theory and practice*, Milton Keynes: Open University Press.

Woodward, C. (1994) 'A qualitative analysis of the psychological effects and coping strategies employed by adult survivors of childhood sexual abuse', unpublished BA dissertation, June 1994, University of Westminster, London.

—— (1995) 'The importance of getting it right: the ethics in researching childhood sexual abuse', unpublished paper, Lancaster University.

Yow, V.R. (1994) *Recording Oral History*, Thousand Oaks: Sage Publications Inc.

Chapter 4

Cultural and sexual identities in in-depth interviewing[1]

Constantinos N. Phellas

Introduction

A number of methodological studies have pinpointed the importance of the differences between the researcher and the interviewee in in-depth interviewing with regard to gender, class and race and the effect these differences might have upon the interview process. In the main, these studies have concentrated on the politics and ethics of social research, with gender and race being the dominating themes in most of the feminists' critiques and Black analysts' criticisms (Carby 1982; Phoenix 1988; Collins 1990). So far, very little work has been done on the various assumptions made by the interviewees regarding the sexual and cultural identity of the researcher and what data there are tend to be impressionistic rather than based on a methodological approach (see Chung 1985; Bhabha 1990; Hall 1988, 1991).

Furthermore, little attention has been given to how the sexual and cultural identities of researchers may shape the research situations when interviewing persons of the same or partially shared racial and/or ethnic and sexual background.

Within this category falls a significant section of the homosexual and bisexual community that is difficult to reach and about whose sexual behaviour we have little substantial or reliable knowledge. This 'hidden population' refers to the category of men from ethnic minority groups who have sex with other men (and often women).

Ethnic minority men who have sex with men share common life experiences. They are all exposed to racial and cultural discrimination. The experiences of racism, identity conflict, oppression and cultural adaptation, as well as the stressful environments in which these men often live, tend to create a tenacious bond among them – a bond crucial to their survival.

This chapter has evolved out of some experiences I had as a researcher on the social and sexual lifestyles of Cypriot men who have sex with men in the Cypriot community living in London. I would suggest that the unfolding of the researcher's and the interviewee's cultural and sexual identities is central to the ways in which the researcher and the researched position themselves in relation to the 'other'. It is also important if the research itself aims to be both emancipatory and anti-discriminatory.

In this chapter, I aim to show that any claims of commonalities or differences by interviewees did not necessarily shape the interview process in any predictable or systematic way. On the contrary, such claims were very much contingent upon each moment in each interview.

By providing some examples of my respective interview experiences I shall try and demonstrate the potentially plastic nature of the relationship between the researcher and the interviewee where they share some sexual, racial and/or ethnic commonality. I shall also attempt to highlight the issue of the way in which the interviewer and the research process itself can be used as an emancipatory tool and a catalyst in redefining and renegotiating one's sense of self-identity. This is especially important in research in sensitive areas such as sexuality and HIV/AIDS within ethnic minority groups where the respondents cannot talk about their experiences and feelings out of fear of discrimination and rejection by the family and the community.

The literature on identity formation of minority persons

Coming to terms with one's identity as an ethnic and racial minority gay man involves a process of awareness of this multiple minority status (Morales 1990). During this evolution the individual tries to reconcile the different dynamics that emerge from his ethnic and racial minority in contrast to those that emerge from his sexual minority status. Cory and LeRoy (1963) were among the first ones to research the conflicts and struggles that ethnic minority gay men and lesbians were experiencing. Their study was based on the lives of gay Puerto Ricans and gay Blacks as being compounded by a rock-bottom social status. The concept of double stigma was first introduced and the personal accounts of those people were viewed from that perspective. Hendin's (1969) study of twelve Black male suicides in Harlem confirmed the earlier findings by Cory and LeRoy that the double stigma can have enormous and destructive consequences on one's mental and physical health. In their study, Cory and LeRoy noted that out of the twelve suicides four related to gay men in reaction to the double stigma of being a racial and sexual minority. Furthermore, they reported that the Black men's attempt to form sexual relationships with White men resulted in an unsatisfactory form of escape from feelings of personal inferiority and rejection.

Over the last two decades various theoretical models have been developed in an attempt to describe the development and formation of the homosexual identity. Troiden (1988), however, has identified a number of similarities between these:

- the importance of the stigma surrounding homosexuality;
- the lengthy time taken in developing a full gay identity and the changes embodied therein;
- the gradual acceptance of the word 'homosexual' as a label referring to one's self; and
- a gradual desire to come out to others.

Troiden used the above-mentioned approaches in conjunction with his earlier model to arrive at the 'ideal–typical' model, which is described below:

Stage 1: Sensitisation – the childhood period which is characterised by 'generalised feelings of marginality';
Stage 2: Identity confusion – the realisation that the person is engaging in homosexual behaviour and that they may be homosexual;
Stage 3: Identity assumption – characterised by the acceptance of the sexual identity, 'gay man' or 'lesbian';
Stage 4: Commitment – presents the adoption of homosexuality as a way of living. Both Coleman (1982) and Troiden (1979) have suggested that entering a 'same-sex love relationship' marks the onset of this stage.

I would like in the following paragraphs to summarise two other models which deal with minority groups: (1) ethnic minorities (Atkinson *et al.* 1979); and (2) ethnic minority lesbians and gays (Morales 1983). These models have been useful in gaining a better understanding of the identity formation process for these groups.

Ethnic minority gay men

Morales (1983) proposed an identity formation model for ethnic minority gays and lesbians that incorporates the dual minority status of this group. This process seems to centre around five different states. Each state is accompanied by decreasing anxiety and tension through the management of the tensions and differences. As cognitive and lifestyle changes emerge, the multiple identities become integrated, leading towards a greater sense of understanding of one's self and towards the development of a multicultural perspective. The advantage of this model is that it proposes different states rather than stages. Therefore, it is possible that persons may experience several states or parts of states at the same time, unlike a stage model in which resolution of one stage leads to another. In the following paragraphs the different states are considered.

State 1: Denial of conflicts

During this state the person tends to minimise the validity and reality of the discrimination they experience as an ethnic person, and to believe that they are being treated the same as others. Their sexual orientation may or may not be defined, but they feel their personal lifestyle and sexual preference have limited consequences in their life. They may identify themselves as gay or bisexual. Morales argues that an idealistic and utopian philosophy of life tends to dominate their perception of reality and their ability to predict how others see them. They tend to attract White lovers, with the central focus of attraction being race or ethnicity.

State 2: Bisexual versus gay

This state argues that there is a preference for some ethnic minority gays to identify themselves as bisexual rather than gay. They sense that they are neither exclusively heterosexual nor exclusively homosexual. Upon examining their sexual lifestyles there may be no difference between those who identify themselves as gay as compared to those identified as bisexual. Can the above cause a conflict in their sexual identity formation? Morales believes not, as the ethnic minorities distinguish a difference in two ways: first, in the way they conceptualise and perceive sexuality; and second, in they way they perceive the gay community as an extension of the White racist society.

Another way sexuality may be viewed by the ethnic minority person is by perceiving the gay community as White, as not inclusive of people of colour, and thereby as racist. The Cypriot gay men may experience the challenges of being racial and ethnic minority persons as extraordinary both in the main-stream society and in the White gay community. As a result, they prefer to socialise with the Cypriot community and to be referred to as bisexual rather than gay.

State 3: Conflicts in allegiance

During this state the member of an ethnic minority becomes uneasy and uncomfortable as he becomes aware of both his ethnic minority status and his homosexuality. The ethnic minority person faces a series of dilemmas (e.g. mixing the different parts of his life; keeping them separate; about taking sides; about betraying either the ethnic minority or the gay community), which cause him a lot of anxiety and cause for concern. His ethnic background dictates to him the importance of the family as a means of survival against the mainstream society. The gay community points to the common struggles of gays as a way to emphasise the need for unity across cultures and nationalities. Morales suggests that such dilemmas provoke uneasiness as the ethnic minority gay man fluctuates among them. He then introduces the notion of multiple identities as a means of reducing the conflict. Enabling the person to prioritise these allegiances and examining the supportive aspects of each community tends to shift the conflict from a monocultural perspective into a multicultural dimension in which his life can be viewed as containing multiple identities.

State 4: Establishing priorities in allegiance

A primary identification with the ethnic community prevails in this state and feelings of resentment concerning the lack of integration among the communities becomes a central issue. There are feelings of anger and rage stemming from their experiences of rejection by the gay community because of their ethnicity. These feelings, coupled with the personal history of the person, encourage a primary identification with their ethnic minority community. It is not uncommon during this state to see the ethnic minority gay man separating White gay friends from ethnic friends and developing relationships with persons who have similar community allegiances. Morales argues that the person has to be encouraged to develop a proactive rather than a reactive or victim perspective in their relationships and allegiances. An example, he continues, of a proactive, affirmative attitude is the reluctance of the individual to be referred to as an ethnic minority person. The term 'minority' carries an oppressive connotation and people should be encouraged to use their ethnic identification (i.e. Cypriot man).

State 5: Integrating the various communities

As a gay person of colour the need to integrate his lifestyle and develop a multicultural perspective becomes a major concern. Optimising the use of social and support groups becomes more important. Adjusting to the reality of limited options becomes a source of anxiety, facilitating feelings of isolation and alienation. The pressure to be the bridge between their ethnic minority community and for the gay community presents a constant challenge to the issues of allegiance and may result in feeling misunderstood. According to Morales, the anxiety and tension around these issues can be minimised if the ethnic minority gay man is encouraged to build his confidence in his judgement in assessing others and to expand his support system to include persons with similar multicultural perspectives.

   These studies show that there are particular problems faced by gay men and lesbians in identity formation, which are not confronted by heterosexuals. The issues highlighted here form the backdrop against which my own research was conducted.

Cypriot men having sex with men

My study involved extensive in-depth interviews with some twenty-six Cypriot (both Turkish and Greek) men who have sex with men (whether gay-identified or not) in the Cypriot community living in London. Interviewees were reached in the main through advertisements in the gay press, the local community paper and through social networks. My first name appeared in all the ads and leaflets and that enabled the respondents to guess in advance that I was of Greek origin.

What they did not know, however, was whether I was born in London or in Cyprus. One of the first questions that I was asked in the original letter of introduction or during the initial telephone conversation concerned my racial identity and, more specifically, my family's residence. That vital piece of information would have indicated to them whether I was classified as an ethnic minority person. Questions about my sexuality were often asked at the beginning of the interview or at different times during the interview, whereas questions about my cultural background were asked during the initial telephone conversation.

This was equally important as for all the respondents it was the first time they had had the chance to talk about how it felt to be Cypriot and have sex with other men as well. They felt comfortable talking to me. It is not surprising that I was asked on numerous occasions to go out on a social basis with them.

It was important for me to find the commonalities and work along with them rather than try and locate any differences. On the other hand, any claims of commonality or difference by interviewees did not necessarily shape the interview process in a predictable or systematic way; such claims were very much contingent upon each moment in each interview.

During the interviews I found myself in situations where interviewees either openly or indirectly claimed points of commonality or difference in relation to me, based upon both known or presumed information about me and my life experiences.

Commonalities

Those with strongly-held Greek identities were also keen to establish: 'How Greek are you?'; 'Can you speak Greek?'; 'Where were you born?'; 'Where does your family currently reside?' All the above served as markers about my own racial background.

All the interviews were conducted in English, although I offered the Greek respondents the chance to talk in Greek if they wished to do so. The language ability (i.e. to be able to speak Greek) served as a marker of cultural identity during the interview.

Language maintenance is an important aspect of identity, and as Taylor and Giles argue in *Language and Ethnic Relations* (1979) language is more than an indicator of ethnicity; it is fairly central to the creation, definition and maintenance of social categories. The fact that a lot of my Greek interviewees could not speak Greek properly made them feel embarrassed and nervous as to how they were perceived by myself. At various times throughout the interview they would throw in one or two Greek words just to show that they had a knowledge and understanding of the language.

However, there were also several ways in which commonalities with me were claimed by those I was interviewing. The fact that my research was academic and I was there to study a subject that has never been studied before gave them the chance to express their dissatisfaction with being Greek or Turkish and sometimes living with their family. All of them have chosen to stress the negative aspects of the Greek/Turkish culture with regard to the tolerance and acceptance of homosexuality.

Furthermore, they have attached to my research work a professional status different from the one that a health authority might have given to it. Academics are well respected in the Cypriot community and enjoy as much status and respect as doctors and religious people do. Their authority carries a certain weight and their work is seldom questioned or challenged. In their eyes, I was like a kind of counsellor who was supposed to have all the answers up my sleeve, hence my decision to research the issue of homosexuality in the Cypriot culture. They assumed that I myself also had had enough of the way Cypriot people regarded homosexuality and sexuality in general with its double standards and hypocrisies.

They assumed that because I had decided to study this particular social issue in my culture I was starting from a negative position and I was there to criticise it and highlight its drawbacks. As a matter of fact, they saw me as a kind of saviour, as they believed that my research would finally change social attitudes towards homosexuality in the Cypriot culture. Common responses as to how they perceived my research were:

> 'I am sure you know how I feel then.' 'It is about time somebody has written something about Cypriots.' 'I would like to see this work published.' 'Hopefully with this piece of work a lot of people would read it and learn something from it.'

As one of my respondents said:

> You know very well, Constantinos, and I am sure I am not the only one to tell you this, that Cypriot families can be very suffocating. I have this terrible fear, and it comes from my childhood that my family are going to swallow me up, because there is a thing about Greek-Cypriot families which is so suffocating, where they want to know what you're doing, who you are doing it with, you know what I mean. (R06)

Criticism about the hypocrisy of the Cypriot culture towards sexuality and homosexuality together with its double standards was a recurrent feature in the interviews. Those talking to me often made sense of their own identities by laying bare their assumptions about mine. They assumed that I was sharing their hostility about the way they felt about their families and community.

Nobody asked me whether I was proud about my identity and about being Greek. On the contrary; not only did they see me as a professional person but also as somebody who was there to spill the beans to the rest of the world about the drawbacks of our culture. Another one said the following:

Most definitely, Cypriots have very strong values and one of the strong values they breed into you from the earliest age is that you will have a family one day, children and wife. That thing has been planted into my consciousness from such an age that it's difficult to shift now. I am sure Constantinos, you have experienced the same pressures from your family, haven't you? (R04)

Sometimes my sexual lifestyle and preferences, marital status and HIV status were far more important to them than my Greekness. It was only after I prompted them to think of what aspects in our culture they like most that they stopped and said:

It's the upbringing. That's just within us; that's one of the many things I like about being Cypriot. When I've been knocking, I've been telling you about the things I haven't liked about the Cypriot way of life. You are right, actually, there's an awful lot of things I do like, the hospitality and there's the nosiness, on the other hand, there's the open nature; there's the intrusion into your space, and there's the tactility and the warmth. The closeness of people; we're very much like Jewish communities in that respect. (R12)

Differences

However, when we touched on the subject of racial harassment and discrimination, experiences of commonality could not have been assumed. 'You are lucky for being born and bred in Cyprus' and 'People who were born in Cyprus had a different upbringing from ours' were common remarks made by my respondents. As a result of that I could not relate to some of the experiences they described to me. Three of my interviewees had been abused because of their colour, and sometimes because of their sexual orientation if they were unfortunate at school and gave away their sexual preferences. I felt I could not help or show a deeper understanding of the situation apart from my usual humane interest.

I can remember being accepted at the age of 10 at an all-boys comprehensive school [name withheld]. I remember being very happy because I knew I was gay then so I must have known before, I've always felt attracted to boys but didn't know what the word was; I just assumed everybody was. When I went to school I realised it was wrong. ... I was bullied at school both because of my cultural background and soft nature. I knew then it was wrong but wasn't aware beforehand. ... I think the other boys at school knew I was gay, they sensed it, I don't know why. No, I do know why, I was more sensitive than they were so I suppose I was an easy target and I never denied it. ... I was an easy target because I was not English and the discrimination felt even bigger. (R06)

> What I am going to tell you now might sound strange to you as you were not born and bred in this country. ... I am not a racist but I had bad experiences since I was a kid with the English people. It's just a different culture, different way of thinking. Different experience. Me and my Turkish, Black and Asian friends sit around and we'll say, 'Do you remember when we were kids and used to go round to White people's houses and they used to say "Sorry, it's time for Johnnie's dinner now, could you go home please", whereas if you go round to an Indian household or Turkish household you'll get fed all the time.' (R07)

> I was speaking to somebody the other day who was Turkish Cypriot and he is thinking of going back and telling his parents. I said, 'It's different for you because you've got a life in this country. You've left your parents there. If I told my parents it would affect my outlook and the way I look on this country ... as soon as you get on that plane you've left your parents, left what you've said and come to this country. You can pick up your life. You've always been known in this country as a gay man. Whereas in Turkey you haven't been so just leave it.' I think there is a big difference between mainland Turks and Turkish Cypriots. The majority of mainland Turks that come over here don't have an established community. The Greek Cypriots and Turkish Cypriots do have an established community. ... You are lucky Constantinos that your family doesn't live here, so you can be your self. (R08)

A further complication arose when interviewing bisexual or heterosexual Cypriot men who happen to have sex with other men. The assumption made here was that I was bisexual/heterosexual myself and that I was enjoying having sex with women and men as well:

> I know I can talk to you because you are a man. I do not like the effeminate gays who are out and about. I like having sex with men like yourself, normal guys you know. (R10)

Again, the assumption was made that because I was appearing to be a 'normal' man, then women and men would fall at my feet. That presented a problem, however, as I could not fully relate to their feelings and experiences. On the other hand, the positioning of me as someone 'Cypriot and born and bred in Cyprus' could be suspended when shared experiences of coming out and bereavement issues were being discussed. So when sexual identity was the subject matter, shared experiences could override attributions of me having lived and having been brought up in Cyprus. A lot of my respondents saw my sexual orientation as a basis for greater mutual understanding. The experiences of being Cypriot and gay were always assumed to be a key point of commonality between the interviewees and myself; to acknowledge and recognise this commonality was important in establishing trust and a safe environment between us. It was my responsibility to provide a context within which comments seen as socially undesirable and unacceptable in the outside world are acceptable in the interview setting.

Interviewees' assumptions about my sexual orientation were central in shaping what respondents chose to disclose to me and in what manner. It seemed to me that the more I disclosed about my own sexual lifestyle, family background, coming out and personal relationships, the more safe they felt to open up to me. The presumptions about my sexual life when I asked about one-night stands ('Everybody does it, don't you?'), the fact that I shared the same sexual orientation with some of them, gave them the presumption that the form of our lives would be the same. How do I explain to them that although the content of our lives might be the same (sexual orientation) the form could be completely different? Again, when I was discussing drugs with them, and more specifically the use of Ecstasy, I was asked directly by one of my respondents whether I was taking any drugs or using any other substance. When I answered that I have never taken Ecstasy, he showed surprise. Again, a presumption is being made that because of my sexual orientation I would have at least tried it.

What my research demonstrated was the complexity of these identifications and dis-identifications; so many dimensions of sameness and difference can be operating at any given moment. And where two people may claim commonality in one dimension, they may fall apart in another.

Relationships

Those who were single would have liked to have met someone and form a relationship. They would have preferred somebody from their own culture but their prejudices and misconceptions made them believe that it was extremely difficult to find such a Cypriot man. They had a negative image of other gay Cypriots. They claimed that most of them are very effeminate. Therefore, they turned to the mainstream gay scene in order to find potential partners. The ones who were in a relationship (all the relationships were with non-Cypriot men) admitted that it would have made a difference to be with another Cypriot man, but due to the reasons mentioned above they had formed relationships with men that they had met in the mainstream gay scene.

Another contentious marker of cultural identity was people's intimate relationships with friends and partners. There were times in a number of interviews when I was asked my opinion on certain problems they were facing with their partners, including the ones that were due to different cultural backgrounds. It felt that unless I disclosed information about myself and my experiences, the interview would not have developed in the way I would have liked it to do.

CP: Do you feel that you are chasing a dream by wanting to have a relationship with a Cypriot man although you are currently in a relationship with somebody else who is not Cypriot?

R: No, no. I would like to believe that I'm a realist. I think that's possible, yes. I don't know. Why do you think it's a dream wanting to have a Cypriot lover and share all the things my culture has to offer us? Did you have a bad experience with a Cypriot lover? (R03)

During the interviews I noticed that there was an interest about me being single or in a relationship. As one remarked, 'I thought you would be with somebody … you have no worries, after all … you have come out to your parents, they don't live here, so nothing stops you from being yourself'. Again, the assumption was made that because I was doing a piece of research on a controversial subject such as Cypriot homosexuality I had full control in all the other aspects of my life. They perceived me as somebody more superior, better than them. In a way I was perceived as being one step ahead of them as I was representing (from the outside) all the things they were not. For these reasons I don't know how much of their responses were subject to the *social desirability effect* – a situation in which respondents say what they think the researcher wants to hear rather than what they believe (Ostrow and Kessler 1993).

Impact on the researcher

Additionally, the interviews presented a dilemma for the interviewer himself. The fact that I was interviewing Cypriots has brought home to me the different connections that one can have and establish with people from one's own culture. I have been living in this country since 1981 and all my relationships have been with non-Cypriot men. I do visit Cyprus very often because of my family but until the start of the research I was not involved with any Cypriot gay men. Getting in contact with other gay Cypriots has brought home a sense of nostalgia about men from my own culture. Admittedly, for me it was somehow difficult to stay unmoved by their individual stories and personal accounts. The contact that I had with my Cypriot respondents in my research profoundly affected my conceptualisation of cultural identity. These shared experiences (problems of accepting one's sexuality, issues of coming out to the family, dealing with family pressure to get married, secrecy, double lives, mental stress, etc.) encouraged me to get in touch with my Greek identity and brought back a sense of belonging.

It made me realise that I have already started coming home after a long period of inner searching. I caught myself wanting to defend my culture when the respondents were criticising it. I found myself wanting to tell them that once the initial period of rejection has passed they would realise that wherever they go they carry themselves with them. I have already experienced what they were going through. It was more of a case of wanting to say to them, 'Don't worry, it's going to be fine in the end. You are a loveable and a good person irrespective of your family's reaction towards your sexuality.' Their experiences served as a reminder to me of how far I have travelled and what I have experienced, and made me realise how fortunate and blessed I am to have arrived at this point and, doing research on a topic that has caused me so much pain and difficulty in the past.

Conclusion

In this chapter I have attempted to convey something of the multifaceted reality of doing research with people of the same or partially shared ethnic and sexual background. As a researcher I was surprised to see the extent to which my sexual and cultural identity was directly or indirectly questioned or commented upon by respondents.

More attention needs to be paid to the assumptions that interviewees make about the sexual and cultural identity of the interviewer and to how and in what ways these assumptions affect the unfolding of the interview: the interviewees may disclose certain kinds of information based on their assumptions about the researcher (social desirability effect); they might decide to give their personal accounts and describe their life stories and identities in terms which compare themselves to assumptions about the researcher. Commonalities and differences are interchangeable throughout the interview process. Markers of cultural and sexual identity, such as language fluency, place of birth, family's residence, coming out to the family, being in a relationship and living with a male partner, can be the basis for claims of either commonality or difference. I would argue that such claims are very much contingent upon each moment in each interview and it is only when each interview is examined separately and individually that some of the debates about sexual and cultural identity and the research process can be further explored in any depth. Sometimes I wonder whether I would have been able to obtain as much information from the interviewees had I still been in the closet myself. Personally, I do not believe that my respondents would have disclosed the same richness of information had I been seen to be heterosexual.

Note

1   This chapter is dedicated to John Christie.

References

Atkinson, D., Morton, G. and Sue, D. (1979) *Counselling American Minorities*, Dubuque, IA: William C. Brown.

Bhabha, H. (1990) 'The Third Space', in J. Rutherford (ed.) *Identity: Culture, community, difference*, London: Lawrence and Wishart.

Carby, H. (1982) 'White woman listen! Black feminism and the boundaries of sisterhood', in Centre for Contemporary Cultural Studies, *The Empire Strikes Back*, London: Hutchinson, pp. 212–36.

Chung, Y.C. (1985) *At the Palace: Work, ethnicity and gender in a Chinese restaurant*, Studies in Sexual Politics, no. 3, Manchester: Department of Sociology, University of Manchester.

Collins, P.H. (1990) *Black Feminist Thought*, London: HarperCollins.

Coleman, E. (1982) 'Developmental stages of the coming-out process', in W. Paul *et al.* (eds), *Homosexuality: Social, psychological, and biological issues*, Beverly Hills: Sage.

Cory, D. and LeRoy, J. (1963) *The Homosexual and his Society: a view from within*, New York: Citadel Press.

Hall, S. (1988) 'New ethnicities', in *Black Film, British Cinema*, London: ICA 7.

—— (1991) 'Old and new identities, old and new ethnicities', in A. King (ed.) *Culture, Globalisation and the World System*, Binghamton: State University of New York.

Hendin, H. (1969) *Black Suicide*, New York: Basic Books.

Morales, E. (1983) 'Third-World gays and lesbians: a process of multiple identities', paper presented at the 91st National Convention of the American Psychological Association, Anaheim, California.

—— (1990) 'Ethnic minority families and minority gays and lesbians', in F. Bozett and M. Sussman (eds) *Homosexuality and Family Relations*, New York: The Haworth Press.

Ostrow, D. and Kessler, R. (eds) (1993) *Methodological Issues in AIDS Behavioral Research*, New York: Plenum Press.

Phoenix, A. (1988) 'Narrow definitions of culture', in S. Westwood and P. Bhachu (eds) *Enterprising Women*, London: Routledge.

Taylor, D.M. and Giles, H. (1979) 'At the crossroads of research into language and ethnic relations', in H. Giles and B. Saint-Jacques (eds) *Language and Ethnic Relations*, New York: Pergamon Press.

Troiden, R.R. (1979) 'Becoming homosexual: a model of gay identity acquisition', *Psychiatry* 42: 362–73.

—— (1988) *Gay and Lesbian Identity*, New York: General Hall.

Part II

The research process and social action

Chapter 5

Gender, 'race' and power in the research process

South Asian women in East London

Kalwant Bhopal

Introduction

This chapter will examine the methodological difficulties encountered when a South Asian woman conducts research on a South Asian community. What difference does 'race', gender and personal experience make to the research process? How do personal experiences affect the research process? I will discuss the use of a feminist methodology in conducting the research and reflect upon the ways in which my structural position, as a South Asian woman, influenced the research process and affected problems of access, the influence of personal experience and issues of power. It will be argued that collaborative, qualitative forms of research may carry advantages in conducting research incorporating a feminist methodology, whilst at the same time issues of 'race', power and status may affect and make us question what a feminist methodology includes.

The research question

The research attempts to critique existing theories of patriarchy (Walby 1990) and argues there is a continuum between two forms of patriarchy (private and public). As South Asian women have different cultural experiences to White women (they have arranged marriages and are given dowries), it is assumed forms of patriarchy that exist for South Asian women in Britain will be different to forms of patriarchy that exist for White women in Britain. Do existing theories of patriarchy apply to South Asian communities in Britain? Do private and public forms of patriarchy exist for South Asian women in Britain?

Methodology

The methods used were sixty in-depth interviews with South Asian women living in East London, and participant observation, which included living with a South Asian community for a period of six months. I wanted my methods to be sensitive enough to allow the categories of analysis to emerge from the data and to use methods which would allow me to investigate the varying significance of difference through which women experienced patriarchy. At the same time, I wanted to present accurate information regarding the numbers of women who experienced different forms of patriarchy and test for the strength of associations between different influences of patriarchy. Hence, a combination of quantitative and qualitative methods were used in the study. Qualitative data is defined as a process used to make sense of data that are represented by words or pictures and not by numbers (Snyder 1992). The processes of qualitative research include ways of conceptualising, collecting, analysing and interpreting data. The use of qualitative data enables researchers to gain insight into the lives of respondents and the meanings they give to their experiences. However, the use of quantitative research allows the researcher to describe the characteristics of a population, as well as to model statistically events and processes occurring within the population.

Prior to constructing the interview schedule, pilot focus groups were carried out with South Asian women in which a number of topics such as arranged marriages, dowries, domestic labour, domestic finance, education, employment and religion were discussed. Issues raised in the focus groups enabled me to construct my interview schedule, allowing for sensitivity for certain questions. This interview schedule was then further piloted to test for wording, order and sensitivity of questions. The data was analysed qualitatively to investigate the meanings women gave to their lives. It was analysed quantitatively to test for the strength of associations between variables.[1] Chi square tests of significance were used to examine the relationships between different influences of patriarchy (religion, education and employment) on women's lives (arranged marriages, dowries, domestic labour and domestic finance). If the chi square value was less than 0.05 the correlation was shown to be highly significant.

The sample

A very specific group of South Asian women was investigated. Here, 'South Asian' was defined as those whose ancestors had originated from the Indian sub-continent: India, Pakistan and Bangladesh. The ages of the women ranged from 25 to 30 years old and they had all been born in the UK. Three groups were investigated to examine the impact of religious difference: women who defined themselves as either Hindu, Sikh or Moslem. Twenty women from each religious group were interviewed to examine the impact of religion on forms of patriarchy experienced by South Asian women. A total of sixty in-depth interviews were carried out with South Asian women living in East London. East London was taken as a specific area to be investigated as it includes a very high population of South Asians from all three religious backgrounds.

The respondents were from different educational backgrounds: 12 per cent had no formal qualifications, 3 per cent had CSEs (Certificate of Secondary Education), 27 per cent had 'O' levels (Ordinary levels), 7 per cent had 'A' levels (Advanced levels) and 10 per cent had HNDs (Higher National Diplomas). Yet others had pursued a higher level of education: 27 per cent of respondents had BAs (Batchelor of Arts degrees) and 15 per cent had MAs (Master of Arts degrees). The occupational background of respondents also varied considerably: 7 per cent were non-earning housewives, 2 per cent were self-employed, 23 per cent were employed in skilled manual occupations and 15 per cent in semi-skilled occupations. Other respondents were from higher occupational backgrounds: 13 per cent were in semi-professional occupations, 2 per cent were in professional occupations and 18 per cent were students.

South Asian women are a very difficult group to study, based on their cultural definitions and strong views regarding male and female roles within their communities. They are a very close-knit group who have and portray a very strong, cohesive sense of belonging and security (Bhopal 1995). There is no obvious sampling frame for South Asian women. The sampling method used was snowball sampling. Once I had made initial contact with a few women, other women were recommended to be interviewed. The respondents were easily accessible as they had already spoken to someone who had participated in the research and I had less chance of being viewed with suspicion. The respondents respected me and felt comfortable, secure and safe that I had entered the homes of other South Asian women they were acquainted with. Other women were contacted through advertisements placed at the local university and in the local student paper to prompt respondents to contact me. In snowball sampling the researcher has no control over the nature of the sample. There is always the danger that the sample will be heavily skewed in favour of particular types of women. I tried to overcome this by using different starting points from which to contact my respondents. On the one hand, the sample may be unrepresentative as it is a snowball sample. On the other, the sample can claim to be representative as different starting points were used to encourage women to participate and there was a diverse approach to contacting respondents.

Feminist methodologies

In carrying out my research, I have been guided by my understanding of feminist methodologies. Whilst most writers on feminist methodological issues agree there is no one method that can be termed *the* feminist methodology, certain characteristics can be drawn out (Cook and Fonow 1990; Harding 1987; Stanley and Wise 1983). There is not necessarily one feminist methodology, but many different feminist methodologies. Feminist critiques point to a male bias within sociology which structures the knowledge base of the discipline and the social relations of production. It is argued that gender bias is introduced through the theoretical frameworks and methods by which empirical investigations are conducted. However, feminist research methodology has certain principles that are considered to be of importance at all stages of research. First, women's lives need to be addressed in their own terms, using the language and categories in which women express themselves to define their own situation. It is important to reflect the language of women who participate in research, so that women's words are not distorted. Second, feminist research should not just be *on* women but *for* women, to provide for women explanations of their lives which can be used to improve their situation. Research should have emancipatory potential. Third, a feminist methodology involves putting the researcher into the process of production, where the researchers can make explicit the reasoning procedures they utilised in carrying out the research and be self-reflexive about their own perceptions and biases which they bring to the research.

Within feminist methodologies the debate between quantitative and qualitative methods includes the claim that quantitative research techniques, involving the translation of an individual's experiences into categories predefined by researchers, may distort women's experiences and result in a silencing of women's own voices. Advocates of qualitative methods have argued that individual women's understandings, emotions and actions in the world can be explored in women's own terms. Jayaratne and Stewart (1990) argue that much of the feminist debate about qualitative and quantitative research has been sterile and based on a false polarisation, and that the solutions offered for methodological problems have frequently been either too general or too constraining to be realistically incorporated into research activity. In the present research I have aimed to incorporate the ideas of a feminist methodology: non-hierarchical, non-authoritarian, non-manipulative and aiming to empower women. This has enabled me to examine and question the differences and similarities (in terms of gender and 'race') which exist between the researcher and the researched and how this affects access, the influence of personal experience and issues of power.

The method

The aim was to build up a detailed knowledge of women's lives, their feelings towards their own roles and what they actually did in the home, their attitudes towards arranged marriages, dowries, domestic labour and domestic finance. As the researcher, I faced the problem of reconciling the discrepancies of differing accounts of participants. For example, there may be a discrepancy between what a woman actually does in the household and what she thinks she does. This in turn may differ from what the community expects her to do. Finally, what she is prepared to admit to an interviewer may also differ, as will what the interviewer perceives to be important enough to report in the study. There are also likely to be further discrepancies of the accounts women give of their partner's behaviour (participation in domestic tasks), accounts which are likely to consist of a mix of facts, expressions of opinion and implicit and explicit value judgements.

I set up the interviews to explore the research questions and to be topically guided, yet informal in style and tone and, in some respects, conversational and free-flowing. I encouraged respondents to discuss what they perceived as the important dimensions of the issues outlined above and to do so in the language and categories they deemed meaningful. I wanted to approximate as much as possible a chat between friends. Due to the instrumental task at hand, however, most visible through the questions, the interviews were different from pure conversations; they were 'conversations with a purpose' (Burgess 1984). The flexibility of the interviews facilitated the emergence of new and unanticipated data and, overall, a diverse range of information was collected. The interviews were tape-recorded, with the exception of five. I sought to preserve as much of the interview situation in the transcripts as possible, including such speech events as respondent's false starts, repetitions and non-verbal expressions, such as laughing and getting emotional. There is no one method for investigating speech and individuals usually decide on the basis of some (often implicit) theory of speech and what set of conventions to use in the creation of transcripts.

The traditional approach to the inclusion of respondent's speech within the text is to polish the speech, for example, by omitting repetition and translating slang into standard English, so that it reads more smoothly than ordinary speech. Whilst I have omitted repetition in participant's speech, I have chosen to reflect the language of the women who participated. As Devault (1990) notes, it is through such translation processes that women's words are often distorted. Language itself reflects male experiences and its categories are often incongruent with women's lives. Devault's understanding of what it means to talk or listen 'as a woman' is based on the concept of 'women's standpoint'. Devault (1990) argues that parts of women's lives disappear because they are not included in the language of the account. In order to 'recover' these parts of women's lives, researchers can develop methods for listening around and beyond words. We can analyse more specifically the ways in which interviewers use personal experience as a resource for listening. Feminist research can be conscious of listening as a process and work on learning to listen in ways that are personal, disciplined and sensitive to differences.

'Woman-to-woman' interviewing – the influence of 'race'

My structural position as a South Asian woman affected my research and has enabled me to examine the many-faceted complexities of the dynamics involved in woman-to-woman interviewing. The feminist approach to interviewing, which is exemplified in the work of Oakley (1981), argues that the research process should include statements and discourses about one's own experiences with the phenomena under question. The goal of finding out about people through interviewing is best achieved when:

the relationship of the interviewer and the interviewee is non-hierarchical and when the interviewer is prepared to invest his or her own personal identity in the relationship.

(Oakley 1981: 41)

This approach is also supported by Finch (1984) who argues that women more so than men are used to accepting intrusions into the more private parts of their lives. In the setting of the interviewee's own home, an interview conducted in an informal way by another woman can easily take on the character of an intimate conversation. Devault (1990) has argued that a feminist sociology can open up standard topics from the descriptive, building more from what we share with respondents as women, than from disciplinary categories that we bring to research encounters:

> women interviewing women bring to their interaction a tradition of 'woman talk', they help each other develop ideas and are typically better prepared than men to use the interview as a 'search procedure'.

(Devault 1990: 101)

I felt women were able to open up, trust and confide in me, which allowed them to reveal very personal and intimate details of their lives; for example, the abusive behaviour of their mothers-in-law. The same information may not have been obtained if the research was carried out by a South Asian male. However, Brah states:

> No matter how often the concept is exposed as vacuous, 'race' still acts as an apparently ineradicable marker of social difference.

(Brah 1992: 126)

Gender may not be enough to create the shared meanings which are necessary to understand the experiences of women's lives. Is it possible a White middle-class woman carrying out research within a Black working-class community may create a situation where there are barriers to understanding? Each individual woman has different cultural experiences. The lack of shared norms about how an interview is organised and unfamiliar cultural themes in the context of the interview create barriers to understanding:

> Gender congruity is not enough to overcome ethnic incongruity, the bond between the woman interviewer and the woman interviewee is insufficient to create the shared meanings that could transcend the divisions between them.

(Riessman 1987: 190)

'Race' infuses itself into the research process and into the interview situation in much the same way that it has been argued that a feminist methodology should do and that shared gender or sex does. 'Race' is a variable that assists both the researcher and the researched to place each other within the social structure and so can have bearings on the relationship between the researcher and the researched. Mies (1991), however, argues that the concept of 'partial identification' is important, that we proceed from our own contradictory state of being and consciousness. This enables recognition of that which binds us to the 'other women' as well as that which separates us from them. Binding us are the experiences of women all over the world, experiences of repression, sexism and exploitation. 'Partial identification' means we also recognise that which separates us, such as forms of oppression that might be rooted in such traits as skin colour, language and education. In these appearances, we see a manifestation of the power relations according to which the whole of society is structured. So 'partial identification', which begins with a double consciousness, means that as researchers we are aware of the structures within which we live and work. However, although our own gender, 'race' and class may enhance 'shared identity' within the research process and affect what we 'see' and how we are 'seen', our experience as competent researchers may also enhance the trust and rapport we seek with the researched. South Asian women who welcomed the opportunity to speak to me enabled this 'partial identification' to surface. I was able to see reality through the eyes of other South Asian women and share a sense of belonging and empathy. If a South Asian woman is able to get another South Asian woman to speak about her life, they not only have 'shared experience', 'shared empathy', but also 'shared identity' (Bhopal 1997).

Access

One of the most difficult parts of the research was finding women to interview. Some women were highly suspicious of my motives. They regarded me as some kind of 'secret investigator', and wanted to know what I intended doing with my tape-recorded information. One South Asian woman regarded me as a 'nosey girl', who had nothing better to do except 'listen to the private lives of respectable women'. Such women chose not to participate in the research. It is possible the research may have attracted certain *types* of women who like to talk about their lives, some of whom may possibly hold different (more progressive) attitudes to those who chose not to participate. The majority of women, however, were extremely friendly and welcomed me into their homes. They were glad to assist me and have someone take an interest in their lives who was willing to listen at great length on an aspect of their life they felt was 'highly trivial and unimportant'. The interview situation made them feel valued. As the women themselves were able to empathise and identify with me, they expected me to automatically understand their situation:

You should know what I mean, being an Asian woman.

In some instances, women did not see their own situation as being 'oppressive', yet I myself felt these women *were* being oppressed. In such cases, it was very difficult for me to stand back and not impose my own views of 'oppression' upon my subjects. For I was aware of my use of White, Western concepts of definition, such as 'oppression' and 'patriarchy'. In these cases, I had to leave aside my own personal views and see reality through the eyes of my respondents. Some respondents were also afraid of revealing personal aspects of their lives for fear of reprisal. In these instances, I found myself assuring confidentiality, to establish trust and rapport, as well as revealing personal details of my own life to develop trust and encourage respondents to participate in the research. The notion of access was extremely difficult. Problems of access were concerned with the difficulty of the group being studied. Such problems and questions help us to think whether we should be conducting research and understand the reasons why there are so few research projects in this area.

Personal experience

In my own research, my personal experiences were affecting my views of my respondents. As a South Asian woman, I felt their lives mirrored those lives of South Asian women I myself had close contact with: sisters, aunts and my mother. I began to question to what extent the lives of these women were different to the lives of my relatives and how their lives were different to my own? In being too close and familiar with the subject matter, there is a possibility that certain aspects may be overlooked. Alternatively, respondents may be aware of our knowledge of the subject matter and may withhold information they see as too obvious in the light of a 'shared reality'. When the researcher and the researched operate from shared realities, there may be a tendency to take too much for granted. Researchers may overlook certain aspects of participant's realities, because of presumed familiarity with those realities. Familiarity with the phenomena under study therefore risks blindness to certain details that may be important. As researchers, issues of 'over-rapport' are apparent. Striking an adequate balance between rapport and distance may overcome this, by being able to 'manufacture distance' (McCracken 1988), to create a crucial awareness of matters with which we may have blinding familiarity. This advice takes on added importance when the issues are highly private and personal. The notion of establishing a 'pretence awareness context', which portrays a message of not knowing or pretending not to know what the informant is talking about, is one possible strategy. Simmel's (1950) discussion of the 'stranger' accounts for intimate disclosures. Furthermore, playing the role of the objective stranger incorporates a structured balance between 'distance and nearness, indifference and involvement'. The implications of this for insiders is clear: to use the nearness and involvement afforded by shared experiences to gain access and establish trust, but maintain whenever possible the distance and mystery of the 'stranger', in order to encourage a full account of the participant's experience.

Power

The balance of power in the research shifted. In some cases, it was evident I had the power, as I was able to control the questions that were asked. I had the pen and the clipboard and I had access to the tape-recorder. In other instances, it was the women who had the power as they were able to decide what they wanted to tell me by withholding information. They could also decide to leave the research unexpectedly. In some instances, women defined the relationship as something that existed beyond the limits of the interview situation. Women wanted to establish an intimate relationship, a friendship. There existed a great tension between these relationships and the goals of the research project. I had the power because it was my decision if I wanted to continue a personal relationship with my respondents. I have decided to keep my relationships with my respondents as professional, research relationships. Because of the familiarity of the researcher with the subject matter and the casual style with which information is shared, the researcher's role may become confused. Informants may perceive researchers as experts who have all the answers. The women began to move beyond the interview questions and the interview situation and, in some cases, began to discuss the more personal and intimate details of their lives. I had to constantly remind myself that I was not a therapist, counsellor or a social worker. In this sense, Reinharz has argued research is:

> conducted on a rape model, the researchers take, hit and run. They intrude into their subject's privacy, disrupt their perceptions, utilise false pretences, manipulate the relationship and give little or nothing in return. When the needs of the researcher are satisfied, they break off contact with the subject.
>
> (Reinharz 1983: 95)

The power relationship between the researcher and the researched is two-way. Cotterill, in writing about issues of power and her own feelings of vulnerability in her research, talks of interviews as:

> fluid encounters where balances shift between and during different inter-view situations.
>
> (Cotterill 1992: 604)

The researcher's goal is always to gather information and thus the danger of exploitation and manipulation always exists no matter who conducts the research or who interviews whom. Finch acknowledges the power the researcher holds when she says: 'I have also emerged from interviews with the feeling that my interviewees need to know how to protect themselves from people like me' (1984: 80).

The relationship of power in the research process can be viewed as a continuum; individuals in the research process are not just passive. The researcher/researched dichotomy is one of power relations. The researcher can be both powerful and powerless in the research process. Issues of power in research are not of course just a question of feminist methodology, but concern all research as a privileged activity. Our status as researchers often gives us the power to initiate research: to define the reality of the 'other', to translate the social lives and language of the 'other' in terms that may not be their own. In the final analysis, the researcher departs with the data and the researched stay behind, sometimes no better off than before. To this extent, the researcher/researched relationship is an inherently unequal one, with the balance of power weighed disproportionately in favour of the researcher. Gender identity between interviewer and interviewee is not always enough to create common understandings or equalise the power relations between the two parties. The researcher, by virtue of having the data, has the power as to what to present.

Conclusion

The results of the research demonstrated that education has a significant impact upon women's lives (see Table 5.1 for the chi square test of significance between education and dowries). Women who had low levels of education were defined as 'traditional' women and experienced private patriarchy inside the household through the practice of arranged marriages and dowries. Women with high levels of education were defined as 'independent' women and experienced public patriarchy outside the household through education and the labour market. By adopting a participatory research strategy (non-hierarchical, non-authoritarian, non-manipulative, and empowering women), I have attempted to incorporate a feminist methodology. I have sought to prevent the repetition of established methodologies which have served to maintain and reinforce women's subordination. The methodology influenced the selection of methods to a great extent. It necessitated the use of methods which would allow me to investigate the meanings the South Asian women gave to their lives. My identity as a woman enabled a 'reciprocity', a sharing of knowledge on the basis of gender identity, to surface. My identity as a South Asian woman enabled me to understand the racism and discrimination my respondents had suffered. My personal experiences and cultural socialisation as a South Asian woman enabled me to understand the experiences of my respondents (arranged marriages and dowries). I was able to account for the power differences between myself and the respondents by recognising that my location in society affected the research relationship. The women themselves also benefited from the research project. They had the opportunity to talk to a 'sympathetic listener' and to tell their story, and for most women the interview process acted as a form of therapy. Many women said nobody had ever wanted to listen to what they had to say. Now they could be heard. To this extent, the research 'gave voice' to a silent group and helped to empower these women. Finally, in my aim to incorporate a feminist methodology, the reproduction of the report was produced in an accessible form where respondents were able to see the results and the final write-up.

However, in incorporating a feminist methodology, I would argue that the notion of woman-to-woman interviewing, as exemplified by Finch (1984) and Oakley (1981), is too simplistic to account for the complexities involved in 'race', power and status differences in the research process. Finch (*ibid.*) and Oakley (*ibid.*) argue that as both parties share a subordinate virtue of their gender, power relations between interviewer and interviewee are equalised. My experience of interviewing demonstrates that same-sex status is not enough to create shared understandings or eradicate power differentials between women. 'Race' is an added dimension which affects the research process. As researchers, we can individually consider which of the many social characteristics at issue are the most important to a particular situation ('race', class, caste, culture) and locate ourselves within a specific critical paradigm. This will enable us to be aware of all these commonalities and differences which exist in the research and acknowledge the very real differences between women. These commonalities and differences can be incorporated within the research process itself, from which we can base our judgements and come to our conclusions.

Table 5.1   The relationship between education and respondents' views on women and the giving of dowries

Relationship	Education (per cent)							Row total
	1	2	3	4	5	6	7	
Burden/disrespected	–	–	–	3	8	21	68	22
Sold to men	–	–	–	10	24	56	10	42
Have to be looked after	10	70	20	–	–	–	–	17
Cultural/historical	26	–	74	–	–	–	–	8
Parents demonstrate love/duty	33	–	67	–	–	–	–	12
Total	12	3	27	7	10	27	15	100

Note
Chi square value (24 degrees of freedom) = 0.00000
1 = None
2 = CSEs
3 = 'O' levels
4 = 'A' levels
5 = HND
6 = BA/BSc
7 = MA/MSc

At the methodological level, an awareness of the double consciousness that arises from being a member of an oppressed class (women) and a privileged class (scholars) enables feminist researchers to explore women's perception of their situation from an experiential base. Feminist researchers can utilise methods and adopt methodologies which best answer the particular research questions confronting them, but do so in ways which are consistent with feminist values and goals.

Note

1   Table 5.1 provides a chi square value for education. Chi square tests of significance were used to test for associations. If the chi square value was less than 0.05, the correlation was shown to be highly significant. The figures in each row add up to 100 per cent. The figures in each column indicate the total number of respondents who had no qualifications, CSEs, etc.

References

Bhopal, K. (1995) 'Women and feminism as subjects of Black study: the difficulties and dilemmas of carrying our research', *Journal of Gender Studies* 4 (2): 153–68.
—— (1997) *Gender, 'Race' and Patriarchy: A study of South Asian women*, Aldershot: Ashgate.
Brah, A. (1992) 'Difference, diversity, differentiation', in J. Donald and A. Rattansi (eds) *'Race', Culture and Difference*, London: Sage.
Burgess, A. (1984) *In The Field: An introduction to field research*, Boston: Allen and Unwin.
Cook, J. and Fonow, M. (1990) 'Knowledge and women's interests: issues of epistemology and methodology in feminist sociological research', in J. Nielsen (ed.) *Feminist Research Methods*, Boulder: West View.
Cotterill, P. (1992) 'Interviewing women: issues of friendship, vulnerability and power', *Women's Studies International Forum* 15 (5): 593–606.
Devault, M. (1990) 'Talking and listening from a woman's standpoint: feminist strategies for interviewing and analysis', *Social Problems* 37 (1): 96–116.
Finch, J. (1984) 'It's great to have someone to talk to: women interviewing women', in C. Bell and H. Roberts (eds) *Social Researching: Politics, problems, practice*, London: Routledge Kegan Paul.
Harding, S. (1987) *Feminism and Methodology*, Indiana: Bloomington.
Jayarante, T. and Stewart, A. (1990) 'Quantitative and qualitative methods in the social sciences', in J. Cook and M. Fonow (eds) *Beyond Methodology: Feminist scholarship as lived research*, Indiana: Indiana University Press.
McCracken, G. (1988) *The Long Interview*, Newbury Park: Sage.
Mies, M. (1991) 'Women's research or feminist research: the debate surrounding feminist science and methodology', in J. Cook and M. Fonow (eds) *Beyond Methodology: Feminist scholarship as lived research*, Indiana: Indiana University Press.
Oakley, A. (1981) 'Interviewing women: a contradiction in terms', in H. Roberts (ed.) *Doing Feminist Research*, London: Routledge Kegan Paul.

Reinharz, S. (1983) 'Experiential analysis; a contribution to feminist research', in G. Bowles and R. Klein (eds) *Theories of Women's Studies*, London: Routledge Kegan Paul.

Riessmann, C. (1987) 'When gender is not enough: women interviewing women', *Gender and Society* 1 (2): 172–208.

Simmel, G. (1950) *The Sociology of George Simmel*, New York: Free Press.

Snyder, S. (1992) 'Interviewing college students about their constructions of love', in J. Gilgun, K. Daly, and G. Handel, (eds) *Qualitative Methods in Family Research*, Newbury Park: Sage.

Stanley, L. and Wise, S. (1983) *Breaking Out: Feminist consciousness and feminist research*, London: Routledge Kegan Paul.

Walby, S. (1990) *Theorising Patriarchy*, Oxford: Basil Blackwell.

Chapter 6

Group inquiry

A democratic dialogue?

Julie Kent

Introduction

In this chapter I outline the features of participatory research and highlight some specific issues that arose when I was involved in *Group Inquiry*. This inquiry aimed to explore the educational experiences of student midwives as part of a national evaluation project carried out between 1991 and 1994 (Kent *et al.* 1994). I examine the work of Seyla Benhabib, whose discussion of discourse ethics and politics seems useful for understanding some of the issues raised by group inquiry and developing feminist participatory research methods.

Features of participatory research

Peter Reason outlines the ideas behind 'co-operative inquiry as an overall term to describe the various approaches to research with people' (1988: 1). He says the use of different terms to describe 'new paradigm' or post-positivist human inquiry highlights features of the method. The term 'co-operative inquiry' points to the importance of *co-operation* in the sharing of research tasks and working together to achieve inquiry aims. 'Participatory research' emphasises *participation* as central to the method. 'Collaborative inquiry' focuses attention on *collaboration*, and 'experiential inquiry' underlines the epistemological basis of the approach and *experience* as the foundation of valid knowledge claims. 'Action research' is underpinned by notions of *agency* and 'dialogical inquiry' uses the concept of *dialogue*. So we are given a view of research where active participants engage in dialogue, which draws on their experiences, and enables them to work together, in partnership. For me this offered exciting possibilities, a critique of traditional research, or what Heron (1981) calls 'orthodox scientific method', and scope for the production of research knowledge that importantly values people as self-directing, thinking and feeling beings, rather than objects to be manipulated or disenfranchised. In addition, participatory researchers often claim this approach has *emancipatory* potential (Maguire 1987). My interest here is to explore the significance of both participation and dialogue as central concepts and to examine their use and limitations. I use 'participatory research' as a generic term to describe this type of research but in my own work I emphasise that dialogue takes place in a face-to-face group. *Group inquiry* best describes the method I used to explore knowledge and power in midwifery education.

Reason says 'the ideology of co-operative inquiry tends toward that of direct democracy' (Reason 1994: 198). Participatory research is premised on a democratic ideal where the concept of participation may usefully be understood with reference to citizenship. So what view of citizens or subjects is implicated here? Who are the participants, and what are the conditions for participation? Much of the discussion in participatory researchers' work (Reason 1988; Heron 1981; Maguire 1987) conceives of the subject as an autonomous, or self-directing agent (Reason 1994). In so far as 'Being' is regarded as foundational, and experiential knowledge as 'the touchstone of the method' (Reason 1988: 5), participatory research inherits a classical liberal tradition that is both contentious and problematic as we shall see. The extent to which principles of equality can operate in the inquiry process requires closer examination. For although Reason acknowledges there may be different skills within the group and suggests that we 'need to be careful that any difference in power or status deriving from organizational or social position do not make it impossible to negotiate an open contract' (*ibid.*, 21) for the research, it is not made clear how this may be achieved. Moreover, Rowan's dialectical research cycle (Rowan 1981) may be firmly located within an Enlightenment project of emancipation and participants are expected to recognise, from the outset, their need for emancipation.[1] Participants are those who enter voluntarily into the inquiry process and who are both willing, and able, to accept the terms of participation. 'Authentic collaboration', says Heron, occurs when 'co-opted inquirers internalize issues to do with both the area and the method of inquiry. They will make the enterprise their own in a vigorous way'; where this does not occur 'any agreement reached is likely to be spurious' (Heron 1988: 55). The reaching of agreements, then, is also of critical importance for the inquiry to proceed and evidently these are accomplished through dialogue.

The importance of dialogue and communication in participatory research points to a number of issues for the legitimation and validation of the method. In effect, the quality of the dialogue, and effectiveness of communication, determines the extent to which agreements, or research outcomes, are to be accepted. In discussing and comparing two studies, one by Robertson (1984), the other by Davies (1986), Reason suggests that the potential for a successful inquiry group is contingent on good matching between members of the group and certain differences, in this case Davies's status as a senior lecturer and feelings of alienation from his work, 'mismatched' him to the students in the group in which he was involved. By contrast, in 'Robertson's inquiry groups there was a good match between her experience and interests and those of the groups she set up, and thus they had the potential of success from the beginning'

(Reason 1988: 21). Successful dialogue is, according to this view, contingent on the strength of similarities between participants and a principle of equality based on sameness. This is problematic, and by adopting a feminist analysis of participatory democratic politics I hope to show how we can move beyond this, by a better understanding of discourse ethics and politics as discussed by Seyla Benhabib. First, an outline of group inquiry.

Group inquiry

As part of a national evaluation project,[2] two groups of student midwives at two sites were invited to take part in group inquiry. The aim of the inquiry was to explore their educational experiences, their views of pre-registration midwifery education and what becoming a midwife might mean. Each group met every three to four months over a period of eighteen months. In the first site, fourteen students agreed to take part in Group 1 and all twelve students at the other site made up Group 2. A workshop style was adopted and seven workshops were held at each site.

At each workshop the group was invited to generate an agenda, or questions for discussion. The students also wrote short accounts of significant events that had happened on the course which would assist in understanding what becoming a midwife meant to them.[3] The workshops were tape-recorded, and notes on a flip chart or A4 paper were kept. In addition, I kept a research diary and field notes. After each workshop I gave the group written feedback, a summary of what had been discussed, the key issues and ideas. We also read and discussed short articles about midwifery. Finally, each group contributed to an account, written by me, of what becoming a midwife meant to them (Kent *et al.* 1994; Kent 1995, 1997). It was agreed that an account of a fictional student would represent the views of each group, by telling a story about what it was like becoming a midwife on each of the diploma programmes. Here, I identify some of the key problems with the inquiry, and suggest that this reveals more fundamental difficulties with participatory research.

Group inquiry 1

My anxieties that this group was too large was not a problem because four students left the course and three subsequently withdrew from the inquiry.[4] The fourth student to exit the inquiry was encouraged to do so. Her unwillingness to comply with the agreed terms of participation may be seen as indicative of a procedure that was far from democratic. Others in the group asserted a view that participants, having agreed to be tape-recorded and to contribute by writing notes and accounts and in other ways, should be excluded from the inquiry if they were not willing to do this. There was no will to try to accommodate this student. This raises important issues about the model of democracy that could be applied to this inquiry. For by adopting a majoritarian procedure, in this instance dissenters were excluded. The difference of opinion about the process whereby the account was to be produced was not examined further and the resolution of this, by the student exiting the group, was in many ways unsatisfactory. This disagreement demonstrated that certain differences would not be tolerated. In effect, the dissident student violated the central premise on which group inquiry was set up – that participants would be willing to enter a dialogue and contribute to discussions that would work towards reaching agreement. So is consensus 'good' or 'bad', i.e. morally justifiable? Does it elide difference and obscure conflict? These questions and the extent to which there could be unity in diversity are critical ones which I shall explore below. Differences did remain within the group, both differences of background, personal characteristics and differences of opinion. I was different from the others because I was not a student midwife and had a nursing background. My role in the group and concerns I had about my contribution highlighted this difference. This in turn raised questions about what it could mean to be 'co-researchers'.

Another theme running through the inquiry was the relationship between theory and experience. Did the subjective experiences of the students provide a foundation for knowledge and was it important that they distance themselves in some way from this in order to analyse critically what they said and what they wrote? Reason (1994) underlines the importance of experience as grounding knowledge and at the centre of a 'participatory world-view'. He deplores the fragmentation of consciousness in the Western world and 'alienated conscious-ness' associated with a separation of self from others. He suggests we need to become 'critically subjective'. According to him we need to test propositional (theoretical) knowledge against experience and so develop a critical self-awareness and extended understanding of ourselves and our connection to 'others'. In their study using 'memory-work', Haug et al. (1987) wrote about their memories in a group, and the process of writing was itself regarded as a critical tool, a means of resistance, a way of rewriting history and articulating theory against experience. Yet in this inquiry writing was a problem. The students had difficulty in writing about 'significant events' and preferred to talk about their experiences. They found this helpful and saw me as a sympathetic listener, but the intention was not to have some kind of 'group therapy'. They valued being listened to more than bringing about change through analysis of their experiences.[5] Did such a view undervalue the potential of writing, talking and listening as forms of collective action? Was the inquiry empowering or had the group been co-opted by a mechanism that enabled them to speak and be heard but which would have little impact on midwifery education? Or did such a view fail to recognise how 'experience' is discursively constructed (Scott 1992; Stanley and Wise 1993) and the ways in which their identities as midwives were actively (re-)constructed through this dialogical process (Kent 1997)? What of the emancipatory claims made by participatory researchers (Maguire 1987)?

Problems of representation, and the extent to which the account produced could represent the views and experiences of the group were highlighted. How could differences be represented? Would the production of an agreed account appear unitary and exclusionary, effecting closure and imply that diversity could be subsumed within this story of a fictional student? The question of style was an issue – should the first person 'I' be used in the account of becoming a midwife since it did not represent a single author but a fictional student who was created by the group? Moreover, although co-authorship was consistent with the participatory approach was it unwise for them to disclose their names? If the conditions for producing the research report could be seen as 'democratic', how would social relations outside the group mediate the outcome? What was my responsibility in this respect? Had I exposed a vulnerable group? Some of the students were anxious that in appearing critical of the education programme they would jeopardise their employment prospects. Clearly the potential benefits to them of producing published papers were not self-evident, or unproblematic. Moreover, for my purposes, another level of analysis was needed which both explored how they constructed their identity as midwives (Kent 1997), and critically examined group inquiry as a method.

Group inquiry 2

Initially, Group 2 appeared to be cohesive and spoke confidently with one voice. I felt at ease with them as they shared a language I understood, about working for women, bringing about change and empowerment. The 'we' of the early sessions seemed unproblematic for it suggested that views were generally similar and any one person could speak for the others. However, over time, what at first appeared as advantages for inquiring together led to certain tensions. In particular, while there was usually a lively discussion it was not always conducted in a way that every student could take a turn in talking. It appeared that some voices were silenced. This was confirmed by a letter to me from one student belonging to an ethnic minority group, who felt unable to express her opinion in the inquiry. My aim was to encourage everyone to talk and to structure the workshops in order that this were possible. In striving to reach some kind of agreement about what is was like on this diploma pro-gramme, it was important that we adopted a procedure where diverse views could be expressed. If not, it could hardly be seen as 'democratic'.

In an effort to ensure that a democratic procedure was adopted, contradicto-rily I sought to control the discussions in two ways. First, to enable each student to participate fully, and second, to develop an analysis of what was discussed. Often the workshops were seen as providing an opportunity to chat about what had happened, to exchange views and opinions on a particular issue but not as part of any effort to produce a coherent analysis. For this reason it seemed that while the group members were happy to produce data, they appeared less willing to analyse it, saying it was tedious looking back over past workshop notes. In practice they seldom did, which added to the difficulty of analysis. On reflection, in the final workshop the students admitted that they had been 'half-hearted' about their participation in the inquiry and had not invested the time or effort that it had deserved. So why was this?

There were at least three indications of what the reasons for this might be. First, the group persisted in seeing the workshops as a chance for a chat, rather than as a systematic inquiry process. As a result, they pointed out that they did not need me to facilitate this kind of discussion. Second, the inquiry appeared to have little relevance to them and they were sceptical about the possibility of it contributing to change. Third, they were already faced with the demands of the course and working in clinical practice, so taking part in this inquiry was an additional burden for which they had little time. In a sense, each of these three explanations related to issues of ownership and control.

This group was concerned about ownership and control of the research. They questioned whether I had a fixed agenda. The extent to which they could 'own' or 'control' the inquiry was, in certain respects, strictly limited and they were conscious of this from an early stage. So they developed a view that this inquiry was for me, that it could serve no useful purpose for them. This created a paradox that remained unresolved. For within these constraints, the potential for the students to set the agenda and ensure that the inquiry had more relevance for them was not realised. They relinquished attempts to direct the inquiry and, instead, left the work of analysis and structuring the discussion to me. While Reason might say simply that I was mismatched with others in the group, or Heron would argue that the members had not internalised the aims or method of inquiry, this implies that the method has a strictly limited application. But I want to suggest that we need to enlarge our understanding of what kind of democratic model might be relevant here to consider whether it is enough to seek like-minded associates to generate knowledge. Do we need to find ways in which diverse views and interests may be represented and included in research and inquiry?

Unable to share the work of analysis, or the responsibility for what took part in the workshops, I felt like an outsider looking in. I became uncomfortable as the inquiry progressed and their anger and frustration with midwifery spilled over into the inquiry. The workshops became more difficult to make sense of, or control, as increased confusion, dissent and feelings of despondency permeated the discussion. The ability to produce agreement in the group was affected. Though beginning with a sense of unity and coherence, the group, through both the educational process and the inquiry process, seemed to become more incoherent and disordered. They clung to their early commitment to midwifery, but their efforts in the inquiry were dissipated. They continued to attend the workshops through a sense of obligation and loyalty to me for which I was grateful. The final workshop seemed a relief for us all and provided a chance to consider whether it had been worthwhile. Perhaps, surprisingly, they felt it had not been a waste of time but that, under different circumstances, it could have been much more.

In summary, then, the inquiry process revealed a number of issues about what being 'co-researchers' could mean. I have identified some of them here. These may be understood as issues about equality, the significance of difference between group members, ownership and control,[6] representation and legitimacy. In short, these were questions about the relationship between democracy and truth, power and knowledge. In order to examine this more closely I now turn to Seyla Benhabib's work which offers a feminist critique of Habermas and development of his discourse model of legitimacy, a model of democracy where discourse ethics is of primary importance. This appears to me to address a number of inherent difficulties in the participatory research approach.

Towards a better understanding of discourse ethics and participatory politics

I find it useful to draw on the work of Seyla Benhabib and her analysis of contemporary ethics and politics in *Situating the Self* even though she does not talk directly about research. Following Habermas, she outlines a revised procedural model of the public sphere that is 'an actual dialogue among actual selves who are both "generalised others", considered as equal moral agents, and "concrete others", that is individuals with irreducible differences' (Benhabib 1992: 169). She proposes a view of democratic procedures which is inclusive, where everyone is regarded as having equal rights to participate in public debate. As we shall see, she is critical of the classical liberal (masculinist) view of participants as abstracted, transcendental, universal subjects and instead argues that we need to see them as concrete, embodied individuals with differences that must be included, rather than discounted, or ignored. Hers is a politics of presence, rather than a politics of ideas (see also Phillips 1994), where individuals are seen as participating in face-to-face dialogue. A closer look at her work helps to clarify the issues relating to group inquiry. It also legitimates the view that it is both politically and morally unnecessary to suggest that we need to become disengaged and disinterested participants in research as Reason and Heron appear to suggest above. They say we need to ensure that power inequalities do not prevent the negotiation of an open contract and suggest that we can somehow 'bracket off the tacit concepts involved in [our] everyday way of identifying the content of the experience' (Heron 1988: 59). In order to prioritise experience and criticise western rationality, Reason says we must 'reclaim the body, to live in the body rather than using it as a tool to carry around the mind' (Reason 1994: 37). It is precisely as embodied selves, or interested persons, that we are enabled to participate in a democratic (inquiry) process that is both just and fair. However, unequal bargaining positions and differences between participants will always construct the inquiry process; all bodies are not the same. Indeed, Reason's reference to 'the body' seems to miss this. Following Benhabib's model, it is important, from an ethical point of view, that a moral conversation takes place, for we are not talking here of unmediated 'experience' but the engagement and interaction of individuals, one with an 'other'. While Reason and Heron are keen to distinguish between the presentational aspects of our engagement with each other, and the experience of inquiring together, my view is that for practical purposes these can not be separated. Experience is always mediated, and an emphasis on experience is empiricist (Scott 1992). It is for this reason that I suggest a better understanding of discursive practice is useful.

In so far then as democratic procedures characterise group inquiry (or feminist participatory research), the rationality of the procedure, according to Benhabib, is of philosophical interest. Group inquiry, as a form of participatory research, is underpinned by certain modernist principles and the aim of reaching an agreement is premised on a model of participatory politics that is rationalist, in spite of the claims which Reason and others might wish to make to the contrary.[7] Benhabib, however, distinguishes between the liberal (Kantian) view of public space, that views participants as unencumbered, free-thinking individuals (the universal subject), from Habermas's discursive view – a discourse model of legitimacy, a politics of communicative ethics (for a brief overview of this model see Habermas 1984). She explains how, according to the discourse model, participation becomes redefined as 'discursive will formation'. Participation is extended to include the realms of society, personality and culture (Benhabib 1992). Participation entails the generation of consensual 'norms of actions', a reflexive process of self-definition and identity formation, and the creative appropriation of meaning (see also Giddens 1991). Habermas's idea of 'practical discourse' therefore draws attention to the conditions for participation and the constraints on how debate is conducted. Benhabib specifies these conditions (for an 'ideal speech situation') as 'universal moral respect' and 'egalitarian reciprocity'. She sees universal moral respect as 'the right of all beings capable of speech and actions to be participants in the moral conversation'. The principle of egalitarian reciprocity is 'that within such conversations each has the same symmetrical rights to various speech acts, to initiate new topics, to ask for reflection about the presuppositions of the conversation' (Benhabib 1992: 29). She says within these rules for debate, the possibility of contesting the rules themselves remains so that there are no limits to what may be discussed or debated (moral reflexivity). According to Benhabib, it follows that communicative ethics 'trumps' other ways of ordering public life and, while not morally neutral, it is more rational for it enables 'validity claims' to be justified.[8] To what extent, then, were these conditions fulfilled in group inquiry? How, in practice, could universal moral respect and egalitarian reciprocity be demonstrated? And how does this discourse model reframe ways of knowing, understanding and being in the world?

A Discourse model of legitimacy

In her analysis of 'the end of the episteme of representation', Seyla Benhabib identifies three critiques of the Enlightenment model:

1   a critique of the modern epistemic subject
2   a critique of the modern epistemic object
3   a critique of the modern concept of the sign

She explains how the substitution of the self as an active agent 'creating conditions of objectivity by forming nature through its own historical activity' (Benhabib 1992: 207) is central to the tradition of German idealism expressed in the work of Marx, Freud, Horkheimer and Habermas's early work. While the self was not seen as fully autonomous, the emancipatory project was to render conscious those hidden desires and needs. The second critique draws attention to the ways in which 'the concept, the very unit of thought in the western tradition ... imposes homogeneity and identity upon the heterogeneity of material' and created a world of 'things' or bounded objects that is 'the triumph of western ratio' (*ibid.* 1992: 208). While lastly, a critique of the sign calls into question the view that there exists a natural relationship (correspondence) between the sign and the signified and instead proposes that systems of social relations determine what signs stand for.

Benhabib maintains that postmodernists focus primarily on the critique of the sign and that they lead us to accept a 'polytheism of values' and a politics of justice beyond consensus. In their view, she claims, there is no longer a subject – therefore epistemology and the philosophical project is finished – and by rejecting Cartesian dualism, there is no independent position from which to judge knowledge claims, only diverse voices that compete to be heard. By contrast, Benhabib provides some basis on which the acceptability of claims may be judged. This *procedural rationality* and Habermas's communicative ethics are *universal* principles which we mobilise in order to allow diverse voices to speak, and divergent views to be expressed, so that political strategy and action may be advanced. What is presented here, by Benhabib, is a model that incorporates the three critiques, that enables us to understand communication as action (practical discourse) and to acknowledge the ontological priority of material beings in a material world. By rejecting the relativist position, Habermas and Benhabib show us a way of being in the world, of knowing and changing it, that, significantly, allows the criticisms of the Enlightenment model to be upheld and also the project of modernity to continue.

According to this model of communicative action, the normative basis of speech is emphasised. In other words, to speak, according to Habermas, is to act,[9] and through speech, agents make inherently moral assumptions which may be universally applied. White explains this 'speech–act–immanent obligation', as 'one which every actor has "implicity recognised", simply by virtue of having engaged in communicative action' (White 1988: 51). While this obligation is insufficient to sort out types of ethical position, discursive rules are necessary for the achievement of a rationally motivated agreement, rules that are not externally imposed but are presupposed by agents who make normative (i.e. rational) claims, says White (*ibid.*). Where agreement that 'generalises interests' is not possible, compromises are necessary. For these to be legitimate – for example, where unequal bargaining positions exist – the burden of proof is on the advantaged agent to justify inequalities. In contrast to some discourse theorists, the Habermasian model sets out the grounds and conditions for dialogue, the circumstances under which different points of view may be articulated and agreement reached.[10]

Tyler (1991) argues that modernism teaches 'the terror of consensus' and that 'consensus is the technology of the fascism of science, democracy and bureaucracy' (*ibid.* 1991: 82). Consensus here is seen as a 'CON', an ideological process that obscures and elides difference, silencing voices and controlling persons. Benhabib distinguishes between 'consensus' as conventionally understood, and consensus from generating an agreement through argumentation and debate. In her view, rather than this closing off further debate, or the conversation ending, there is a possibility of it continuing ad infinitum where there is the political will to do so. This Habermasian position, according to Benhabib, is distinguishable from classical liberalism and from relativism, or nihilism, because it provides a way forward, by bringing forth order from chaos and allowing it to change, then to be revised again. Agreement enables us to proceed. And though Tyler maintains that this subsumes differences in a quest for 'totalisation', Benhabib outlines a way in which there can be unity in diversity, where differences and a willingness to take the view of the 'other' does not lead to uniformity, where autonomy and solidarity are two sides of the same coin, mediated by discourse, and where 'facts' and values are reintegrated through a process of moral justification.

Beyond method?

In group inquiry I was faced with these ideological dilemmas. How could the different experiences and views of participants be accounted for? On the one hand, I could take the role of analyst and examine the variability between individual accounts, looking for the ways in which these were structured, the discursive rules that were played out in the way students told their stories – a discourse analytic approach. But would this not set my interpretation above theirs? How could I justify my position as analyst?[11] What values were intertwined with the 'facts' of 'becoming a midwife'? How could I ensure that I was accountable to them – that my account was subjected to scrutiny and dispute by them? As analyst I could appear to have the last word. Although Woolgar (1988), Ashmore (1989) and other reflexive discourse analysts do not set stable boundaries around their research accounts, but seek to open them up, to invite dispute (by using new literary forms), I wanted to invite the students to dispute my view, to be accountable *to them* for the claims that I might make, and this seemed possible only within the confines of face-to-face dialogue – as actual selves in actual dialogue.

Accountability was important in order that we could arbitrate between different accounts or validity claims. It seemed that only then could claims to 'know' what becoming a midwife might mean be legitimated. A discourse model of legitimacy is useful so that the authoring of a research account is not seen as an exercise of power, that knowledge produced is not the product of exploitative and oppressive social relations, the control of one over an 'other'. In short, group inquiry was seen as a method that could, potentially, give voice to differences, but that could also recognise common concerns. It was not intended as a means of control but as a procedure where communicative rationality

> carries with it connotations based on the central experience of the unconstrained unifying consensus-bringing force of argumentative speech, in which different participants overcome their merely subjective views and, owing to the mutuality of rationally motivated conviction, assure themselves of both the unity of the objective world and the intersubjectivity of their lifeworld.
>
> (Habermas, quoted in White 1988: 43)

Through dialogue we could therefore construct narratives of 'ourselves' as participants in the research and as authoring accounts of 'becoming a midwife' via programmes of pre-registration midwifery education.

According to Tyler, 'TRUTH, in modernism, is subborned by METHOD' (Tyler 1991: 85). So can we go beyond method and abandon 'truth' altogether? Criticisms of modernist concerns with 'truth' are premised on the belief that there are normative constraints on what will be accepted as a 'true' account of the world. In other words, that certain other accounts are rendered 'false' and the supremacy of one claim to truth over another can only be disputed by challenging the method, rather than the position of the knower. It follows that this position remains unaccounted for, uncontested and intact. While counter claims to 'know' may be put forward on the basis of other 'standpoints' (e.g. feminist standpoint theory), this can lead to a situation where 'truth' is read off from experience, or the social position of the knower. What is then highlighted is *who* knows and attention is focused reflexively on the position of knower and circumstances of knowing. Yet, if there can be no agreed position from which to judge claims to know or the 'facts' of the case, does anything go? Are all comers accepted as having a legitimate or valid claim? It is this effect that critics of epistemological relativism and much postmodern writing argue leads to charges of moral bankruptcy. For, in practice, we do adopt value positions in order to judge the adequacy of accounts and it is a procedure for enabling us to discern between these value positions that Benhabib (and Habermas) advocate.

At the level of research practice this amounts to an exhortation to adopt an ethical position and research procedure that enables participants in the research to have the opportunity to validate their claims to 'know' as morally justifiable and, more radically, to set the terms/rules under which such judgements will be made. So, in order to arbitrate between accounts, any dispute is re-framed as a question of moral principles and political practice, rather than an epistemological debate about the relationship between knower and known (subject and object). The terms of a debate about 'truth', then, may be adjusted as we discard worries about the stability of the subject and object world and how we may know ourselves. Instead, the creative possibilities of negotiating who we are and how to act in the world extend before us through engagement with others. The will to enter into this dialogue is the will to become a person, to define a 'self' and to make sense of (know) our place in a world shared with others. That is not to suggest that an agreement provides any kind of ontological guarantee, but it can provide a direction in which to proceed.

From this discussion of discourse ethics and politics I hope to have shown that we need to adopt what Benhabib, following Arendt, calls 'an enlarged mentality' (Benhabib 1994: 33) for a feminist participatory research approach. In effect this means that we can go beyond notions of equality as sameness, that differences between co-researchers may be recognised as integral to the inquiry process rather than seen as invalidating it and that we need to adopt the standpoint of others when considering our own point of view. Then, rather than assuming we can deny some aspect of ourselves in order to adopt some kind of neutral position (or at least aspire to this), we can acknowledge our own interests and the interests of others and include them in our discussion. In group inquiry, then, the differences between myself and the student midwives and the differences between them can be seen as contributing to, rather than detracting from, the accounts produced. The legitimacy and validity of group inquiry rests on the willingness to participate in a dialogue to reach agreement and a deliberative model of democracy (and knowledge production).

Conclusions

In this chapter I have suggested that we need to examine in detail the concepts of *participation* and *dialogue* as central to participatory research methods. In order to do this we need to ask ourselves what model of democracy underpins such a research approach? From my discussion I have concluded that certain assumptions about Reason, Heron and Maguire's views of participants as citizens and subjects are problematic. In particular, the idea that we must somehow 'match' the researchers in participatory research seems to imply that successful research is contingent on similarities between participants in a group. Not only does this gloss over inevitable and irreducible differences between participants, it is in danger of excluding the voices of some members and denying the relevance and significance of those differences. What seems to be invoked here is a notion of equality based on sameness and a view of communication where differences are distorting and to be somehow minimised. Such a view appears to be based on a form of classical liberalism which is highly controversial.

By referring to the work of Benhabib my intention has been to highlight the relevance of a discourse theory of democracy for participatory researchers. In her revision of Habermas it seems to me that Benhabib offers a valuable insight into how we might understand the dialogical features of participatory research methods. Benhabib shows how differences may be included in public debate (inquiry) and provide the very conditions for dialogue. It follows that participants in group inquiry may be recognised as interested, embodied individuals who are equal moral agents with symmetrical rights to participate in discussion. Moreover, it is precisely by debate around their differences that agreement becomes possible.

There were other obstacles to participation in group inquiry which I identified here. I suggested that certain skills, additional to linguistic competences, were prerequisites for the inquiry and indeed are needed to participate in democratic policy formation. Reason and Heron appear to have neglected this in their discussion of successful inquiry, though Maguire does refer to this issue. Resources of time and access to diverse forums were unequally available to participants in group inquiry and the membership of the group was limited by external constraints. Moreover, it appeared that there is an optimum size for inquiry groups if the research process is to be manageable and efficient.[12] It follows therefore that a number of problems remain for participatory researchers about the extent to which the inquiry process may be seen as a democratic dialogue and how we might extend that dialogue to those outside the inquiry group in the context of an unequal world.

Acknowledgements

This chapter refers to research funded by the Department of Health and the ESRC. The opinions expressed are those of the author. Thanks to Charlotte Hooper and Judith Squires who commented on an earlier version of the chapter and to Maggs Research Associates.

Notes

1 Thanks to Charlotte Hooper for drawing my attention to this.
2 In 1991 the Department of Health funded *Direct but Different – An Evaluation of the Implementation of Pre-Registration Midwifery Education in England*. Pre-registration midwifery is the preparation as midwives of those who are not already registered nurses. Courses are a minimum of three years in length and may be at either diploma or degree level. Maggs Research Associates were contracted to carry out this research and I was the Research Officer/Project Manager on the project.
3 This was based on critical incident technique and 'memory-work' (Haug *et al.* (1987).

4 It seems likely that inquiry groups do need to be quite small and I think ten people is most realistic. This is important for it does indicate that a participatory model of democracy rather than a representative one is appropriate.

5 So this may suggest that the value of this inquiry method was precisely this – to provide a forum for debate and discussion and being heard, rather than making decisions or effecting policy change.

6 Reason (1994) does discuss this briefly.

7 In his discussion of 'future participation' as a participatory world-view, Reason (1994) does seem to want to reject modernist principles, but the democratic ideals which underpin the participatory approach do not, in my view, make this either theoretically coherent or morally desirable.

8 For an elaboration of 'validity claims' see White (1988). He explains:

> when a speaker orients himself [sic] toward understanding — that is, engages in communicative action – his speech acts must raise, and he must be accountable for three rationality or 'validity claims': truth, normative legitimacy and truthfulness/authenticity. Only if a speaker is able to convince his hearers that his claims are rational and thus worthy of recognition can there develop a 'rationally motivated agreement' or consensus on how to coordinate future actions.
>
> (*ibid.* 1988: 28)

9 Speech–act theory is usually attributed to Austin (1962). See Potter and Wetherell (1987), Habermas (1984) and Thompson (1984).

10 For a critical assessment of Habermas's work see Thompson (1984).

11 See Fairclough (1989) for suggestions on this point in relation to discourse analysis.

12 In this regard there appeared to be similarities between the inquiry process and Chambers' (1995) account of the 'discursive experiment' at the UK Women's Peace Camp, where she concluded that discourse theory was less useful for understanding decision-making processes but should be seen as relating to the formation of public opinion. Certainly, constraints operating in group inquiry limited the extent to which students could influence or participate in executive decision-making about the future of midwifery education.

References

Ashmore, M. (1989) *The Reflexive Thesis: Writing the sociology of scientific knowledge*, Chicago: University of Chicago Press.

Austin, J. (1962) *How To Do Things With Words*, London: Oxford University Press.

Benhabib, S. (1992) *Situating the Self: Gender, community and postmodernism in contemporary ethics*, Cambridge: Polity Press.

—— (1994) 'Deliberative rationality and models of democratic legitimacy', *Constellations* 1 (1): 26–52.

Chambers, S. (1995) 'Feminist discourse/practical discourse', in J. Meehan (ed.) *Feminists Read Habermas: Gendering the subject of discourse*, London: Routledge.

Davies, G.G. (1986) 'Student intentions and institutional experience: an evaluation of different psychological explanations of student behaviour', PhD dissertation, University of Bath.

Fairclough, N. (1989) *Language and Power*, Harlow: Longman.

Giddens, A. (1991) *Modernity and Self Identity*, Cambridge: Polity Press.

Habermas, J. (1979) *Knowledge and Human Interests*, Boston: Beacon Press.

—— (1984) *Theory of Communicative Action*, vol. 1, *Reason and Rationalisation of Society*, Boston, MA: Beacon Books.

Haug, F. *et al.* (1987) *Female Sexualisation*, London: Verso.

Heron, J. (1981) 'Philosophical basis for a new paradigm', in P. Reason and J. Rowan (eds) *Human Inquiry: A sourcebook of new paradigm research*, Chichester: Wiley.

Heron, J. (1988) 'Validity in co-operative inquiry', in P. Reason (ed.) *Human Inquiry in Action: Developments in new paradigm research*, London: Sage.

Kent, J. (1995) 'With women: knowledge and power in midwifery education', PhD dissertation, University of Bristol.

—— (1997) 'Constructing accounts of becoming a midwife: a politics of identity', *Self and Agency, Journal of Applied Sociology* (forthcoming).

Kent, J., MacKeith, N. and Maggs, C. (1994) *Direct but Different – An Evaluation of the Implementation of Pre-Registration Midwifery Education in England*, A research project for the Department of Health, vols 1 and 2, Bath: Maggs Research Associates.

Maguire, P. (1987) *Doing Participatory Research: A feminist approach*, Boston, MA: University of Massachusetts.

Phillips, A. (1994) 'Dealing with difference: a politics of ideas or a politics of presence?' *Constellations* 1 (1): 74–91.

Potter, J. and Wetherell, M. (1987) *Discourse and Social Psychology: Beyond attitude and behaviour*, London: Sage.

Reason, P. (ed.) (1988) *Human Inquiry in Action: Developments in new paradigm research*, London: Sage.

—— (ed.) (1994) *Participation in Human Inquiry*, London: Sage.

Robertson, G. (1984) 'Experiences of learning', PhD dissertation, University of Bath.

Rowan, J. (1981) 'A dialectical paradigm for research', in P. Reason and J. Rowan (eds) *Human Inquiry: A sourcebook of new paradigm research*, Chichester: Wiley.

Scott, J. (1992) 'Experience', in J. Butler and J. Scott (eds) *Feminists Theorize the Political*, London: Routledge.

Stanley, L. and Wise, S. (1993) *Breaking Out Again*, London: Routledge.

Thompson, J.B. (1984) *Studies in the Theory of Ideology*, Cambridge: Polity Press.

Tyler, S.A. (1991) 'A post-modern in-stance', in L. Nencel and P. Pels (eds) *Constructing Knowledge Authority and Critique in Social Science*, London: Sage.

White, S.K. (1988) *The Recent Work of Jurgen Habermas: Reason, justice and modernity*, Cambridge: Cambridge University Press.

Woolgar, S. (1988) *Knowledge and Reflexivity: New frontiers in the sociology of knowledge*, London: Sage.

Chapter 7

Participatory research

Whose roles, whose responsibilities?

Grindl Dockery

Introduction

This chapter is a reflection on the role of participatory research (PR) in empowering local people and their communities. My focus in this chapter is not only on *how* one does PR, but also on the important question of *why* do PR at all; that is, *what* is different about PR from conventional research, *who* benefits from participating in the research process and *who* is exercising power? It is not about a tool kit or a set of techniques that provide quick or easy solutions to produce an effective outcome, nor is it an automatic alternative to conventional approaches to research – in fact, it may be ill-advised in certain contexts. Supporting or enabling participation in the strongest sense becomes a political act through establishing partnerships between the researcher and the researched, whereby ownership, empowerment and responsibility for accountability are shared throughout the research process. PR can play an important role in fostering or stimulating community activism at both the individual and collective levels.

Critical discourse on the concept and nature of participation fundamentally challenges conventional ideologies (Wisner 1988). Through their promotion of the Enlightenment values of neutrality and objectivity, and of the notion of absolute truth, conventional approaches to research (paradoxically in some eyes) foster disempowering and discriminatory practices. PR, in the critical sense, challenges the status and power that is exercised by professional researchers and emphasises the demystification of the research process. Thus, participants make a commitment to work together to enable a process of education and empowerment and to facilitate ways of sharing power and ownership. Generally, participation as a basic principle is important and should not be seen as a concept only relevant to research (Maguire 1996).

The level of participation in practice may vary from mere tokenism or manipulation by researchers and sponsors to a radical process where researchers form an alliance with those being researched (Braidotti *et al.* 1994). As a PR facilitator I actively support and attempt to enhance local people's sense of ownership and control over the research process, with a commitment to enabling the education and empowerment of those participating. This means making alliances, taking sides with those who are normally marginalised from the exercise of power in our society and sharing knowledge and skills in a partnership that aims to avoid practices that exacerbate inequality.

In this context, PR challenges the power currently exercised by statutory-sector agencies such as the National Health Service (NHS) in the UK. It is concerned about these agencies' accountability to the public, for whom they make major resource decisions, and it challenges where they stand in relation to the rights of and injustice towards those who do not have equitable access, who are marginalised from the political, social and economic processes, who do not enjoy a decent quality of life or achieve full citizenship. It is problematic for bureaucracies like the NHS to enable the less powerful to participate and be empowered to play a major role in the decision-making process. In describing typical bureaucratical and hierarchical organisations, Mark Easterby-Smith puts it very succinctly:

> [A] combination of power culture and highly centralized controls, with rigidly designed systems and procedures, produces behaviour amongst managers that makes learning almost impossible. In particular, the tendency to make scapegoats out of those who made mistakes leads to a general aversion to taking risks, and managers, afraid of being punished as harbingers of bad news, tend to concentrate on providing only good news to their superiors.
>
> (Easterby-Smith 1992)

Hilary Rose, in her discussion on activists, gender and community health movements, makes the point about separating what are government and professionally initiated programmes, which want to encourage public participation in health and welfare projects based on the objectives of the powerful, from those social movements concerned with health and welfare, which are spontaneous social movements from below. These social movements do not necessarily exclude professionals and intellectuals,

> but it does suggest that they have placed themselves on the side of the environment, of women, peace or of people's health. The social projects of such movements are essentially open, they are made, and this is a strength not a weakness, with the stuff of dreams.
>
> (Rose 1990: 211)

Aligning oneself with those 'being researched' will often draw criticism from those academic or professional researchers who believe that research can be and should be totally objective, and that the researcher is able to be neutral and value free. There will also be critics who say that the PR approach to research will bias the project and, therefore, invalidate the findings. This type of critique is often based on what paradigm a practitioner is allied to. There are fundamental differences between the conventional paradigms and those which take a more critical stance, e.g. feminist and participatory paradigms, in defining knowledge and truth. The debates around objectivity and bias in research methodologies have been expressed predominantly through a polarised argument about the value of quantitative and qualitative methods. In PR, concern about research methods is secondary, whereas concern about the research process is dominant, and Cornwall and Jewkes suggest this polarisation of arguments marginalises the real concerns about knowledge and process:

> Locating the debate about PR within the controversies of the qualitative–quantitative divide obscures issues of agency, representation and power which lie at the core of the methodological critiques from which the development of participatory approaches stem.
>
> (Cornwall and Jewkes 1995: 1667)

Many conventional research methods that are described as objective, e.g. direct observation and questionnaire surveys, may be used in PR, as are qualitative methods that are described as more subjective, e.g. individual interviews, group discussions, participant observation and diagrammatic models such as those developed in rapid appraisal (*PLA Notes* 1994–7). A multi-method approach provides options for answering a variety of questions, which in turn generates a rich, comprehensive set of data and information. It also enables a process of triangulation to be applied, thus increasing and verifying the validity of the final analysis. This is in contrast to how PR approaches may be perceived by others. In Jules Pretty's words:

> [i]t is commonly asserted that participatory methods constitute inquiry that is undisciplined and sloppy. They are said to involve only subjective observations and so respond just to selected members of communities. Terms like informal and qualitative are used to imply poorer quality or second-rate work. Rigour and accuracy are assumed, therefore, to be in contradiction with participatory methods. This means that it is the investigators relying on participatory methods who are called upon to prove the utility of their approach, not the conventional investigator.
>
> (Pretty 1995: 178)

There is not an automatic loss of quality or validity in PR, nor does this approach mean there is an introduction of bias into the research. Rather, it may improve the quality of the research, providing a more accurate and valid representation of local people's experiences. For example, validity can be further improved by feeding back the preliminary analysis of responses to those who have been interviewed, enabling them to make further comments or changes and thereby verifying what will be presented as the final analysis. Sharing editing responsibilities of reports is also an important way of supporting joint ownership of the data and provides an opportunity for further educational experiences to take place.

The knowledge generated through PR is particular and specific knowledge, what Donna Haraway terms 'situated knowledges'. Without abandoning the notion of objectivity, she argues that 'objectivity turns out to be about particular and specific embodiment and definitely not about the false vision promising transcendence of all limits and responsibility. The moral is simple: only partial perspective promises objective vision' (Haraway 1988: 582–3). The planning and conduct of the research is informed by the knowledge and experiences of those who are simultaneously researchers and researched. They offer views that are both objective (in Haraway's sense) and subjective and thus produce situated knowledges, knowledge from somewhere. In doing so, they challenge the conventional idea of pure knowledge which is uncontaminated by the conditions of its collection. The 'outsider' is no more able to offer value-free or neutral knowledge than the 'insider'; rather, they speak from different positions.

Proponents or facilitators of participation are active in countries of both the North and South, although much of the development in critical theory and practice in PR, including innovative research methods, has been in countries of the South (De Koning and Martin 1996). This chapter draws on two case studies where community groups, consisting of predominantly women, conducted research with the aim of bringing about changes in the delivery of local health services. One case study focuses on the struggle by community groups to keep a local community health centre open and the other case study looks at issues related to women's sexuality and sexual health services.

Participation and bureaucracies

Having addressed the general or broad overview on PR in the previous section, I will move to the more specific environments where 'hands-on' activity is taking place at public sector level and within local communities.

The reforms or transformations that have occurred within the NHS in the UK have led to the division of the NHS structure, often in the belief that the new parts can operate as separate entities and in isolation from each other, whilst at the same time competing against each other. For example, the split between purchasers and providers of services has meant that the various health trusts (providers) compete against each other to win contracts from health authorities (purchasers) for providing services. A similar competition exists between fundholding and non-fundholding GPs in gaining access to services for their patients or clients. Despite the rhetoric on 'choice' by politicians, concerns regarding equitable access and accountability are widespread amongst users. Where are the public, or, as they are usually called now, 'consumers', situated in these policy changes and what difference have the changes made to the quality of services? At present it appears that the consumers have little involvement in or power over the decisions being made on their behalf.

In the UK there have been a number of political directives handed down from national level to district operational levels of the NHS to implement or apply the concept of 'public participation or involvement' in providing services (NHS Management Executive 1991), and on the formation of 'healthy alliances' (Mersey Regional Health Authority 1994). How the notion of public consultation and participation, as referred to in the policy statements made by the different health authorities and trusts, is interpreted and applied in the planning and implementation of health services is not necessarily clear or consistent. The rather ambiguous interpretations of public participation also present problems for any research projects which purport to be participatory but are sponsored or funded through the NHS. Can the NHS, or sections of it, politically, economically and professionally afford to support the PR approach which is grounded in empowering and accountable processes? If so, in what contexts would this be possible? Is it, in fact, possible in any statutory or bureaucratic organisation?

One fears that although behind the policy and rhetoric of public participation participants may be *involved*, there is no political commitment to their having *control* over, or a real stake in, the ownership of the process and its outcome or outputs. Power usually remains within those structures which fund and direct such processes. The interpretation and application of such a potentially radical concept as participation is often left to individual institutions or organisations to interpret, and to apply those concepts handed down from the political policy-making levels as they see fit. This often leads to managers rushing around asking, 'How do we get the public to participate?' and at the same time setting the parameters in how far this should happen, thus applying a less radical interpretation of the term 'participation'. This could be interpreted as a reluctance to really share power with the public or the users of services.

On the other hand, some health managers and health authorities have attempted to consult and involve local people and community groups in decisions that affect how and what services are provided. An understanding of how communities work, and respect for those who are normally marginalised from the decision-making process, is crucial for those professionals who are trying to consult and involve local people. They must have a commitment to listening and learning as well as talking, and to respecting views which may differ from their own, as priorities and solutions to addressing needs are often different. This is not an easy process for many professionals.

In my experience, local people often express feelings of disbelief, cynicism and mistrust towards those professionals who dare to venture forth into their community on the premise that they are there to consult. The negative feelings are usually based on previous experiences of the 'consultation process' and the less than positive outcomes of a consultation exercise. There is also the belief that health services are increasingly being diminished and that this is about saving money. It is against this groundswell of feelings that professionals face the challenge of being accepted, proving their credibility and deciding how far they are prepared to align themselves with the disempowered. Despite these challenges, in my experience there are sympathetic individuals at all levels of management who have supported the PR approach and have been excited by the outcome (e.g. Project I in the case studies). However, as Papadakis says:

> A major problem facing radical reformists is the general suspicion and fear of the bureaucracy. Any change in this area would require a change in attitudes based on a better understanding by the projects of the complexity of the bureaucratic process, and on greater transparency of these processes. However, initiatives for change will have to come from outside the bureaucracy. Progress in 'debureaucratization' has been limited probably because of the 'absurdity of asking bureaucrats themselves to develop plans for debureaucratization' (Grunow 1986: 203).
>
> (Papadakis 1993: 97)

Exclusion/Inclusion

The use of language or jargon by professionals often excludes or confuses others, and bears little resemblance to the sort of language which is inclusive of the users of services. Indeed, I have been in meetings where even some professional members attending have had to ask for a clarification of terms being used by managers. Terms and words used by local people to express what they perceive or feel may differ from, and yet have a similar meaning to, concerns raised by academics and professionals. This situation relates particularly to those groups who are least able to exercise power and who are disadvantaged, marginalised and discriminated against by society. Factors such as poverty, class, race, gender, disability, sexuality and age influence the language people use, but, furthermore, relations of power influence what they will say and to whom (Bhavnani 1988). Language can be a means to exclude, thereby limiting 'others' access to debates and consultation on the very issues that are of concern to those 'others', i.e. disadvantaged users of public services. In recent times there has been more emphasis on intersectoral collaboration and co-operation and healthy alliances, such as promoted in the Healthy Cities initiative. It is imperative, therefore, that language and communications are accessible between the various sectors as well as between professionals and local people if such initiatives are to succeed.

There is also a belief amongst many professionals that these 'others' – local people – would not understand the complexities of planning and running a health service and, therefore, the sharing of information should be kept to a minimum so as not to cause confusion amongst those outside the health professions. Yet, as Stacey discusses, local people, especially women, are unpaid health workers who take on responsibilities in caring for families and should, therefore, be seen as not only consumers but as producers, and part of the whole health team: 'Historically, however, they have been treated as 'the other', the people out there, the people that can create a nuisance when they don't conform, when they don't comply with the latest professional ideas' (Stacey 1994: 89). Their particular knowledge and its potential contribution to service planning is usually devalued or ignored.

Rhetoric, needs and manipulation

The danger in seeking the participation of people, such as carers, who normally do not have access to influencing service planning decisions, e.g. local people and community groups, is that without a commitment to the political concept of empowerment by those facilitating the process, participation becomes merely a process of manipulation, a way of coercing local support and reducing expenditure. Papadakis, in a critique on social movements, writes about the risks of uncritical interventions in the name of emancipation:

> Erasaari posits a general trend towards increasingly sophisticated techniques for manipulation, particularly in therapeutic forms of power which encourage people to 'become instruments of power over themselves through themselves' (1986: 239). Self-help is simply a smokescreen for self-manipulation in the interests of the state, for a reduction in state expenditure on welfare programmes.
>
> (Papadakis 1993: 97)

Insincere rhetoric and manipulation can cause long-term damage to future relationships or contact between researchers and those being researched. Research which is not participatory, other than through local people giving their time and knowledge to researchers who then extract this knowledge and information without further contact, has created feelings of frustration and anger within those communities left behind. In one instance, I turned up to conduct a group discussion with members of a community organisation only to be met at the door by a group of very frustrated men who wanted to know who I was and who I worked for. On explaining that I was a freelance researcher who had been contracted to do this work for the local health authority, but was not actually an employee of the said authority, they responded with, 'Oh, that's all right then, but if we knew you were an employee of theirs coming here to ask questions again about what our needs are, we would have given you an earful and sent you packing.' Their reaction was based on previous experiences, where there had been no response or sign of any benefit to them from the numerous meetings and health-needs assessments that had been conducted in their area. It is clearly not cost-effective or efficient, and is manipulative to conduct repeated needs assessments or other research, when there has been little attempt to use existing data in policy formulation and planning or implementation of services. In many cases it is breathtakingly obvious what the needs are, but as one local person said to me, 'We've been needs-assessed to death with nothing to show for it!'

These examples raise the question of why local people should co-operate with research projects which they have not initiated and where they do not have control over the process and its outcome, let alone the analysis and ownership of the data generated through the research. Nor is it, I suggest, a democratic way of conducting research; instead, it reinforces the inequality of a conventional research approach.

Case studies

The following discussion will address some of the key questions and issues relevant to PR and how these change the way the research process is approached:

- Who has initiated or requested the research to be done?
- Who decides what the focus or key questions are in the research?
- Who is in charge or controls the planning and conduct of the research?
- Who identifies the specific recommendations based on the research findings?
- Who owns or has control over the findings, including the final research report?
- Who has control over, or power to respond and act on, the findings of the research?

I will attempt to respond to these questions using examples from PR projects I facilitated in Merseyside (UK), during 1995 and 1996. In addressing these questions I will refer to Project I and Project II, which are briefly described below.

Project I

This research project was based in a disadvantaged area in North Liverpool, involving two wards (West Everton (Ward A) and Breckfield (Ward B)), with a high level of unemployment (32.3 per cent and 45.1 per cent, respectively). Both areas have low house ownership, and they are mainly dependent on rented accommodation from local council and housing associations. They have the lowest level of car ownership in the city (75 per cent and 86 per cent) (Liverpool City Council 1991). In Ward A there is a resident-led community council with several community workers attached, which acts as an umbrella for most other local organisations in the area, e.g. tenants' groups and a local health forum. In Ward B there is a more limited development of local groups and organisations and they do not have a community council, although this may change in the near future as local pressure for community development workers to be appointed in the area increases.

In both wards, especially Ward A, there has been a high level of activism on various issues which are seen to affect the well-being and quality of life of the wider community. Much of the hard work is dependent on small groups of local individuals motivating, involving and informing local people on decisions that have been made regarding services or other development plans in their area. There is also a history of campaigning by local people to improve the quality of their living environment on such matters as housing, street safety for children, public transport and health services.

The research project conducted in these wards in 1995 followed a request to the health authorities in the previous year from the local health forum in Ward A to conduct research as part of their development plan for health services in the area. In response to the proposed closure of a community health clinic that served both adjacent wards, they initiated a campaign to keep the clinic open and approached Ward B to join them. This was the first time that both wards had undertaken such an activist movement together.

The health services in both wards were not seen as adequate or of good quality by many local people and the activists were aware of the severity of the poor health status that existed in these wards, especially in Ward A. They had the highest prescription rate per GP practice in the city and a high standard mortality ratio (SMR) of 168 compared to many other areas in the UK, as well as a high level of limiting long-term illnesses (18.6 per cent and 23.5 per cent), higher than the national (13 per cent) or city average (17 per cent) (Liverpool City Council 1991). The number of GPs working in the area was also below the city average per capita of population.

Public meetings were organised and held by the campaign group to inform and discuss with other local people the issues surrounding the decision to close the community health clinic. As a consequence, personnel from the health authorities and health trust were challenged by local people about the absence of research to justify their assumptions that the clinic was not being used by local people and that the policy of moving all community clinic services into GP practices would not lead to the same level of quality care. The community health clinic had a drop-in, open-door policy for people wanting to access the various organised specialist clinics, e.g. community dentistry, hearing and child health surveillance, family planning, etc., which was better than waiting for appointments with a GP, of whom only half were qualified to do childhood surveillance. The community health clinics were usually overseen by specialist staff in their field, who also worked in other parts of Liverpool. The health trust had in fact already started reducing the clinic services, to the point that many local people in both wards thought the clinic was already closed and therefore had stopped going.

Under pressure from local people, the health authorities agreed to research being conducted in both wards with the provision of some funding, and further funds were procured from the Liverpool Community Voluntary Service. A research group was established and they worked together, forming a united front in both the research project and currently as the health advisory group for their respective wards, which is known as BECHAG. The Save the Children Fund (SCF) Child Health Project operating in the area provided administrative back-up for the research.

I was approached by the campaign group, having met some of the members on previous occasions, and was assessed by local people as to my suitability and appropriateness to assist them in the planning and conduct of the research at a specially organised meeting with the campaign group. My appointment was on the basis that they would have joint control and ownership over the research process and the resulting research report.

Project II

The SHADY Research Project on the sexual health concerns of women who have sex with women was based in Liverpool, but it covered much of Mersey-side and part of Cheshire, in areas defined as 'city', 'small town' and 'rural' within the North-West region of the UK (SHADY 1996). The research was initiated by a small group of women who identified themselves as lesbians and bisexuals, and who were concerned about how well sexual health services were meeting the needs of lesbian/bisexual women in Merseyside. There was a feeling that these health services, through their marginalising and discriminatory practices, rendered women who have sex with women invisible. The group initially met informally, outlining what was required to be able to plan and conduct a research project which would address issues around sexual health, sexual health risks and use of sexual health services. Tasks such as fund-raising, networking amongst local lesbian/bisexual groups, collecting secondary data and developing the research methodology were shared amongst the group.

On further investigation it was found that there had been very little research within the UK on issues related to sexual health for women who have sex with women (Dockery et al. 1997). The steering group, as it became known, expanded as funds from various health authorities and trusts were received, following a long eighteen months of canvassing. During this preliminary stage, a series of open meetings for women who had sex with women were held so that women in the study areas had the opportunity to contribute ideas on the aims and issues to be addressed in the research. At these meetings an open invitation was extended to women to get involved in various ways with the project, such as signing up to be co-researchers, steering group members or interviewees. The steering group and research team ultimately included working-class and middle-class women, those present in personal and professional roles, employed and unemployed women, Black and White women, lesbians and bisexuals, and disabled women, covering a range of ages, coming from across Merseyside and Cheshire. The basic principles of equal opportunities were applied in the appointment of a co-ordinating researcher and in how the project was managed.

Differences and similarities

The approach to both projects was based on the philosophy and concept of participation for education and empowerment. As the co-ordinating researcher, my major roles were facilitation and forming partnerships with those participating in the conduct of the research. My appointment to these projects was on the basis that the *ownership* of and *control* over the research process and the data or information that was generated by these projects would be the joint property of all participants.

In response to the question *Who has initiated or requested the research?*, it is apparent from these two projects that they were initiated by members of the same communities or groups who were to be researched. Through expressing their concerns and protesting about the standard and provision of health care in their relevant areas, they had raised awareness of the key issues in a wider community. In this process of resistance to bureaucratic decisions and through sharing their concerns about future access to quality health care, they also identified what action should be taken, i.e. research, in response to what were seen as important health issues affecting many in their own communities. In demanding such action they also demonstrated a confidence which enabled them to make a commitment to undertake the research in their respective communities.

The initial difference between these two projects is that in Project I there was an existing, geographically-placed working-class community with active, established local groups from which to draw participants in the planning, organising and conduct of the research. They were White women of different ages and educational backgrounds, with a few men providing some support and input at steering-group level.

In Project II, the steering group was not linked to active, established, geographically-placed local groups, but had to identify and establish a community with which to conduct the research, through networking and public meetings. Homophobia and heterosexism made the creation of this temporary community the first challenging aspect of the research. The geographical research area was not a fixed or specific site in Merseyside, but access to participants was by snowballing via social and professional networks to identify any lesbians and bisexual women who might be interested in participating.

In both research projects the steering groups decided on the final focus and specific questions and issues to be addressed by the research. This was achieved through participatory planning sessions that provided opportunities for all participants to share information or knowledge and develop further skills that would enable them to complete the research. The planning sessions not only provided a space for dialogue to take place but became a training and learning experience for both the members of the steering groups and the researchers. Brainstorming, with the introduction of a practical planning framework (Dockery 1996) outlining the key stages of the research process, and the delegation of shared responsibilities amongst members were the main activities in the planning stage. The recruitment of more co-researchers for further training was one of the responsibilities shared by everyone, with specific duties such as gathering more information for a secondary data review being assigned to individual members who were able to get access to the required information identified in the brainstorming sessions. Financial arrangements were agreed by the groups and the management of the research funding was assigned to those members who had either been involved in generating the funds or had the knowledge and time to follow through the administrative arrangements put in place to ensure accountability for the funds.

In both projects, the research teams, who were separate from the steering group in that they would be specifically collecting the data, had separate training sessions after the initial planning phase with the steering groups, where consensus had been reached on the key questions to be addressed in the research. In the training sessions the research objectives and issues were refined by the teams and used as a focus in the exercises to develop the required skills for collecting the data.

After considering all the options, it was decided the methodology for Project I would be a randomised household questionnaire survey, with the questionnaire being developed through the analysis of semi-structured interviews and group discussions conducted with local people who were seen to be the main users and most affected by the threatened closure of the community health clinic, e.g. women with young children, older people. Due to the time scale, I conducted the qualitative interviews and from the analysis prepared a preliminary report for the whole group to edit, comment on and share ideas for the development of the questionnaire. The research team field-tested the questionnaire and made comments on the editing process before the final version was ready for starting the survey. A geographical area for the survey was decided and agreed upon and then the streets with households were randomly selected for the survey. The stages in the research where local people were not directly involved, such as doing the random selection of streets and households, were carefully explained so that everyone knew what was involved and how it was done.

The success of the survey was confirmed with a 73.3 per cent response rate, the high rate due primarily to the fact it was local women who were conducting the survey, which involved many hours of tramping around local streets and encouraging residents to participate. Most team members expressed how much they had learnt about their own community by visiting people's homes, finding many in need of support and often very lonely. It also provided time for the team to update local people on the status of the community health clinic. Almost without exception, people thought the clinic was already closed.

In Project II it had been decided the emphasis would be on qualitative semi-structured interviews and group discussions, with a later decision to develop a questionnaire to be snowballed in the various social networks or other contacts to whom women had access. A checklist was developed by the research team who were trained to conduct the interviews, and the questionnaire was put together on the basis of issues raised in interviews. We also drew on work developed by other colleagues doing similar research who allowed us to adopt parts of their questionnaires. A few members of the research team conducted the analysis of the 54 qualitative interviews.

Ethical issues relating to sensitive topics such as sexual abuse were discussed by the whole research group. It was decided that in interviews, unless the interviewees raised the topic themselves, the researchers would not do so. Experienced, independent facilitators were identified to offer confidential support to both interviewers and interviewees if required. (However, we did collect information on sexual violence and abuse in the questionnaire.) These decisions were determined by the balance between the level of skills achieved by interviewers and the counselling support available if women being interviewed requested it, and the need to recognise the high level of abuse many women have faced. It should be more widely acknowledged that interviews can raise painful issues, potentially causing harm or distress in the absence of appropriate support.

In both projects, the combined use of qualitative interviews with a question-naire, in a climate of scepticism towards non-quantitative data, was seen as a powerful way to convince purchasers and providers in the health services of the research findings. It also enabled a process of triangulation to take place for the final analysis. In Project II, the questionnaire was especially important in providing women with anonymity and confidentiality in their responses to the personal questions being asked. From the analysis, both research groups then identified recommendations for the final reports to be presented to the purchasers and providers of health services. Open meetings were held in both communities to ensure that the findings were shared outside the research groups, and to enable further comments on the recommendations. Sharing of information by researchers with those being interviewed was seen as a small contribution towards the time and effort people had put in to the research and relevant information leaflets were distributed where required. The research findings continue to be used by both research groups in their ongoing efforts to influence the quality of care being provided to their relevant communities.

In Project I, the group's success in preventing the closure of the community health clinic and their subsequent involvement in the recruitment of two new GPs for their community has motivated, inspired and given a sense of individual as well as collective empowerment to all those involved in the project. On completion of the research and the production of a final report, participants in the research decided not to disband, but are now the health advisory group with a holistic health agenda. It is already racing ahead, in some instances ahead of the health authorities, with new ideas for improving and introducing new health initiatives in their local communities. The group has insisted on a partnership arrangement with the local health authorities and health trusts, which includes consultation on all aspects of planning present and future health services in their area.

In Project II, there have been ongoing requests for project members to present the findings and recommendations of the research in seminars for purchasers and providers of sexual health services and, in some instances, health promotion units have been instructed to implement the SHADY report recommendations. To date, the final report has provided both users and professionals with comprehensive information on women's views about sexual health in the UK. Although the research group has now disbanded, many of the team maintain contact and continue to use the skills they gained through the research project.

Concluding remarks

There is a need for professionals to be clear about what they mean by the terms 'participation' and 'empowerment' to avoid confusion and to establish how these concepts will be applied in practice. The more radical interpretations of participation and empowerment have been hijacked by dominant, powerful groups and redefined to eliminate what is seen as a potential threat to the *status quo*, setting the scene for what Humphries calls 'contradictions':

> We are living in a period of profound contradiction. The rhetoric of empowerment drops on our heads at every turn like confetti, its mention directly or by implication *de rigueur* in articles, books and political statements. It has become a key objective in the training of professionals of all kinds, particularly in the 'caring' professions.
>
> (Humphries 1996: 1)

To be empowered within the context of these case studies was to challenge the dominant norms and values of conventional research which perpetuate discriminatory practices and yet be able to achieve a high-quality and professional output. Through the research process, the information, knowledge and confidence gained enabled participants to challenge the assumed rights of professionals to be solely responsible for planning and making decisions about how and what health services are provided to local communities. Participants in Project I, through their confidence and skills, were able to make a difference by changing the way the system makes decisions for the many at a local level.

Investigation into the causes of health inequalities that exist in less egalitarian societies compared to others where inequalities are much less has established strong links between positive health status and social cohesion in community life. The perpetuation of inequalities between individuals and groups is an expensive process for a society as a whole, resulting in decreased health and quality of life for all its citizens. Richard Wilkinson states that,

> [w]hen looking at the nature of the pathways which are most likely to link physical disease to inequality, there are good reasons for thinking that psychosocial pathways are most important. Simply the fact that we are dealing with the effect of relative differences, rather than of absolute material standards, points strongly in that direction. ... What it means is that the quality of the social life of a society is one of the most powerful determinants of health and that this in turn, is very closely related to the degree of income equality. ... The indications that the links are psychosocial make these relationships as important for the real subjective quality of life among modern populations as they are for their health.
>
> (Wilkinson 1996: 4–5)

PR has the potential to strengthen social bonds and thus contribute directly to a decrease in health inequality and an overall improvement in health status. A participatory approach, where the process is owned and shared by all participants, generates much more than just data; it brings about positive changes amongst individuals and groups as a whole. Participating in an empowering process can even improve your health!

Acknowledgements

I would like to thank friends and colleagues who worked with me on both of these projects, with special thanks to members of BECHAG and SHADY. A thank you also to the European Commission, health authorities and the voluntary sector who funded the projects.

References

Bhavnani, K. (1988) 'Empowerment and social research: some comments', *Text* 8: 1–2, 41–50.

Braidotti, R., Charkiewicz, E., Hausler, S. and Wieringa, S. (1994) *Women, Environment and Sustainable Development: Towards a theoretical synthesis*, London: Zed Books Ltd, in association with INSTRAW.

Cornwall, A. and Jewkes, R. (1995) 'What is participatory research?', *Social Science and Medicine* 41 (12): 1667–76.

De Koning, K. and Martin, M. (eds) (1996) *Participatory Research in Health: Issues and experiences*, London: Zed Books Ltd.

Dockery, G. (1996) 'Rhetoric or reality? Participatory research in the National Health Service, UK', in K. de Koning and M. Martin (eds) *Participatory Research in Health: Issues and experiences*, London: Zed Books Ltd, pp. 164–76.

Dockery, G., McDermott, L., Price, J. and Shaw, L. (1997) ' "We just have normal sex": the perceptions and experiences in sexual health of women who have sex with women in Merseyside and Cheshire', *The Journal of Contemporary Health* 5, Spring: 42–6.

Easterby-Smith, M. (1992) 'Creating a learning organisation', *Personnel Review* 19 (5): 24–8.

Erasaari, R. (1986) 'The new social state?', *Acta Sociologica* 29: 225–41.

Everton Road Clinic Campaign and Research Group and Dockery, G. (1997) *Final Reserach Report: Community Led Research on GP and Clinic Services in the Everton/Breckfield Areas of Liverpool*, Liverpool: BECHAG.

Grunow, D. (1986) 'Debureaucratization and the self-help movement', in E. Oyer (ed.) *Comparing Welfare States and their Futures*, London: Gower.

Haraway, D. (1988) 'Situated knowledges: the science question in feminism and the privilege of partial perspective', *Feminist Studies* 14 (3): 575–97.

Humphries, B. (1996) 'Contradictions in the culture of empowerment', in B. Humphries (ed.) *Critical Perspectives on Empowerment*, Birmingham: Venture Press Ltd, pp. 1–16.

Liverpool City Council (1991) *1991 Census: Key Statistics Liverpool Wards 1971/81/91*, Liverpool: LCC.

Maguire, P. (1996) 'Proposing a more feminist participatory research: knowing and being embraced openly', in K. de Koning and M. Martin (eds) *Participatory Research in Health: Issues and experiences*, London: Zed Books Ltd, pp. 27–39.

Mersey Regional Health Authority (1994) *Strategic Statement: Improving health in Merseyside*, Liverpool: Mersey Regional Health Authority.

NHS Management Executive (1991) *Local Voices: The views of local people in purchasing for health*, Leeds: NHS Executive.

Papadakis, E. (1993) 'Interventions in new social movements', in M. Hammersley (ed.) *Social Research: Philosophy, politics and practice*, London: Sage Publications Ltd, pp. 83–104.

PLA Notes (formerly *RRA Notes*) (1994–7) London: IIED.

Pretty, J. (1995) *Regenerating Agriculture: Policies and practices for sustainability and self-reliance*, London: Earthscan Publications Ltd.

Rose, H. (1990) 'Activists, gender and the community health movement', *Health Promotion International* 5 (3): 209–18.

SHADY (1996) *Final Report of the Research on the Sexual Health Needs of Lesbians, Bisexual Women and Women who have Sex with Women in Merseyside/Cheshire*, Liverpool: SHADY, c/o MASG.

Stacey, M. (1994) 'The power of lay knowledge: a personal view', in J. Popay and G. Williams (eds) *Researching the People's Health*, London: Routledge, pp. 85–98.

Wilkinson, R.G. (1996) *Unhealthy Societies: The afflictions of inequality*, London: Routledge.

Wisner, B. (1988) *Power and Need in Africa: basic human needs and development policies*, London: Earthscan Publications Ltd.

Chapter 8

Deaf and hard of hearing people in court

Using an emancipatory perspective to determine their needs[1]

Donna M. Mertens[2]

> *Relay interpreter:* He was in court. This is while he was in the actual court-room he stood in front of the judge and he was told don't use communica-tion. Let the interpreter take care of the communication, and all you are allowed to answer is yes or no. He was told to keep your hands to the side, don't sign.
>
> *Moderator:* This was in court when you were on the stand, when you were on the stand?
>
> *Deaf participant:* I had to admit to doing what I was charged with. But most of it was just yes, no questions. You know, they asked me questions and I an-swered if I was guilty.
>
> (Real time transcript, March 30, 1996, Chicago, IL)

The opening quotation is taken from a real time transcript of a focus group that was conducted to ascertain the nature of court room experiences for deaf and hard of hearing individuals in the United States of America. A multitude of concerns about obtaining a fair judicial process for people who are deaf or hard of hearing are captured within the text of this short quotation. Concerns such as these gave rise to the project undertaken by the American Judicature Society to improve access to the courts for deaf and hard of hearing people.[3]

The evaluation plan for this project was based on the assumption that program evaluation is a process that can provide information to decision makers and program participants throughout the entire scope of a project. An emancipatory perspective was brought to the program evaluation design in order to highlight concerns about social justice and fairness throughout the evaluation process.

Scholars writing from the perspectives of feminists, ethnic minorities, poor people, and people with disabilities have commonly expressed dissatisfaction with both the post-positivist and interpretive/constructivist paradigms of inquiry, arguing that an emancipatory framework is more appropriate to stop oppression and bring about social justice (Lather 1992; Mertens 1998; Mertens *et al.* 1994; Oliver 1992; Steady 1993). Definition of what it means to conduct research or evaluation within the emancipatory paradigm is somewhat problematic in that it is associated with multiple meanings, and various scholars tend to emphasize different dimensions of this approach. In an effort to define what I mean when I describe this work as emanating from the emancipatory paradigm, I focus on providing explanations and examples of the four following characteristics:

1   it places central importance on the lives and experiences of diverse groups that have traditionally been marginalized;
2   it analyzes how and why inequities based on gender, race/ethnicity, and disability are reflected in asymmetric power relationships;
3   it examines how results of social inquiry on inequities are linked to political and social action (i.e. empowerment of marginalized groups); and
4   it uses an emancipatory theory to develop the program theory and the evaluation approach.

In this chapter, I examine the application of the emancipatory paradigm to the first stage of the development of a training program for judges and other court personnel to improve deaf and hard of hearing people's access to the court system in the United States.[4] This example is particularly appropriate because of the traditional power held by judges and court personnel as contrasted with the relatively powerless position of deaf and hard of hearing people. The project began with a year-long assessment of the needs and concerns of the deaf and hard of hearing people who had previous contact with the judicial system. In the second year of the project, the results of the needs assessment were translated into training materials for judges and other court personnel, and the training was conducted. The impact of the training in the court systems was assessed in the third year of the project. This chapter focuses only on the needs assessment phase of the project.

Methodology

The evaluation began with needs assessment activities designed to 'listen to the voices' of the deaf and hard of hearing people in order to develop training that is validly representative of experiences of those with the least power. The design incorporated sensitivity to the heterogeneity in the deaf and hard of hearing communities in terms of cultural identification, degree of hearing loss, age, gender, presence of additional disabling conditions, race/ethnicity, level of language functioning, socio-economic class, and status with the judicial system (e.g. victim/offender/jurist). Five focus groups were conducted in four regions of the country, and one individual interview was conducted with a deaf-blind woman.

Participants

The criteria used to select the participants for the focus groups and the interview exemplify the application of the emancipatory paradigm in the sense of placing central importance on the lives of diverse groups that traditionally have been marginalized, and in the development of the evaluation approach. First, it should be noted that the individuals whose opinions were solicited were members of the deaf and hard of hearing communities themselves. Thus, the perspectives of the least powerful were solicited to form the basis for the training materials for the judges and other court personnel.

Second, a description of the characteristics of the participants provides evidence that the diversity within the deaf and hard of hearing communities was represented in the data. The preferred mode of communication is one of the key characteristics that is indicative of the representativeness of the diversity of the target population.

A brief explanation of the various communication modes provides the background necessary to understand the criteria that were used to select the groups. These are explained in Table 8.1, along with a grid that depicts the way in which diversity within the communities was represented. In addition, diversity was included in terms of gender, race/ethnicity, presence of additional disability, and status with the court. These characteristics are summarized in Table 8.2.

Emancipatory researchers have tried to debunk the myth of homogeneity in oppressed groups, i.e. that everyone who shares a particular ethnicity or disability or gender is the same (Stanfield 1993). By focusing attention on the diversity of people who are labeled deaf or hard of hearing, it is possible to effectively debunk the myth that all problems can be solved in courts by the provision of sign language interpreters or a particular assistive listening device.

Achieving appropriate representation of interests in deaf and hard of hearing communities was not unproblematic. When research or evaluation is conducted within the emancipatory framework, the goal is to provide access to those who have traditionally been marginalized. Typically, focus groups are constructed to be homogeneous in order to lessen the feeling of intimidation that might result from groups with differential levels of power (Krueger 1988). However, the criteria to use as the basis for determining homogeneity are not necessarily simple and clear. In this project, the determination was made that the preferred mode of communication and hearing status would form the primary criteria for forming groups. This meant that other characteristics were mixed within groups, such as offenders, victims and jurists. Although this mixing had the potential of creating tensions within groups, the focus group moderator tried to defuse this problem by cautioning people to avoid discussing the specifics of their cases. Rather, he asked the participants to focus on communication problems they encountered in the courts.

Table 8.1　Diversity in communication needs and abilities

	Interpreter type	*Able to read captions*	*Assistive listening devices*
Group 1 (*deaf*)[2]	ASL[1]	yes	personal hearing aids
Group 2 (*deaf*) deaf/blind[3]	ASL; relay[4]	limited/no	no
Group 3 (*hard of hearing*)	n/a	yes	personal/room assistive devices
Group 4 (*deaf*)	MSL[5]	limited/no	no
Group 5 (*oral deaf*)	oral[6]	yes	personal hearing aids
Interview	deaf/blind	at close range	no

Note

1　American Sign Language (ASL) is a visual–gestural language that has its own grammatical structure.

2　One man was 'oral deaf' and relied on voicing, lip reading, and the real time captioning.

3　A deaf/blind interpreter uses ASL, but signs directly into the hands of the deaf/blind individual so they can 'feel' the signs.

4　A relay interpreter is a person who can translate from ASL to a simpler form of visual–gestural communication, usually involving some pantomime and explanation of complex concepts in simpler terms.

5　Mexican Sign Language (MSL) is a unique visual–gestural system of communication that has its own signs and grammatical structure.

6　An oral interpreter uses careful enunciation of speech instead of signs to convey the information to the deaf or hard of hearing person who then lip reads the interpreter.

Table 8.2　Demographic characteristics of focus group participants

Gender	Male	15
	Female	17
Race/Ethnicity	Caucasian	17
	African American	6
	Latino	9
Additional disability	None	30
	Deaf/blind	2
Status in court[1]	Victim	10
	Defendant	11
	Witness	12
	Party	3
	Jurist	9
	Other (advocate)	3
Total in each category		32

Note:

1　Participants could choose multiple responses for this item.

A second issue associated with running focus groups in this study is that participants in a marginalized community often live in closer social circles than those in the mainstream.[5] Thus, the participants may be known to each other. Indeed, we did find this to be true in our focus groups. The caution to discuss only communication problems was again used to allow participants permission to reveal only personal experiences that they were comfortable sharing.

Data collection process

An emancipatory framework was used to develop the evaluation approach. First, the American Judicature Society established an advisory committee that included deaf and hard of hearing judges and attorneys, and other representatives of the courts and judicial education. Second, the evaluator shared the evaluation approach with the advisory committee and agency staff to explain the concept of an emancipatory approach to evaluation, as well as to solicit their input into the evaluation plan itself. Their comments were used as a basis for the development of the plan, which is viewed as a 'work in progress', to be amended as needed during the course of the project.

The key to the first year's work was to use the focus groups as a needs assessment tool for obtaining data concerning the needs and concerns of deaf and hard of hearing adults in the judicial system. The focus group was viewed as being an appropriate vehicle for this purpose because focus groups are structured to elicit the issues that are most salient for the participants (Billson 1996). It is a forum in which the participants are viewed as the experts on their own experiences. Thus, the data that are generated are reflective of the concerns of the marginalized group, and not those of the researcher.

Data were collected during the focus group sessions by means of observation, video recording, real time reporting that resulted in transcripts, short evaluation forms completed by the participants, and debriefing with the agency staff, focus group moderators, observers (including available Advisory Committee members), and the evaluator at the end of each session. Data were analyzed by means of a temporal pattern of activities, from the time of first contact with the judicial system until resolution of the judicial matter (e.g. sentencing, dismissal, etc.).

The focus groups yielded information by means of the substance of the participants' comments about their needs and concerns, as well as by insights gained from observing the process of and problems with communication in the groups. These insights have implications for fair practices in the courts, as well as revealing problems and challenges in trying to conduct inquiry within an emancipatory paradigm. The need for technical equipment and trained personnel represents a high cost in terms of money and access to appropriate equipment and people. The exact needs varied from group to group; some of the variations are described in the following three examples that serve to illustrate the 'lived learning' that occurred during the focus groups.

First, in the second focus group, deaf individuals were sought who represented the less-educated, limited-language part of that population. In anticipation of the need for accommodation to achieve effective communication, two American Sign Language (ASL) interpreters, one relay interpreter and a real time reporter were hired. Even with this network of support, communication was challenging, suggesting that the conduct of research with the appropriate support systems is problematic. With the best knowledge available regarding appropriate communication supports and the resources to provide those, perfect communication was not achieved.

In this less-educated group, one deaf man did not understand basic concepts such as who a lawyer is or who a judge is. This person was unable to process the messages communicated by the sign language interpreters. Therefore, the relay interpreter pantomimed and described in greater detail the situations that were being discussed. For example, instead of using the sign for 'judge', the relay interpreter signed: 'You remember the man in court; the man who wore the black robes?' This man with limited language skills is the same person featured in the opening quotation of this chapter who was told to admit to the charges, keep his hands at his sides, and only shake his head 'yes' or 'no' during his court hearing. Yet it was clear in the focus group that he would not have understood the signs, or the concepts that would have been presented in the court room.

Second, in the focus group for late-deafened and hard of hearing adults, efforts were made to provide appropriate assistive listening devices. A real time reporter was hired to provide written captions during the focus group, and the staff consulted with the Advisory Committee members and an FM Accommodations consultant in order to arrange an effective communication environment. When the focus group moderator began the session, he explained that assistive listening devices were available, and asked if everyone could hear him and understand what was being said. At the beginning of the session, everyone said 'yes' that they could hear and understand. However, during the first break, two of the participants started talking and one indicated that she was unable to hear the conversation during the focus group because she used a cochlear implant and needed a cable that would allow her to make use of her personal device. These two participants brought this to the attention of the staff before the second half of the focus group, and the FM consultant indicated that people with cochlear implants should bring their own cables. The following comment clarifies the importance of using the emancipatory 'lens' when choosing an evaluation approach and in the interpretation of results:

Participant 2.1: Maybe you should know that Jill is now using my cochlear implant cable. I'm not being critical of the gentleman that provided the equipment. But I mentioned before that people with cochlear implants use that cable and the system today did not have any cables. And he erroneously assumed that all people with cochlear implants have their own cables. But we don't. They cost $60 to us from the manufacturer, and many people cannot afford them. And Jill does not have a cable. So she took her cochlear implant out, and she was trying to hear with a hearing aid and a neck loop. And it wasn't working very well for her. So I lent her my cable, and I'm doing fine. I'd rather she used it. But you should be aware of that because I think it's important in providing accessories like cochlear implant cables and personal receivers. Then I mentioned I could hear myself better when I unplugged it. The personal receivers have an external microphone on them so you can hear your own voice when you're speaking. And we don't have those either today. And I think it's important to meet the different aspects of hearing loss, the kinds of accessories that we need.

So, in using this approach, an environment was created in the focus group that provided the participants with the opportunity to express their communication needs in a way that revealed insights into what is required for effective communication in this group. This underscores both the complexity of the assistive listening devices that are required, and provides information that can be shared with court personnel concerning the need for a range of devices they should have available for this population.

The third example involves a comparison of the late-deafened adults and the Mexican Sign Language (MSL) users in terms of their ability to describe their experiences in court. The Advisory Committee members had reminded the staff that the purpose of the focus group was to obtain information to be used for developing the training for judges and other court personnel, and that the focus group moderator should try to steer the conversation toward their experiences in the court itself. To this end, he opened the focus group for the late-deafened adults with the request that participants describe 'difficulties in finding where you need to go, whom you need to meet, what you need to do, all of that, that are related, of course, to your hearing.' The participants then proceeded to relate their experiences of trying to obtain appropriate assistive listening devices after they had received notice that they needed to appear in court.

The moderator then made a similar request at the beginning of the focus group for the users of MSL. He said, 'Okay. Let's start with when you go into court. Tell us about any problems you had finding your way around.' The response was quite different from the late-deafened group, as is seen in this MSL user's initial comment that followed the request:

> I was arrested for stealing. I went to jail for three days. While I was in jail, I was trying to tell the officers that I needed to make a telephone call to have someone bail me out. The officers took my number or my request three times on paper. All the other hearing individuals could make phone calls. I couldn't. I need an interpreter. An interpreter was never called to jail. I was not bailed out. So what happened was I went to court.

The moderator tried to re-focus the person on the court experience, but he was interrupted by another respondent who wanted to 'tell his story' from the time of his first encounter with the police on another charge. And so the stories continued throughout the focus group, each person starting their individual story at the beginning, unable to begin toward the 'end of the story', describing the court experience itself.

During the first break in the focus group, the interpreter explained that this way of telling the story is necessary in this population because their mode of communication is visual–gestural. In order to tell the story, they have to set up the context in which the actions occurred. In a culture that is print-based, a person can jump to the end of the book, so to speak. But, in a visual–gestural culture, the context has to be established in order to tell the conclusion. This is a point that was made at the very first meeting of the Advisory Committee by several of the deaf attorneys who serve on the Committee.

The staff and the moderator expressed frustration about the communication – it seemed slow and difficult to control. One could guess that the reaction of court personnel to this type of communication system might be similar. The complexity of the communication issues is compounded by the cultural practice of telling the individual stories from beginning to end with enough details to establish the 'picture', i.e. the context in which the actions occurred. With time pressures in court, it might be anticipated that a cultural clash could occur between a deaf persons' ways of expressing themselves and the court's desire to have an expeditious proceeding.

From these experiences, one might conclude that focus groups were an inappropriate vehicle for obtaining information about this populations' needs and concerns. However, if the focus group is viewed as an attempt to provide an ideal setting for communication to occur, and problems such as these occurred anyway, then one might infer that the courts (a far less ideal situation) might need to make accommodation to insure fair trials and appropriate judicial experiences for this population.

Results

The purpose of this section is to illustrate two basic principles of the emancipatory approach, rather than give a comprehensive report of the study's results. First, selective results are used to explain how and why inequities based on disability are reflected in asymmetric power relationships. Then, I explore the link between the results and social and political action.

Asymmetric power relationships

Many characteristics are associated with higher power status in our society, such as being male, White, able bodied and wealthy. In this chapter, I focus on differences in power that arise from hearing status, as well as position in the court. The contrast of experiences within the deaf and hard of hearing communities themselves provides one illustration of power differences and their consequences. The group of late-deafened/hard of hearing adults explained that they had little difficulty in maneuvering around the court house, finding where they had to be and who they had to meet. They explained that they brought their written notice to the courthouse, read the signs, voiced for themselves, read people's lips, and, if they had additional questions, they wrote them down and handed them to the court personnel. Their one complaint was that they had to bring the paper and pen themselves, and they thought it would be more appropriate for the court personnel to have paper and pen at hand.

In contrast, one user of MSL described arriving at the court house with his paper in hand – he had received a citation for a seat belt violation. He said that he showed his paper to people in the court house, but being unable to read, speak, lip read, write English or Spanish, or understand ASL, he finally became frustrated and left. He was unaware that the consequences for nonappearance in court was a bench warrant being issued for his arrest. A short time later, he reported that he was detained because he did not have the correct change to purchase a train ticket, and so he jumped the turnstile to gain entry to the train station. When the security officer ran a check on him, he found that there was a bench warrant out for his arrest. A bench warrant is a much more serious issue than a seat belt violation, and so he was taken to jail. From there, his situation degenerated as no interpreter that understood MSL was available to him. No TDD telephones were available near the jail. Thus, the 'power' of being able to communicate in a more-close to mainstream manner is illustrated in the contrasting stories found in these two groups.

The initial quotation that started this chapter can also be analyzed in terms of the power relations that exist. A deaf man with low-language functioning is instructed to admit to what he was charged with, not to sign, and only to shake his head 'yes' or 'no' in the court room. McAlister (1994) noted that 'Problems surface when a trial court confines its inquiry to mostly 'yes/no' questions to elicit the defendant's understanding of the rights she waives and to determine whether the waiver was constitutional. A colloquy in which a defendant answers only 'yes/no' questions is generally insufficient upon which to find a competent waiver of constitutional rights' (p. 190).

Other examples of asymmetric power relations related to ability to hear and standing in the court abound in the focus group transcripts. One deaf woman reported that she had been violently raped. No interpreter was present with her in the police station when she first tried to report the crime. She said she did have an interpreter when she met with her lawyer. However, when the accused man's lawyer entered the discussions, he did not work with the interpreter so that she could understand what was being said. She said that when they did go to court, the accused rapist was released, and to this day she does not know why. Her lawyer told her it had something to do with the way she reported the crime.

The deaf and hard of hearing persons who could voice for themselves reported that they all had been initially denied accommodation for their hearing loss because the judge and other court personnel said that if they could speak that well, they did not need an interpreter or other accommodation. The judge and court personnel have the power to deny access to appropriate accommodation. They decided that if they could hear the deaf or hard of hearing person then there was no problem, despite the fact that the deaf or hard of hearing person could not understand the proceedings. In addition, this group of individuals also reported that court personnel had hung up on them on the telephone when they had attempted to make contact through the telephone relay service.

Link to action

The participants in the focus group were asked to express their ideas about what kind of changes were needed in the court system. The following ideas for action were generated by the participants during the focus groups, staff and others in the debriefing sessions, and a review of literature related to deaf and hard of hearing people in the courts. The ideas can be categorized as relating to communication support services or cultural issues.

Communication services

The communication support services that are needed vary according to the needs and capabilities of the deaf and hard of hearing people interacting with the court. First, there is a need for a relay interpreter for deaf people with limited language or users of a sign language other than ASL. As was mentioned previously, the relay interpreter needed to pantomime or simplify legal concepts so that the deaf man with limited language could understand. As McAlister noted:

> If the deaf person does not understand the concept that a particular sign is meant to convey, the method of communication used is irrelevant because the deaf person will not understand the meaning of the communication. For adequate comprehension, *a deaf person must understand both the method and the content of the communication*. Individuals with minimal language skills typically do not have the conceptual framework for legal concepts, just as they do not have the linguistic skills necessary to convey those legal concepts.
>
> (McAlister 1994: 181)

The responsibility for the relay interpreter is then to translate the concepts into signs and concepts that are familiar to the deaf person. McAlister used the example of the word 'subpoena', which might be translated into ASL signs equivalent to the English words: 'paper require you show-up court later' (*ibid.* 183).

Court systems need to be able to provide the appropriate type of interpreter in a timely fashion. Depending on the deaf person's preferred mode of communication, this might be an ASL, MSL or oral interpreter. Other types of interpreters that did not arise in the current study might include a Signed Exact English interpreter, or a cued speech interpreter.

For hard of hearing people, appropriate assistive listening devices are needed. Often, courts would offer to provide a sign language interpreter when contacted by a late-deafened or hard of hearing individual. However, they did not use sign language, and therefore that would not have been an appropriate accommodation for them. One respondent described a variety of assistive listening devices that courts could have available, recognizing that one system will not be appropriate for everyone. For example, people who wear one kind of hearing aid can benefit by using the FM loop that they wear around their necks. Other people use a silhouette, which is a hearing aid that is shaped like a little thin disc that fits behind the hearing aid and plugs into a personal receiver. Then there are people who have cochlear implants who need a cable that can plug into a receiver and external microphone. The complexity of the technology was previously discussed in this chapter in terms of the need for the special cable for the cochlear implant users.

Another type of communication support that was used and discussed in this study is the use of real time captioning. Courts could use a system such as this for individuals who are deaf and hard of hearing and able to read English. The participants in our study reported difficulty in obtaining real time captioning, being transferred from office to office, with no one claiming to know about it or how to obtain it in a court room.

Appropriate accommodations such as those that have been included in the above commentary must be available to deaf and hard of hearing individuals in a timely manner. In one situation, a request for the appropriate listening support system resulted in notice that the case would have to be delayed for six months (if the deaf woman insisted on having the appropriate support). As this was a child custody case, a six month delay could have disastrous consequences. Therefore, the woman chose to go to court without appropriate technical support.

Cultural issues

Four issues of a cultural nature arose that relate to providing improved access to the courts for deaf and hard of hearing individuals. First, the 'telling of the story' that was mentioned previously is a cultural way of expression that is at odds with general court procedures. In a visual–gestural mode of communication, it is necessary to establish the 'picture' in which the action occurs. This is a bit time-consuming and could be viewed by the court as information that is 'off the point'. Nevertheless, it is necessary for the deaf person who uses this mode of communication in order to adequately express their experiences. It might be necessary to establish a mediator who could get the information accurately from the deaf client and then convey it more succinctly to the court.

Second, the participants reported being arrested or witnessing others who were arrested because the police misunderstood their sign language as being indicative of aggressive behavior. One participant described her experience when the police came to arrest her husband as follows:

> But then when the officers arrested him, he was asleep. The police woke him up. And he started saying to the officers, leave me alone, leave me alone, in sign language, waving his arms, thinking it was his brother both-ering him. The police thought he was waving his arms to attack them, and they jumped him. When I tried to get involved, the cops told me to stop and pushed me out of the way. There was not communication between the officers and him except for the fact that they communicated with him with their fists that they were going to beat him up and arrest him. I said why are you going to arrest him? They said, well, someone said spousal abuse. ... There was no communication. The police seemed too busy arresting him. And I'm trying to get involved and tell the officers, no he's deaf. And they never communicated. I never did say anything about spousal abuse. ... So when it came time for trial, all of this was dropped.

Third, participants reported that judges sometimes look at a person and see only the person's disability, not their capabilities. One participant described a case involving child custody as follows:

> A lot of time some of the decisions made by the judge and the lawyers because of lack of training and lack of knowledge of what a deaf or hard of hearing person can do and an understanding of deafness. ... Especially in a situation where the deaf mother who was almost going to lose her child, I mean the judge looked at the girl (deaf mother), looked and thought deaf, didn't believe it, he had no idea. He felt that the mother of the deaf woman should have the child because this girl, she's deaf, she's not able. They looked at her as if she was disabled, that she was incapable of raising a child, and that was a frightening situation for the deaf community.

Fourth, judges and other court personnel sometime mistakenly assume that because a person cannot hear that he or she is stupid. This last vignette describes such an experience:

This is a kind of proceeding, where you had to go in to the judge and meet with him and make sure that everything that was on the statement was true and this kind of thing. And my attorney was with me. And we were sitting about that wall to this wall distance [indicating about six feet]. And the judge was talking, and he was talking to me. Of course, I wasn't aware of it. I thought, well, it must be my attorney that he's talking to. But my attorney didn't respond. And I finally realized that he was talking to me. So I said, I'm sorry, your honor, but I am hearing impaired. Would it be okay if I approached the bench? And he finally allowed me to do that. And he still started going, speaking very, very quickly. And I – when it was my turn, I said, I am really sorry, but I just did not understand what you said. He immediately started talking to me like I was a child of five. The vocabulary. There was anger in his voice because I didn't understand him, I'm a grown woman and I was not – and I already told him I was hearing impaired. So again, I had to stop him and say, no. I can understand your words. I can't understand your voice. I could not hear your voice. And so that happens frequently. People think because you can't hear you have no brain.

Conclusion

Although the action-oriented recommendations that resulted from this study seem obvious, such as not trying to fit the same size or type of hearing aid on everyone, it does not appear to be obvious to the courts that there is a need to be responsive to individual needs. Two further examples serve to illustrate the need to increase communication between the courts and the deaf and hard of hearing communities. In one instance, a hard of hearing woman was asked to attend a public hearing on assistive listening systems in the courts. She said:

> They invited me to use the assistive listening system. And I was so glad that I did because it gave me the opportunity to criticize it. Because what they had provided was a big box for maybe fifty headsets. ... I told them that there are a variety of accessories available. ... And I told them they should seriously consider a variety of accessories so that people with hearing loss could pick the accessory that enables them to use the system.

A second recommendation grew out of a link between the deaf and hard of hearing communities and the courts. A woman who had been successful in obtaining the real time captioning for her court experiences was invited back to the court house to speak to the court reporters during their lunch break about the experience. She was able to dialogue with them and answer their questions. She expanded on that experience with the following suggestion:

Have you ever – has the recommendation been made in the past that it might be beneficial to have community advisory committees for the courts of local people who have all kinds of disabilities to listen to some of the situations and problems that have come up locally and make recommendations?

... And that they would allow people with disabilities to give input, but it would also be a pool of resources for court personnel to contact people if they have a question pertaining to how to accommodate a person with a disability.

Framing an inquiry within the emancipatory paradigm does not guarantee that emancipation or empowerment will occur. What does emancipation or empowerment of deaf and hard of hearing people mean in this study? The needs assessment phase of this project was designed to obtain input into the needs and possible courses of action from the members of the deaf and hard of hearing communities. The deaf and hard of hearing people's views were integrated into the design of training for the judges and other court personnel to improve access to the courts in terms of both communication and cultural accommodations. A videotape, entitled 'Silent Justice', was made that featured some of the focus group participants telling their own stories. The focus group participants were also invited to participate in the consumer panels at the court training workshops and on planning teams for improved court access in their states. Thus, they have been given access to power through these means. Documentation of changes in the court systems themselves represents the next stage of the project.

Notes

1   Paper presented at Essex '96, Colchester, England, July 3, 1996, as part of the Emancipatory/Anti-Discriminatory Research Theme.
2   Dr Mertens was chosen to be the evaluator for the project because she has 25 years' experience in conducting evaluations, 14 years' experience teaching deaf and hard of hearing university students, and an advanced rating of competency in sign language. For further correspondence, Dr Mertens can be contacted at: 4600 Marie St, Beltsville, MD 20705 USA, (202) 651–5202, or Donna.Mertens@Gallaudet.edu
3   Funding for the project was provided by the W.K. Kellogg Foundation.
4   This chapter includes a description of the methodological implications of working within the emancipatory paradigm. For further reading on the epistemological and ontological assumptions that underlie this paradigm, see Mertens (1998).
5   My thanks to Carole Truman and members of the AJS Advisory Board for raising this issue concerning confidentiality and micro-politics in a marginalized community.

References

Billson, J.M. (1996) *Focus Groups for Social and Market Research: A training manual*, Alexandria, VA: Group Dimensions Research.

Krueger, R.A. (1988) *Focus Groups: A practical guide for applied research*, Thousand Oaks, CA: Sage Publications.

Lather, P. (1992) 'Critical frames in educational research: feminist and post-structural perspectives', *Theory into Practice* 31 (2): 1–13.

McAlister, J. (1994) 'Deaf and hard of hearing criminal defendants: how you gonna get justice if you can't talk to the judge?' *Arizona State Law Journal* 26 (1): 163–200.

Mertens, D.M. (1998) *Research Methods in Education and Psychology: Integrating diversity with quantitative and qualitative approaches*, Thousand Oaks, CA: Sage Publications.

Mertens, D.M., Farley, J., Madison, A.M. and Singleton, P. (1994) 'Diverse voices in evaluation practice: feminists, minorities, and persons with disabilities', *Evaluation Practice* 15 (2): 123–9.

Oliver, M. (1992) 'Changing the social relations of research production?', *Disability, Handicap and Society* 7 (2): 101–14.

Stanfield, J.H., II (1993) 'Methodological reflections: an introduction', in J.H. Stanfield and R. Dennis (eds) *Race and Ethnicity in Research Methods*, Thousand Oaks, CA: Sage Publications, pp. 3–15.

Steady, F.C. (1993) 'Women and collective action', in S.M. James and A.P.A. Busia (eds) *Theorizing Black Feminisms*, London: Routledge, pp. 90–101.

Chapter 9

Ethnography in the form of theatre with emancipatory intentions

Jim Mienczakowski

'People Like Us'

Dora: In my own warped way I thought that what I had with my husband was love. Even the violence. I thought that was an expression of love. ... I always got into fights with my husband. That's the only way I knew how to get a response. I'd push him to the edge and then I'd get beaten or hit over the head. I knew myself I'd done wrong but I just wanted to get punished – and my husband was quite cruel at times with that. I used to drink to get into a fight so that I could get punished. I knew what I was doing and my husband would always hit me. ... *(Pause)* I keep pushing and pushing and pushing. *(Pause)* My husband stuck a broken glass in my neck once. *(She shows her scar.)* He was a drinker too – but he wouldn't admit it. Not even to himself. A bloody accountant. People thought we had it made. You can't possibly understand people like us.

(*Busting*, Act II, Scene ii)

Wayne: I was nearly married once. Couldn't last, but. Not with people like us. ... But either your woman drinks and you just go down hill together or she doesn't drink and can't understand yah. Either way you're frigged from the start.

(*Busting*, Act I, Scene iii)[1]

Overview

The body of work described as critical ethno-drama in this chapter seeks to provide reflexive insights for care givers, health agencies and others into the worlds of certain health consumer communities, specifically those relating to experiences of schizophrenic psychosis and institutionalised detoxification processes. In telling the stories of groups of health consumers and health professionals to health and student communities via the medium of ethnographically-derived theatre (in which the meanings and explanations of the performances are negotiated with audiences in forum discussions at the close of each performance), the potential to share insights and negotiate explanations and meanings (Bakhtin 1984) is created.

As an ethnographer and teacher of social science research methodologies and the performing arts, I have been only too aware of how small the readership of most academic ethnographic reports can be and how receptive and yet *unchallenged* the audiences of most theatrical productions remain. Moreover, it is most uncommon for the informants of a given research project to be able to access and comment upon an ethnographic account, to which they have contributed, once it has been constructed and objectified as an academic report (Cherryholmes 1993). The processes of critical ethno-drama attempt to offer emancipatory insights by telling informants' stories, largely narrated in their own words, to wide audiences inside and outside the confines of the academy. By combining research process with theatrical narratives constructed by informants, it is hoped that research becomes relevant to both its informants and those outside the academy. For me, the idea of assisting health informants to establish their own agenda and criteria for empowerment and then giving them the means to publicly voice such an agenda is an entirely appealing notion. Blending ethnographic research and critical pedagogy in order to give voice to those arbitrarily marginalised by the nature of their health constraints, I believe, has the potential to create a *worthwhile theatre*.

As the explanations, meanings and insights generated by ethno-drama performances are consensually controlled and constructed by informant groups, they represent not only an opportunity for informants to voice their under-standings, explanations, experiences and emotional location within the circumstances of their health, but opportunities for student nurses and health professionals to reflect upon their own professional practices (Coffey and Atkinson 1996). The ethno-drama process neither reflects a recidivistic return to an idealised form of critical–emancipatory practice nor an embracing of postmodern fragmentation. Far from it. If we view the postmodern fracturing of meta-narratives not in Lyotard's (1984) terms of 'shattering' but more as dislocation, segmentalisation, specialisation and localisation (Bernstein 1996), then we might see postmodern stories not as a disheartening rupturing of human understanding but as a more useful micro-minutia discourse on what is going on. Essentially, in ethno-drama, we are polyphonically voicing the health agenda of informants in a 'public voice' (Agger 1991) to wide audiences who might otherwise be disadvantaged or inhibited from accessing and interpreting the micro-minutia discourses of research data presented in a traditional academic form.

Background

Since 1992, two major ethno-drama productions have involved funded research shared between the Faculties of Nursing and Health Sciences and Education and the Arts, Griffith University, Australia, and a third student-led ethnoperformance project has involved a community group of persons with acquired brain injuries and able-bodied student actors. The cross-faculty productions, both two-act full-length performance pieces, entailed casts and production teams of around thirty-five and were used as coursework elements for student assessment for the nursing and theatre students involved in them. The research is ongoing and a follow-up data-gathering tour of the production Busting[2] took place in 1998. As part of the research process, the ethnographically derived scripts are published and circulated to health authorities and community groups for comment and amendment; they are also made available to audiences throughout the performances. After careful validation of contents and representations made, the scripts are performed to invited groups of health consumers, health professionals and health agencies and are forum workshopped (Boal 1985 [1979]) in order to continually add data to the process. Perform-ances, typically sponsored by health education agencies, are also performed to general audiences of school and tertiary students and interested others as part of an overt attempt to influence understanding and attitudes towards given health issues (Mienczakowski et al. 1993).

The full-length plays, Busting[3] (which describes alcohol detoxification processes) and its predecessor, Syncing Out Loud (an ethnographically-based play concerning experiences of schizophrenic illness), were born out of a desire to meld theatre and ethnographic research into a reflexive, reflective teaching tool. The pilot project, Syncing Out Loud, performed by nursing students and actors in theatres and a residential psychiatric setting to health informants and health professionals, followed a well-established heritage of psychotherapeutic nursing strategies intended to promote insight and discussion amongst nursing students and health consumers (Cox 1989; Price 1992). The use of professional actors to assume the role of patients in order for medical students to practise nursing interventions has been described by Cox (ibid.). Watkins (1990: 47–8) extends the role-playing use of actors in depicting the enactment of 'critical incidents' from nursing–patient histories in order for students to explore the emotional experience of patient/family and health professional relationships. The Busting and Syncing Out Loud projects further develop the function of role-playing real-life scenarios for vicarious training purposes by dramatising informants' life experiences and involving student nurses and others in both the characterisation and researching of the roles. Here, student nurses not only play the parts of professional nurses in the scenarios, they are also engaged in the characterisation, research and prolonged representation of the experiences and perceptions of health consumers and their families, and ultimately take responsibility for their performed representations during forum interactions[4] (Boal 1985 [1979]). During the forum sessions informants are able to reflect upon the actor's interpretation and representation of self (Turner 1986; Conquergood 1988, 1991) and audiences, in general, may realise how particular social and mental health issues are experienced (Mienczakowski 1996). Essentially, forum elements involve audiences questioning and debating the representations made on stage with the actors, informant representatives and project writers and directors. Forum validation sessions, which supply each audience member with a copy of the script and a supplementary questionnaire, are recorded on audio tape. Data drawn from the forum discussions may be added to the performance script, which is periodically revised and amended as the representations given during performances change meaning. In this way the script is always under revision and remains open to amendment and change. It is never finished and the understandings generated within it are never closed.

The guiding principle leading this critical theory-based ethnographic approach[5] is to attempt to accurately give voice to groups of health consumers who otherwise consider themselves to be disempowered or disenfranchised in some way. In voicing their arguments in their own words we intended to compare and contrast their explanations of the circumstances surrounding their health consumption with the impressions and perceptions of their life-worlds accepted as health explanations by the general public as well as by health professionals. Thus, through an extension of the forum theatre techniques of Boal (1985 [1979]) in which the representations of the plays are debated with audiences, an intentional 'collision of cultures' (Bharucha 1993) between the worlds of alcohol dependency and schizophrenic psychosis, for example, and their parent cultures can be engineered. At all times, consensus with the contributors is paramount (Habermas 1971, 1984, 1987) and the scripts are permanently subject to amendment and revision to ensure that the representations made are recognisable to, and offer the insights desired by, informant groups. It must be noted here that informants include health consumers, care givers and health professionals working within the research settings.

Health promotion voices

The remit of the *Busting* project's funding bodies was to create community understanding and awareness of alcohol and drug issues. The theatre spaces selected for performances to school and university audiences were consequently used as health education arenas by community health agencies. During *Syncing Out Loud*, psychiatric support agencies provided health promotional literature to all audience members. At every performance, intermission and forum discussion counsellors and psychiatric nurses were on hand. In *Busting*, free drinks followed by 'penalty-free' alcohol impairment breath tests were provided for audience volunteers by community police during the play's intermission. Again, social services and AA counsellors were present at each showing, as were other health support agencies. Packages of health education support materials were supplied to participating schools and copies of the scripts/project report, funded by community health agencies, were made available to audience members. (The script versions of the performances have subsequently been included as teaching materials for nurse education students in a number of university nursing departments.)

Who gets a voice? How research does or does not become representation

No representation, either written or performed, is added to the overall production until it has been vetted, discussed and validated by informant groups or their representatives present at every scripting and rehearsal session. This typically involves nursing staff who confirm that the physical and semiotic representations of their professional settings, made by the actors, are authentic and relevant. In both the *Busting* and *Syncing Out Loud* projects, informants were invited to participate in the rehearsal process to guide actors whilst actors reciprocally undertook periods of immersion within clinical settings. In these circumstances, pairing involved partnerships between students and nurses already working in the environment under study. The extract below, taken from a nursing informant during a group scripting session, is typical of data gathered by researchers involved in these reciprocal arrangements and reflects the overt voicing of both health and nursing agendas.

> Lisa: (*Slow fade until the level of lighting has been reduced sufficiently to overlay the actors' faces with slow sequence of slides showing people in drinking situations – including the collage sequences from Act I. Lisa checks the contents of the drugs trolley and writes up her observation notes as she talks.*) We need people in this unit who can offer women support. The women in here are silent drinkers, just like all women with dependency problems must be silent. And there are so many of them out there. Thousands and thousands of women in every city of this country are raging Valium addicts or Serepax addicts or temaze-pam addicts – and they don't know where to go to get help. Most of them don't even know that they need it: because they are women and women aren't supposed to be seen 'out of control' or using something to 'get by'. ... And though we might get a few women through detox, not many can stay to get rehab and the kind of help they really need – because they've got kids and other responsibilities to deal with apart from themselves. So they come in more and more often just to clean up and then they slowly drift into chronic alcoholism. Just because there isn't anyone else to care for the kids and nowhere for them to go with their kids where they can get the help that they need – until the social welfare takes the kids off them.
>
> (*Busting*, Act II Scene iii, p. 76)

The stage setting of the play *Busting* replicated that of the research setting, containing nursing stations and medical equipment, etc., so that nursing and health informant behaviours/routines could be accurately portrayed. Besides informing actors of the perceived veracity and worth of their scripted dialogue, their *physical representations* of health and nursing behaviours within the setting were also subjected to close scrutiny and consensual change.

Before being shown to general audiences, the entire report/script and ethno-drama production is validated by groups of health informants who are bussed to special closed validation performances. At this stage, if informants object to representations being made in the play (and no consensual solution can be found) then the offending scenarios are deleted from the performances. By way of example, the following field notes/script were part of the *Busting* Research Project. Drafted from field notes and combined with informant anecdote the scenario was to be scripted for performance. In the final analysis none of the following data were added to the *Busting* performance script but the incident did add to the overall understanding of the phenomenon being studied. Seen from an informant point of view, the data fails to capture the informant's perspective in a form which will prove emancipatory when performed to an audience. However, in a nursing context, the incident clearly demonstrates the demands and complexities of the nursing role within this health area. These field observations were rejected by the scripting team and other informants as reinforcing stereotypical perceptions of alcohol abuse. Although both health and nursing participants strongly related to the account, they were also aware that these particular observations, translated into a performed episode, would not advantage public understanding of alcoholism as an issue. As health informants control the construction of representations and general content of the scripts, this scenario was 'culled' from the project.

Here there is a tacit tension between the values of *pure research* and the researchers' *self-identities and values* and the goals of emancipatory theatre. The tension cannot be long-lived. The task, as I see it, 'is to create critical citizens who are no longer content in occupying furtive spaces of private affirmation but who possess the will and knowledge to turn these spaces into public spheres' (McLaren 1997: 9). If data demonstrates stereotypical and popularised understandings of health consumption, then to reify such understandings in text and performance would be to disadvantage and constrain further our informants' *explanations of their other selves*. Assuredly, we every day see the results of abusive drinking on the streets, in social gatherings and in the media and have no difficulty in recognising the antics of those who are inebriated. This is known. What remains unknown are the explanations behind and from within such behaviours. Accordingly, the following scenario was culled from the script and treated as potentially discriminatory as it did not adequately explain informants' perspectives. This is the 'critical factor' of critical ethno-drama seen in operation.

I walk from brilliant sunlight through dark tinted glass doors into the gloom of the narrow entry hall, I am late. I stand in front of this security screen so that Angie, the duty nurse, can peep through and identify me. The screen, which guards the admissions nurses from the outside world, is smaller than I remember. To its left – the entry door, to its right – Geordy. Geordy, forty-ish, scowling, slight, unshaven, matted hair, is dressed in a once pale blue cotton shirt and soiled, torn shorts. He sits on a narrow bench parallel to the reception desk. A strong, stale odour of alcohol and sweat wafts over me. I notice that one of his bare feet is caked in dried blood. … He repeatedly attempts to light a cigarette, seemingly unaware that his orange plastic lighter has no flame. He is becoming agitated. He dashes his lighter to the ground.

'Bitches won't let me in!' he bellows, as Angie arrives at the screen. 'And that attitude won't get you back in here any quicker!' retorts Angie as she opens the double security doors to let me through. Suddenly the screen vibrates loudly as Geordy bashes it with his head. 'Stop that, you silly bugger,' Angie commands. Geordy walks away, pauses, and, bare-toed, kicks the wall hard in anger. He stands stock-still for a second then hops in agony as his already battered foot fails to impress the masonry. He is now clutching his head in one hand and his toes in the other. If he were Buster Keaton or Oliver Hardy I might laugh. Angie does. 'Geordy, behave!' she orders, trying to stifle her giggles. Meekly he sits once more on the bench and nurses his head then his toes.

'We only discharged him this morning. Busted before you could blink. Thinks it's tomorrow already!'

Cardinal rules 1 and 2: no admission for persons known to be violent or for persons who have been through detox within the previous 24 hours. She laughs again then quietly adds, 'I'll let him in when the piss and bad manners are out of him.'

(Field notes/Scripting scenario, Urban Detox Unit, Summer, Queensland 1993)

Multi-perspective narratives

In order to provide opportunities for audiences and informants to gain emancipatory insights, it is essential that the explanations given in ethno-dramas are true to the informants' perspectives and do not reinforce observers' uninformed observations.[6] This intentionally angular slant to story telling adopts elements of Kurosawa's multi-perspective narrative (as seen in the film *Rashomon* 1950) and extends Boal's (1985 [1979]) use of individual perspective in performance construction. In this way, a real-life story or series of actual events may be interpreted and explained from the contrasting perspectives of each participant. Boal's work often further involves rehearsal activities in which an informants' story of experiencing oppression is re-enacted from the perspective of each character involved: victim, perpetrator or witness. A 'spectactor', an audience member who has contributed to the work by telling a story of personal oppression, may then be physically drawn in to the action in the forum elements of a Boal-style performance. By helping reconstruct the enactment of their real-life scenario of oppression, even the eventual outcome may be fictionally role-played and altered to conclude in the spectactor's favour when in real life it disadvantaged them. In this way, the victim (vicariously) becomes 'victor' and experiences a de-historification of past events (Mienczakowski 1995; Mienczakowski *et al.* 1996).

Ethno-drama does not, as yet, *fictionalise* medical outcomes (reconstructing utopian scenarios so that persons with schizophrenia find total cures or persons within the experience of alcoholism gain absolute total control over their addictive behaviours). It simply seeks to voice and explain informant perspectives which are otherwise silenced. Boal's work seeks political solutions to social and political oppression and focuses informant objectivity upon the causes of informant experiences of oppression in order to provoke collective, political action (Schutzman and Cohen-Cruz 1994: 13). Critical ethno-drama seeks to emancipate audiences and informants from stereotypical and oppressive understandings of illness, and in so doing free informants from the historified perceptions of their health constraints. The following data extract reveals an informants' personal (non-political) perspective of oppressive experiences and offers immediate insight into the informant's life-world and the circumstances of oppression he wishes to change.

Glen: We don't want to be laughed at. When you see a bloke falling down 'pissed legless' people laugh. They laugh and stare. It's not funny. He's ill, not just drunk. He's ill!

Interviewer: What would you like to say to young audiences about your experiences?[7]

Glen: I'd like to say that an alcoholic has absolutely no control over his disease.[8] Absolutely none whatsoever. We shouldn't be looked at the way we are in the community. ... Like the lowest of the low, probably just above a drug addict.[9] We want public understanding; education.

(Interview, April 1993, Yalkara Detox Centre)

Some of the above data were added to the body of the *Busting* script (given as dialogue for composite characters within the play to reveal),[10] but elements were also used as agenda headings for the categorisation of other data. The next passage, almost entirely verbatim transcription, was approved for inclusion in the *Busting* script because it was an explanation of self that informants identified with, understood and which, in performance, deeply moved both themselves and other audiences. Although Jason was portrayed as a sad character with little self-hope within the *Busting* text, the physical semiotic performance of his explanation nightly brought audiences to tears and caused health informants to reflect deeply upon their own circumstances. The representation of Jason partly provoked the responses and insights that the informant Glen wished audiences to receive, and informants viewed Jason as depicting 'disempowerment' rather than being a 'disempowering' representation. Ultimately, the portrayal of Jason is not about producing sympathy but empathy.

Jason: G'day, my name is Jason and I'm an alcoholic. Thankfully I haven't had a drink today nor have I taken any drugs. Drinking has been my life since I was twelve. Both me mum and dad died through drink and my brother was killed in a suicide smash last year. He took his wife and child with him but. He was an alcoholic but.

I'm 21 and I've been through detox in Kakuri, Cairns and a couple of Salvo places and now here. Sometimes I think that it's all too late for me now. I did a stretch in jail up north but I couldn't dry out there. You can get drugs in some prisons easier than on the street so I couldn't really get it together. I don't really want to talk to people unless I've had a drink and I'm sorry about me shakes today. But we all know about withdrawals here so I expect you'll understand if I don't make much sense.

I am nobody to give advice – I can't show youse how to be but I have something to say: I want to make something of my life, but I just can't seem to make it. I've been drinking that much, I can't get up for work. You just get lazy. All I want to do is just get drunk. I think that it's all too late for me now. I feel it is you know, yeah. I should have taken me chances. I tried to get into the navy but they wouldn't accept me, you know? I got a job in a gold mine, but I turned that down an' all. I'd like to say, and I mean this for kids like Maria who are only getting pissed for fun now, I want to say to them, 'I can't help youse out, you know, I can't show you how to be. Just don't end up like someone like me, you know. 'Cos I just like getting drunk, like partying, having a good time, but I tend to go overboard; don't know when to stop. I'd like to say that, you know, keep going in this kind of life and you've signed your own death certificate. *(Tears are welling in his eyes)*

The first few years, when I started, I said to myself, 'I'll just do this for a while, then I'll start doing something else' and then before you know it you're just that much in a rut, you can't get out of it, you know? So I ended up keeping going a few more years, you know, and I ended up a dole bludger you know, no friends, no family, except me drinking partners and all they do is go live their lives in detox centres, go to rehab and get their dole cheques.

If you don't bust you've 'made it'. Yeah, that's it. That's what it's about – you've 'made it', 'the big win'. Just don't bust. *(He is crying so much that Chrissie helps him from the stage. Mark takes the lectern. Long pause)*

(*Busting,* Act II, Scene i, Alcohol Anonymous Youth Disclosure Meeting)

The eliciting of emotional responses (Ellis and Flaherty 1992; Ellis 1991) through such performed representations is intended to connect and confront audiences (Conquergood 1992, 1993: 342–3) and participants with the realities of informants' lived experiences. The desire to emotionally engage audiences is upheld by the audiences' understanding that the staged representations they are seeing are documented, informant-worded research narratives based upon real lives. Hence, Jason demonstrates the potential of the ethno-drama process to give voice, in their own words, to the health concerns of disenfranchised, or subordinate (Fraser 1990), health consumers. This 'voicing', to audiences of health professionals, care givers and others, is essentially reflexive in nature as it informs those officially responsible (Apple 1993) for determining health provision of their consumers' needs and experiences. Health agencies, government representatives, health professionals and health educators are all invited to ethno-drama performances, and surveying of our audiences (and audiences of other health-based plays) reveals that health theatre predominantly attracts health audiences. The implications strongly suggest that at the least such research-based performances hold the potential to offer insight and provoke change amongst those who play a part in the construction of health provision.

Ethnography: emergent trends of representation and textual practices

The development of ethnographic narratives into a staged, performance form is clearly an elaboration and enhancement of ongoing, world-wide interest in evolving ethnographic constructions and practices (Ellis and Bochner 1996: 26–31). In terms of textual challenges to ethnographic construction and ethnographic report writing there have been many. Oscar Lewis (1965) contested narrative representation with *La Vida: A Puerto Rican Family in the Culture of Poverty*. Here, monologues and conversations were transcribed as a novel without a framework of distinction between fictional and verbatim elements. Susan Krieger (1983: 195) in *The Mirror Dance*, an ethnographically-based novel set in a women's community, moots that ethnographic realism is enhanced by 'writing-up' research in a fictionalised form. Apart from the opening chapter, the ethnographer's voice is silent and we hear only the counterplay of the voices of her informants. Ethnographic research is also written and disseminated in formats which have embraced poetry and biography (Richardson 1994; Ellis 1995) and interpretative interactionism (Denzin 1989, 1995) in an attempt to use ethnographic and social science practices to question the usefulness of boundaries between literature, arts and social science explanations of the world (Ellis and Bochner 1996). Partially, this thrust lies in the recognition that explanations of the world made through literature and the arts are closer to understandings gained through anthropology and the social sciences than those made via the physical sciences (Rorty 1980).

Theatrical ethnography: theatre approaching research

Ethnography's theatrical heritage also has an obvious but boundary-blurring history. In performance terms, Turner (1986) envisaged a development of ethnographic practice in which the *performance* of ethnography could be seen as a means of investigating channels of reception and human understanding. This implies a connection between the traditional values of textual, academic presentation and those of performance. It is a position which Conquergood (1991: 190) sees as 'deeply subversive and threatening to the text bound culture of the academy'. The challenge arguably lies with the proposition that performed ethnography may provide more accessible and clearer public explanations of research than is sometimes the case with traditional, written report texts (Mienczakowski 1996). The public performance of ethnography in the idiom and language of its informants may be argued to de-academise the report construction process. Not insignificantly, ethno-drama also returns 'the ownership, and therefore the power, of the report to its informants as opposed to possessing it on behalf of the academy' (Mienczakowski 1996: 255).

The genre described by Paget (1987: 317–18) as 'verbatim theatre' uses performances in which 'oral histories' (Cheeseman 1971) are enacted on stage. There is a vast catalogue of verbatim theatre productions, from the late 1960s to today, dealing with subjects as varied as the 1926 General Strike and coal mine disasters (*Close the Coal-house Door*, Nottingham Playhouse), earthquakes (*Aftershock*, Newcastle, Australia) and conflict (Joan Littlewood's *Oh What a Lovely War*), which have political and social ambitions and also rely upon oral history and documentary accounts. However, where documentary techniques and ethno-drama part company is in the critical attempt inherent in ethno-dramas to act reflexively upon audiences and in the adherence of ethno-dramas to research protocols and informant control. Moreover, ethno-dramas are always set in 'time present'. Frequently verbatim (oral history) performances remain trapped in their own historification. The communities and circumstances depicted in ethno-dramas are intentionally asserting influence over their identification in wider society whilst also offering insights and explanations into otherwise closed but continuing worlds. Verbatim theatre pieces often locate their discourses in specific past events (wars, disasters and union activities) and whilst they seek to explain they do not necessarily seek their informants as respondents or audiences of the work.

Scripting

Our ethno-drama research is conducted by the entire project team: academic researchers, nursing informants working in the setting under study and student nurses participating in the project. Scripting is also the result of a team approach. Working to an informant agenda derived from analysis of interview and observation data, scenarios are constructed from the database by a team which includes informants and researchers. Normally, one of the project leaders takes responsibility for drafting scripted dialogue which is then workshopped in rehearsals until it 'fits' the needs of the project. The overt intention of this approach is to present an informant-led research piece rather than an 'authored' product.

The nature of the ethno-drama performance is strongly mentored by informant preferences. Whereas informants in *Syncing Out Loud* wished for an explanation of self which involved sharing and demonstrating the parameters of schizophrenic psychosis, and allowed for the fictionalising of scenarios, scripting sessions in *Busting* involved an informant preference for verbatim dialogue. Informants expressed the view that 'unnecessary' literary and plot fabrication would render the play 'a fiction' instead of being interpreted as 'a truth'. Geertz (1988), Atkinson (1990) and Richardson (1992) point out that the self-reflexive potential of an ethnographic representation and its construction frequently depends more upon the literary ability of its authors than the validity claims made of its data. However, for the informants of *Busting*, it was important that the audience tacitly understood that the play's authority rested upon the project's factual research status and verbatim narration which could not be dismissed as authorial invention. This was partly in response to the numerous misrepresentations of alcohol-related behaviours informants had encountered through the media and because of an understanding that the research performance process was *about them and their lives* and not about the lives of some *fictional other*.

Acceptable fiction

Fictional inclusions were inserted into the *Busting* script to link plot and sub-plot. These were fictitious in the sense that they were combinations of separate elements of informant data and were not the product of single interviews. Most often they were informant scenarios seen as 'typical' of interactions experienced within the field of study. Fictional links were always based upon informant accounts or anecdotes and were agreed *as real* and *plausible* by informants (Mienczakowski 1994, 1995).

The following passage from *Busting* (Act II, Scene ii) was taken from a nurse's account of informing a detoxee that his liver was seriously malfunctioning. The dialogue remains largely unaltered from the anecdote related to a researcher by the nursing informant. However, it has been fictionalised in the sense that other characters have been added and the setting has been changed from that described by the informant to a public detox ward. What was a private moment between a long-term health consumer well known to the nursing informant has become a public moment of explanation and levity. This revelation serves several purposes within the script. It accentuates the long-term health implications of abusive drinking whilst also dealing with nurse–patient relationships and the role of the nurse within such circumstances (Cox 1989; Watkins 1990; Jennings 1992). Most poignantly, it demonstrates health consumer humour, dignity and resignation in critical health circumstances. Glen, a veteran of over forty acute detoxification sessions is in no doubt as to the implications of the test results. This is not just a moment of light relief for the audience but an insight into the world of alcohol abuse beyond the perception of comical 'falling down drunks' referred to earlier. Here, Glen controls the humour, all be it self-mockingly, but he is laughed with rather than at.

Glen: Is my wife after me? She'll have guessed where I am by now. Has she phoned for me?

Lisa: No Glen. It isn't about your wife. It's about your test results.

Glen: I know. Me liver isn't in such good shape is it? ... I was warned last time. But I'm not going to bust again.

Lisa: I hate having to say this Glen, but your liver is in pretty bad shape.

Glen: Getting bigger is it?

Lisa: I'm sorry, Glen. We can't treat you here.

Glen: (Whispering) Shot is it? Me liver? (Pause) How long then? You know? ... before it packs up?

Lisa: I don't know – but they'll do some more tests at the R.C.H. They're much better equipped ... there.

Glen: (Still whispering) I reckon I knew it was coming, but. Been warned enough. Seen this happen plenty – had to be my turn sooner or later. (Pause) Don't want to depress me mates before I go, though. Don't tell them will you Lisa? (Pause) I knew when they pulled me into the R.S.L. [Returned Servicemen's League] that night that this could be me last bender. Don't tell them, but. It's pointless scaring them and all. Most of us boys have been going through detox a dozen times a year since school. I don't have a single mate who hasn't busted. Me Dad went the same way. Scotch drinker he was. Bottle a day man. Cremated last year – took three days to put the fire out. (Laughs with Lisa) Will you let my wife know where I am, if she asks that is?

Lisa: (Squeezes his hand) Of course I will, Glen. It might not be that bad after all.

Theoretical basis

The critical theory-based emancipatory intentions of these projects involves a theoretical relocation of Habermasian (1971, 1984, 1987) communicative consensus within Alberoni's (1984) vision of 'the nascent state'. Here, emancipation is signified by perhaps no more than the achieving of a nascent moment in which insight and critical reflection prompt individuals towards objectivity or even *latent* objectivity. Alberoni describes nascency as the advent of an advent, the moment in which an individual first fully comprehends their self-conscious location within the circumstances of oppression. Provocatively, marxist critical theory is alleged to mobilise the masses 'in the name of their interests, their resentment, and their desire for revenge' (Alberoni 1984: 229) and hence to perpetually construct new enemies against which to move. Consequently, Alberoni redefines the search for truth and enlightenment as the individual discovery of a form of self-consciousness 'which appears at a certain point as consciousness of one's own historicity' and allows the individual to acritically moderate his/her understanding of the past into prehistory. Within the nascent state, 'all of history is the history of errors; it is one-sided and incomplete and, to use the Marxist term, is prehistory' (*ibid*.: 64). For health consumers, oppression may not be politically defined but shares synergies with its historicised public perception.[11] Similarly, emancipation cannot be guaranteed from the constraints of physical illnesses which are individually experienced but collectively defined. Therefore, within the ethno-drama process, individuals are offered (potential) emancipatory opportunities via voicing their unique agendas of concern to those who are responsible for constructing the conditions and material provision (Apple 1993) of their daily health care. As the informants involved in the ethno-drama process are specifically disenfranchised through both their experience of illness and through the institutional and public (historicised) disposition towards their medical conditions, voicing their agenda is seen as a form of emancipatory action.

Conclusion

Though the ethno-drama process is not claimed to collectively bring about emancipation, it retains the potential to effect instrumental change through the insights it gives to audiences. Examples of audience members (parents, general practitioners, human resource managers and others) responding to the plays' representations with increased awareness and emphasis upon alcohol-related issues have been much evidenced in the research. Undoubtedly, the greatest level of insight, and subsequently potential emancipation, has been gained by nursing students working on the projects, many of whom expressed profound changes in their understanding of, and dealings with, persons involved in these health issues (Rolfe *et al*. 1995).

Habermas (1984) guarantees that there will only be participants on the journey towards enlightenment; the ethno-drama process also cannot guarantee enlightenment or emancipation as a direct outcome of its processes. Nor can it, authoritatively, establish that the insights it gives will be beneficial to those who receive them. However, by offering insights, it moves participants (whether they are oppressed by circumstances of health or otherwise) towards potential (individuated) emancipation and therefore gives rise to opportunities for informants to be heard where previously they were not.

Notes

1 Verbatim transcription used as dialogue in the play *Busting* (1993).
2 'Busting' is the term frequently used by detoxing alcohol and substance abusers to describe a return to substance abuse after a period of abstinence or sobriety.
3 *Busting: the challenge of the drought spirit* (1993) focused upon the status of women in the world of alcohol and drug abuse.
4 Augusto Boal is the founder of a form of emancipatory theatre in Brazil which allows participants to reconstruct and overcome the circumstances of their political and social oppression. In 'forum' theatre the themes are devised by audiences who participate in the construction of solutions to their given problems.
5 Critical ethno-dramas reinterpret not only ethnography but critical theory. Within our context of health education drama, critical theory seeks to be emancipatory by giving its subjects the means by which they can politically and socially locate, understand and influence the conditions of their existence. We have specifically chosen to work with persons with schizophrenia and persons undergoing detoxification for alcohol dependency, singularly to voice their opinions.
6 See note 4.
7 This question was standard in all interviews.
8 There are competing theories of how alcoholic identities are constructed. Glen's understanding of alcoholism as a disease is often alleged to take the responsibility for recovery away from the health consumer.
9 Conversely, drug abusers in the research felt their perceived status to be slightly higher than that of alcoholics whom they frequently referred to as 'methos' (drinkers of methylated spirits) and 'derros' (derelicts).
10 Composite characters are constructed from the anecdotes, transcriptions and behaviours of several informants.
11 For example, Rich (1993) points to anecdotal evidence used to support such notions as the moon's cycles influencing mental disorders. Luce (1971) highlights the tendency of seventeenth- and eighteenth-century physicians to report, as fact, regular monthly cycles in case studies of epilepsy and other lunacies, and the continuation of psychiatric staff and police to associate divergent behaviours with the cycles of the moon. The notion that because animal biology is affected by lunar cycles, human biology must also be affected is a persistent and recurrent misconception.

References

Agger, B. (1991) 'Theorising the decline of discourse or the decline of theoretical discourse?' in P. Wexler (ed.) *Critical Theory Now*, New York and London: Falmer Press, Chapter 5.

Alberoni, F. (1984) *Movement and Institution* (trans. P. Arden Delmoro), New York: Colombia University Press.

Apple, M. (1993) *Official Knowledge: Democratic education in a conservative age*, New York: Routledge.

Atkinson, P. (1990) *The Ethnographic Imagination: Textual constructions of reality*, London: Routledge.

Bakhtin, M. (1984) *Problems of Dostoevsky's Poetics* (ed. and trans. Caryl Emerson), Minneapolis: University of Minnesota Press.

Bernstein, B. (1996) *Pedagogy Symbolic Control and Identity: Theory research critique*, London: Critical Perspectives on Literacy and Education.

Bharucha, R. (1993) *Theatre and the World*, London and New York: Routledge.

Boal, A (1985 [1979]) *Theatre of the Oppressed* (trans. C.A. and M.L. McBride), New York: Theatre Communications Group.

Cheeseman, P. (1971) 'Production casebook', *New Theatre Quarterly* 1: 1–6.

Cherryholmes, C.H. (1993) 'Reading research', *Journal Of Curriculum Studies* 25: 1–32.

Coffey, A. and Atkinson, P. (1996) *Qualitative Data Analysis*, Newbury Park, CA: Sage Publications.

Conquergood, D. (1988) 'Health theatre in a Hmong refugee camp: performance, communication and culture', *TDR – The Drama Review – A Journal of Performance Studies* 32 (3), 174–208.

—— (1991) 'Rethinking ethnography: towards a critical cultural politics', *Communication Monographs* 58: 179–94, June.

—— (1992) 'Ethnography, rhetoric, and performance', *Quarterly Journal of Speech* 78: 80–123.

—— (1993) 'Storied worlds and the work of teaching', *Communication Education* 42: 337–48.

Cox, H. (1989) 'Drama in the arts lab', *Australian Nurses Journal* 19 (1): 14–15.

Denzin, N. (1989) *Interpretive Interactionism*, Newbury Park, CA: Sage.

—— (1995) 'Performance texts', paper delivered to the American Education Research Association, San Francisco, April.

Ellis, C. (1991) 'Sociological introspection and emotional experience', *Symbolic Interaction* 14: 23–50.

—— (1995) *Final Negotiations: A story of love, loss and chronic illness*, Philadelphia: Temple University Press.

Ellis, C. and Bochner, A. (1996) 'Talking over ethnography', in C. Ellis and A. Bochner (eds) *Composing Ethnography: Alternative forms of qualitative writing*, Altamira, CA: Sage, pp. 13–45.

Ellis, C. and Flaherty, M.G. (1992) *Investigating Subjectivity: Research on lived experience*, Newbury Park: Sage.

Fraser, N. (1990) 'Rethinking the public sphere: a contribution to the critique of actually existing democracy', *Social Text* 25/26: 56–80.

Geertz, C. (1988) *Works and Lives: The anthropologist as author*, Cambridge, UK: Polity.

Habermas, J. (1971) *Knowledge and Human Interest* (trans. T. McCarthy), London: Heineman.

—— (1984) *The Theory of Communicative Action* (trans. J. Shapiro), Boston: Beacon Press.

—— (1987) *Philisophical Discourse of Modernity: Twelve lectures* (trans. F. Lawrence), Boston: Beacon Press.

Jennings, S. (1992) *Dramatherapy in Families, Groups and Individuals: Waiting in the wings*, London: Kingsley.

Krieger, S. (1983) *The Mirror Dance: Identity in a women's community*, Philadelphia: Temple University Press.

Lewis, O. (1965) *La Vida: A Puerto Rican Family in the Culture of Poverty*, San Juan and New York: Random House.

Luce, G. (1971) *Biological Rhythms in Human and Animal Physiology*, New York: Dover.

Lyotard, J.-F. (1984) *The Post-modern Condition: A report on knowledge*, Minneappolis: University of Minnesota Press.

McLaren, P. (1997) 'Unthinking Whiteness, rethinking democracy: or farewell to the blonde beast; towards a revolutionary multiculturalism', *Educational Foundations* (Spring) 11 (2): 5–39.

Mienczakowski, J. (1994) 'Theatrical and theoretical experimentation in ethnography and dramatic form', *ND DRAMA, Journal of National Drama, UK* 2/2: 16–23.

—— (1995) 'The theatre of ethnography', *Qualitative Inquiry* 1 (3): 360–75.

—— (1996) 'An ethnographic act: the construction of consensual theatre: ethnography in the form of theatre with emancipatory intentions', in C. Ellis and A. Bochner (eds) *Composing Ethnography: Alternative forms of qualitative writing*, Altamira, CA: Sage, pp. 244–64.

Mienczakowski, J., Morgan, S. and Rolfe, A. (1993) 'Ethnography or drama?', *National Association for Drama in Education (N.J.)* 17 (3): 8–15.

Mienczakowski, J., Smith, R. and Sinclair, M. (1996) 'On the road to catharsis: a framework for theoretical change', *Qualitative Inquiry, USA* 2 (4): 439–62.

Paget, D. (1987) 'Verbatim theatre: oral history and documentary techniques', *New Theatre Quarterly* 12: 317–36.

Price, N. (1992) 'Theatre for health', *The Queensland Nurse*, October.

Rich, D. (1993) 'Lunacy – a valid concept?' *The Australian Journal of Mental Health Nursing* 2 (6): 251–6.

Richardson, L. (1992) 'The consequences of poetic representation: writing the other, rewriting the self', in C. Ellis and M.G. Flaherty (eds) *Investigating Subjectivity: Research on lived experience*, Newbury Park, CA: Sage, pp. 125–37.

—— (1994) 'Writing as a method of inquiry', in N. Denzin and Y. Lincoln (eds) *Handbook of Qualitative Research*, Thousand Oaks, CA: Sage, pp. 515–29.

Rolfe, A., Mienczakowski, J. and Morgan, S. (1995) 'A dramatic experience in mental health nursing education', *Nurse Education Today, UK* 15 (3): 224–7.

Rorty, R. (1980) *Philosophy and the Mirror of Nature*, Princeton, NJ: Princeton University Press.

Shutzman, M. and Cohen-Cruz, J. (1994) 'Introduction', in M. Shutzman and J. Cohen-Cruz (eds) *Playing Boal*, New York: Routledge, pp. 1–16.

Turner, V. (1986) *The Anthropology of Performance*, New York: Performing Arts Journal Publications.

Watkins, P. (1990) 'All the world's a stage', *Nursing Times* 86 (21): 47–8.

Chapter 10

Disabled women in El Salvador reframing themselves

An economic development program for women

Joanie B. Cohen-Mitchell

Disability in El Salvador

Very little has been written about disability in Central America. Documentation tends to be of a statistical/census nature that lists numbers, gender, location and nature of disability. A comprehensive study of disabled women in El Salvador does not exist, although UNICEF has begun compiling data about those disabled by the war, both men and women. Smaller studies, conducted by private organizations such as FUNTER (*Fundacion Teleton Pro-Rehabilitacion*), have touched on the rehabilitation aspects of disability: special education for children, centers for the blind – but always focusing on 'this health problem,'[1] and ignoring the multiple ways disability affects other parts of an individual's life.

ACOGIPRI de R.L.

ACOGIPRI de R.L. is the acronym for *Asociacion Cooperativa del Grupo Independiente Pro-Rehabilitacion Integral de Responsibilidad Limitada* (The Cooperative Association of the Independent Group for Integrated Rehabilitation with Limited Responsibility).

In 1981, in the home of Eileen Giron, a group of approximately fifteen disabled people began to discuss ways of creating an income-generating project run exclusively by the disabled. Without any formal tools of analysis for feasibility studies, the group began to examine different types of vocational training and skills available to the disabled population of San Salvador through educational and training opportunities. After much inquiry and proposal writing, and with the help of different connections in San Salvador development circles, initial funding came from Catholic Relief Services to open two small workshops. One was a ceramics workshop and the other a sewing and tailoring workshop. Set up as a co-operative, these workshops were operated and managed exclusively by disabled individuals, a first in El Salvador. The sewing workshop functioned until 1984, and then closed, due to a plethora of tailor shops in San Salvador that accounted for its small profit margin.

The ceramics workshop, Shicali, one of three in El Salvador and the only co-operative that employed only disabled persons, continued to show a small profit margin. With funding from USAID, ACOGIPRI was able to purchase more equipment and move into a building that provided space for a bigger workshop and a salesroom.

With the motto '*nosotros tambien podemos*' ('we can also'), ACOGIPRI is an excellent example of a grassroots development effort that employs its philosophy in all aspects of its business. As a legal co-operative, ACOGIPRI has a monthly membership fee, a revolving loan program for members, ongoing training and education for its membership and employees, and is involved in advocacy for disabled persons and development efforts with other non-governmental organizations (NGOs) and governmental programs in El Salvador and in the North.

In 1987, ACOGIPRI began a 'Disabled Women's Program' to address the issues of lack of education and training for women with disabilities.[2] As a means to 'discover' the hidden disabled women of San Salvador, ACOGIPRI began outreach into the community and began holding training sessions on aspects of functional literacy, self-esteem, gender issues, communication and community advocacy. Additionally, ACOGIPRI began to organize and host 'Central American Training Programs for Disabled Women' for women from the region, and, most recently (with funding from the Canadian Coalition on the Disabled), has begun sending women from El Salvador to neighboring countries to visit their programs and provide training for the development of other disabled women's groups mostly in Guatemala, Nicaragua and Honduras. ACOGIPRI's goal is to act as a catalyst in order to create permanent programs and networks to meet the various needs of disabled women in El Salvador and Central America.

Rather than using the deficit model for program development which often focuses on rehabilitation, the Women's Program of ACOGIPRI chooses to draw on women's existing strengths and augments these inherent strengths with much needed educational and vocational training.

Who is the disabled woman in El Salvador?

El Salvador (*el pulgarcito de las Americas* (the thumb of the Americas)), although the smallest country in Central America, is the most densely populated. With a population of 5.5 million inhabitants, almost one million have some sort of disability. According to the same source, 65 per cent of these one million are women (CONAIPD 1994: March).

After twelve years of war, El Salvador has moved into a more stable climate, conducive to broader economic and social development. After the first 'democratic' elections, the new government released its official national policy on disabled persons in El Salvador. This included a study and list of recommendations for the handicapped, both children and adults. There are a series of government and non-governmental programs of education and training under way that have been set up to address issues of disability, especially in the areas of special education and rehabilitation. However, there is a marked tendency for the programs created for adults to serve only war veterans and other men. Most disabled women (including those who fought in the war) are not included in the majority of development efforts, and severely disabled women are rarely included in the majority of development efforts. Additionally, most funding agencies that support development efforts for the disabled in El Salvador at the present time have a pre-set agenda that usually focuses on vocational skills. Using what I refer to as a 'deficit model', these programs focus on physical rehabilitation in areas where the disabled person is lacking (as assessed by the funders and governmental studies), rather than drawing on the strengths, interests and needs of program participants and their social realities.

The process as alternative paradigm research

My research design was developed in response to a set of broad headings and categories developed by the Inter-American Foundation. The Inter-American Foundation was interested in how *grassroots development strategies can have an impact on poor people*. In my research model the focus shifted slightly. My research was designed to create a process of inquiry into the skills necessary so that 'poor people' themselves can have an impact on and meaningfully interact with grassroots development strategies. By focusing on disabled women in El Salvador, and examining their social reality, I hoped to prove that a collaborative process could be developed that would help these women learn the skills necessary to be protagonists. I wanted to show that these women could access, alter and/or create development programs in their immediate environment (community) in ways that would potentially impact their lives.

Appropriating participatory and feminist research and thought

Although I am loathe to label what I do as a researcher as strictly participatory research, participatory action research or feminist research (mainly because it places me in a box), I feel comfortable articulating the tenets on which alternative paradigm research is based as most in line with my beliefs about why and how I should operate as a researcher. The alternative research paradigm is concerned with what is possible rather than what is (Burrell and Morgan 1979: 17) and clearly articulates a stance: research can be tied to the emancipation of people from oppressive structures. I believe, as do most researchers who subscribe to this alternative view of research, that everything we do has a political nature and therefore cannot be neutral.

One alternative paradigm approach from which I appropriate tenets and methods is participatory research (PR). As I understand PR, it allows a way for me to 'openly demonstrate solidarity with oppressed and disempowered people through our work as researchers' (Maguire 1987: 28). Participatory research combines investigation, education and action to reinforce the bond between research and action. It also challenges the dominant research paradigm's beliefs about the purpose of knowledge creation which, for those who operate within the dominant research paradigm, focuses merely on interpreting social reality. In participatory research, the goal of knowledge creation is to change and alter social reality and this goal must be realized through a systematic change process where critical consciousness (for both the participants and the researcher), improvement of the lives of those involved in the process, and, finally, a transformation of societal structures and relationships can take place.

Collective inquiry is another key element that draws me towards participatory research. In participatory research, collaborative data collection and collective inquiry with all involved is desirable and sought out by the researchers. The other piece of participatory research that is important for me is collective action. As I interpret participatory research, the goal is transformative collective action to effect social change. Not only is it hoped that personal transformation will occur, but also that group energy will be created that leads to collective transformation. The act of 'doing' participatory research itself can be seen as action and transformation. However, other types of action can and often do result as the group continues to reflect and analyze the larger structures of the problem. Becoming technically skilled or creating an intervention may be the beginning of the struggle to face the political structures that oppress.

Finally, how the knowledge generated by this collective inquiry process is used forms another key element of participatory research. As Peter Park states:

> In the traditional social science research model, especially the 'pure' type, knowledge that the researcher produces is deposited in the scientific store-house from which, supposedly, policy makers, corporate executives, and other would-be social engineers draw requisite techniques for administering to, managing, and manipulating unwitting pacified populations. ... Participatory research restructures this relationship between knowing and doing and puts the people in charge of both the production and the utilization of knowledge.
>
> (Park 1992: 3)

Another source from which I have drawn to shape and develop my alternative research methodology is some feminist research and theories. Most feminist researchers realize the importance of dialogue in order to tap into and validate women's knowledges and experiences. This is not new thinking. Throughout the 1960s and 1970s small grassroots consciousness-raising (CR) groups formed in order to give women a safe space to share their thoughts, feelings and experiences as women. From the well-known slogan 'the personal is political,' we have come to understand the role that CR groups played in helping women re-examine what they thought to be individual problems, and, in a group setting, begin to analyze them as broader social problems. By using dialogue to analyze and construct understanding and knowledge that would transform their own social reality, CR groups fomented political action for the purposes of liberation from existing oppressive structures.

More recently, feminist theorists exploring knowledge creation have begun to revisit the 'master narratives' of social and critical theory. These theorists are interested in exploring the interconnections between feminisms, feminist and liberatory pedagogy, and a truly empowering and emancipatory feminist research paradigm. One assumption they share is that by examining and understanding these 'master narratives', we, as feminist researchers, are more free to pick and choose how we want to shape our own praxis and practice as researchers. Coupling some feminist research concepts with tenets on which participatory research is based seemed natural to me, a way in which to develop a research methodology that embodies my beliefs about research, women and inquiry and the truly emancipatory possibilities of the alternative paradigm. As Lather puts it:

> my argument is in no way a collapsing of all these theoretical moments into some spurious synthesis. I cannot but believe that it is in both our parallels and our differences across the various feminisms, Marxisms, and poststructuralisms that we can begin to move forward towards a future that transcends our present limitations.
>
> (Lather 1991: 49)

And:

> critical inquiry is needed to empower the researched, build emancipatory theory and move toward the establishment of data credibility within praxis-oriented, advocacy research. ... My goal is to move research in many different, and indeed, contradictory directions in hope that more interesting and useful ways of knowing will emerge.
>
> (*ibid.*: 69)

Another useful 'theory' for me and my thinking about my role as it relates to the disabled women I would be working with is the socialist feminist 'standpoint theory'. Appropriating insights from Marx, Engels, Lukacs and others, standpoint theory 'refers to a position in society which is shaped by and in turn helps shape the ways of knowing, structures of power and resource distribution' (Hennessy 1993: 67). However, this does not mean that conceptualizing reality from the perspective of women's lives, interests, activities and values makes us see and understand the world clearly. Material forces, social positioning and the social construction of a person's role play an important part in shaping our various ways of knowing. When approaching research from the viewpoint of liberation and empowerment of the most marginalized, it appears to me that we must take into consideration not only the positionality and location of our co-researchers but also their socially constructed view of women. For most disabled women, simply being a woman does not signify access to nor alignment with the 'feminist perspective' and its ways of viewing the world. We cannot use women's lives as reference points to define women because women do not all share the same perspective. To suggest that we all operate from the same standpoint is only to fool ourselves.

Finally, I will mention some key concepts that I have taken from feminisms of Women of Color that will be used throughout my chapter.[4]

1   *The concept of voice*: In order for counter-hegemonic knowledges to exist, women must be free to name their own realities in an authentic voice; that is, a voice rooted in their own experience. Women must be able to use their own forms of expression and convey ideas in their own ways. This means that to name those realities is considered valid. Since knowledge is constructed, it is important to allow different groups of women to speak for themselves in order to create their own knowledge.

2   *The idea of contextuality*: Counter to the idea of a universal concept of 'Truth,' knowledge about and an understanding of the world are culturally and historically specific. This idea is important in the area of development since a 'successful' project created in one place cannot necessarily be re-created in another cultural context.

3   *The multiplicities of social identities*: Your identity – your gender, race, class, ethnicity, sexual orientation, religion, urban versus rural, etc. – affects how you interpret the world. The multiplicity of identity leaves no room for the idea of a universal 'we' who might claim to speak on behalf of all women or on behalf of all disabled people.

Literacy and reframing: a critical literacy approach

Literacy is not defined primarily as a condition where someone 'has it' and is literate or does not 'have it' and is illiterate. Literacy is a dynamic entity situated within the social and power dynamics of a society and is much broader than just the skills of reading and writing. As defined by Paulo Freire, literacy involves a 'reframing' of one's reality through conscientization:

> To acquire literacy is more than to psychologically and mechanically dominate reading and writing techniques. It is to dominate those techniques on terms of consciousness; to understand what one reads and to write what one understands; it is to communicate graphically. Acquiring

literacy does not involve memorizing sentences, words or syllables – lifeless objects unconnected to an existential universe – but rather an attitude of creation and re-creation, a self-transformation producing a stance of intervention in one's context.

(Freire 1973: 48)

However, it is not as easy as saying 'I think I will reframe myself in the eyes of society today.' I use the term 'reframe' because it is my belief that the disabled women in this study had been framed by society. They had been assigned a fixed identity and with that identity their possibilities in the world were determined. I say reframe when I speak of this group of women because they redefined themselves according to their own desires, needs and possibilities as women who were disabled. Also of concern are the theoretical and ideological bases of literacy and the acquiring of literacy skills. In the broader understanding of literacies as knowledge, it is important to examine what the nature of knowledge and of learners (or knowers) is in society, and how the life experiences of these knowers is socially constructed in relation both to power and social control in the society. Most positivist theories of knowledge, which tend to focus on rationality, separate the nature and knowledge of an individual from his/her life experiences, actions, and social context. From this kind of theorizing comes the belief that there are standards and norms of knowledge based on scientific, 'rational' norms rather than acquired through living life and gaining experiences. In her book *The Everyday as Problematic* (1987), Dorothy Smith argues that dominant social science and what is believed to be knowledge cannot be separated from real people and their perspectives based on the geographical, historical location of their real lives. The problem with positivist knowledge is that the norms for determining valid knowledge are not based on *all* real people and *all* their specific lives, but are based on those with power and control.

As Michel Foucault (1980) pointed out, in knowledge itself are relations of power and control. This power does not only exist between those who know (the knowers) and those who do not, but is part and parcel of the conditions which make those that know the ones with power. Knowledge cannot be separated from the social, political, cultural or economic conditions of society. The way society maintains this knowledge of the dominant interests is through its institutions, the places where these norms of society are reproduced in order to perpetuate domination.

A critical approach to literacy attempts to counter this domination by developing active forms of resistance and reframing positivist knowledge production. In the Western world, this discourse of critical literacy is most closely associated with Paulo Freire. Seeing literacy as a political act, Freire requires people to 'theorize' about their everyday world, 'reading the world' as he calls it as well as 'reading the word' (Freire 1973). The ultimate goal of this kind of literacy is empowerment and social transformation.

A critical approach to literacy also makes it possible to reframe not only our own experiences but also to reframe and theorize about the ways others see the world. The possibility also exists for participants to gain an understanding of how race, class, gender, ability and disability all participate in the interplay of power relationships. A critical approach to literacy can also illuminate the role that oral and written literacies can have in helping participants express their understandings of their world. Giroux sees literacy as

> inherently a political project in which men and women assert their rights and responsibility to read, understand and transform their own experiences, but also to reconstitute their relationship within the wider society. In this sense, literacy is fundamental to aggressively constructing one's voice as part of a wider project of possibility and empowerment.
>
> (Giroux 1988: 64)

By linking literacy to knowledge and power, a critical approach aims to emancipate individuals so that they can participate in 'the unveiling of reality.'

The research process

The research model described below was shaped by the disabled women I was working with at ACOGIPRI. My original research design was very close to the one below; however, the reality of doing research altered a few parts of the original research model.

Component I: Interviews and visits

Before I could begin with interviews, it was necessary to build an environment of trust and confidence with the women I would be inviting to work on a collaborative research effort for the next five months. Without the formal connection to ACOGIPRI, this type of inquiry activity would never have been possible. Since people were constantly streaming in and out of the office and the ceramics workshop, my presence there and willingness to engage in spontaneous conversation was important. This allowed the women to sound me out and decide for themselves whether or not I was someone they felt comfortable inviting into their lives.

To begin the project formally, Eileen invited all women who had, at one time or another, been connected to the Women's Program at ACOGIPRI to an informal meeting where we would all become acquainted. At this initial meeting, I extended invitations to anyone interested in talking with me, adding that a commitment of four to five months (a few times a month) would be preferable after the initial interviews and home visits.

After the initial meeting, I began the home visit/interviewing process, setting up appointments with all those interested in participating. I started with very open-ended interviews and informal home visits, trying to find answers to the following research questions that would help me understand a bit more about the disabled women in El Salvador:

- How are the basic family/household unit and its variations defined in the socio-cultural context?
- How do disabled women in El Salvador understand the inter-relationship between their social context and the literate and/or abled environment in which they operate?
- What tasks are these Salvadoran women required to negotiate in their daily lives that require literacy?[4]

The following is the list of interview questions that led us into an in-depth discussion:

- What problems do you face daily as disabled women?
- What kind of support from your family members have you received in order to overcome obstacles presented to you? (After a few interviews, it was obvious that not all women received support in the positive sense, yet felt obliged to answer that they did because of the way the question was asked. This question was later changed to: Do your family members support you in order to overcome obstacles presented to you?)
- What problems do you think exist for disabled women in El Salvador?
- Do you think that disabled men and women face similar problems in Salvadoran society?
- Why do these problems you mentioned exist?
- What causes these problems?
- What can be done to change these problems?
- Can a group like ACOGIPRI help work to solve these problems?
- Would you be interested in participating in a group that discussed and examined these problems?

Ten women approached me. The women varied in their abilities and disabilities: some of the women were in wheelchairs, some had lost limbs, some were deaf.[5] Their educational levels also varied. Three of the women either had a university degree or were currently pursuing one. Three women had primary school experience. Two had finished high school. Two had no formal school experience.

It was soon obvious after a few interviews that the first question had to be a lead-in for a woman to describe her 'disability' and then explain her life in relation to it. By responding to this question first, each woman explained what had gone 'right' for her in her life as well as some of the broader problems she felt she was facing. Although when asked directly about problems and possible causes of the problems facing disabled women in El Salvador, some women could not answer. Responses to initial questions about the woman's life and disability are what helped me find the answers and opinions about possible causes, and were easily picked out while transcribing.

These interviews/home visits were of varying length. Some women were initially interviewed for two hours and then additionally interviewed during a follow-up lasting anywhere between one and three hours. Other women were harder to interview on tape (with frequent stops and requests to turn off the tape recorder) although more time was probably spent with them in an informal setting.

Ann Oakley, in her article 'Interviewing women: a contradiction in terms,' suggests that a feminist interviewer will often have trouble 'justifying' her interviews if they are compared to and critiqued by the traditional interview paradigm created by predominately male sociologists (Oakley 1981). She summarizes the traditional literature on interviewing as valuing: (1) the interview as a one-way process in which the interviewer elicits and receives, but never gives information; (2) an attitude towards interviewees that views them as an objectified function of data; and (3) interviews as having no personal meaning in terms of social interaction, thus negating anything except the statistics and data gathered through the interviewing process.

Oakely suggests that all of these traditional paradigms of interviewing are problematic for the feminist interviewer whose primary orientation and stance is towards the validation of women's subjective experiences as women, people and knowers (author's addition). I found this all to be true as I fumbled with my tape recorder, and wondered if this 'chatting' would 'count', or worried that I needed to be trying to set a more formal mode for this interviewing business. However, upon returning home and listening to the tapes and reconstructing the conversations, I realized that this informal chatting and reciprocal conversation style were exactly how interesting and essential concepts were formed. Many of these ideas would later play key roles in our group research.

I found that once I could let go of the male model of interviewing that I had in my head, it was easier for me to trust my intuition and just go with what felt appropriate and right. The other part of this interviewing I found to be imperative was the notion of operating from the subjective. I had to operate on the assumption that these women were the knowers and the creators of intimate knowledge about disabled women in El Salvador and that only they could inform me. This assumption freed me from the constraints placed on an interviewer conducting interviews from within the dominant interview paradigm.

After every interview and/or visit, I would return home or to the office to listen to and transcribe (in Spanish) the interview. Often, conversations were incomplete and had to be examined in the context of a previous thought or theme we were discussing before I could make sense of the text. Many times a woman would ask me to turn off the tape recorder in the middle of a comment because she had begun to cry or was telling me something she didn't want recorded. This process of transcribing and reconstructing conversations took between eight to twelve hours per interview. Because I knew I would need to re-examine these interviews again as I began my writing, I made copious notes about the setting, the time of day, any contextual clues I thought would later help me to better understand what was going on. Additionally, upon returning to Amherst, I had to translate my Spanish transcriptions into English for the writing up of the research.

After about seven weeks, I had interviewed ten women in the greater San Salvador area. All of them except one had a pre-established relationship with ACOGIPRI which made an enormous difference in terms of trust, confidence and the ability to conduct the kind of investigation I was hoping for.

At this stage of the project I also began to visit other disabled people's organizations (mostly rehabilitation centers), women's groups, feminist organizations and other government and non-government groups whose insights might help me better understand the location of disabled women in Salvadoran society. I also visited special education programs to look at what some of the women I was working with had experienced during their childhood. Additionally, I started accompanying my friends on their trips into the outside world: the world of having to figure out a way to step up into a bus, how to get across the street, how to communicate with the outside world if you are deaf, how to convince someone on the street to lift up your wheelchair into a taxi, or how to ignore the odd glances and more often disbelieving stares received as they entered into public life. Although these were not specifically my personal issues, the frustration I felt at not being able to solve a problem, create a solution, or have the entire society listen to an educational talk became my issue.

Component II: Gathering information, constructing analysis

Before we could meet as a group to examine mutual issues and decide what kinds of actions we would or could take, I had to analyze the interviews, transcripts, discussions and observations that I had been gathering during this time. I listened to and looked for answers to my research questions, hoping to better understand the context of disabled women in El Salvador. At the same time, I listened to the tapes and read the transcripts in the hopes of discovering key concepts, generative themes, and issues. What did these women believe to be the root causes of the problems they experienced in their daily interactions, both with their families and with the broader Salvadoran society?

Transcribing the interviews made it possible to visually pluck out words and/or generative themes that were often repeated in my discussions with these ten women. From this list of generative words and themes, I used a process based on problem posing, and analysis. During the first step, I presented the generative themes I had gleaned from my interviews and observations (presenting them as small sections of direct quotes). This was done using flip charts and small pieces of cardboard and, for those who were not able to read, verbally reading the quotes to them. Then, the group did small group activities to analyze and examine these statements. At this point small groups were given guiding questions:

- What ideas, themes or learning did you pick up from these quotes?
- Are there other issues you feel need to be discussed that are not presented here?

Second, over a longer period of time, we used problem-posing to examine some of the generative themes as they arose in the context of the meetings.

This group approach to analysis was important in order to help the women see that I was not there to be the 'gringa expert,' and that it was their experiences as disabled women in El Salvador that made *them* the knowers and the experts. Also, I thought the group could more readily identify the structural, systemic causes of problems they encountered in their everyday lives if we began by looking at the individual and then moving out towards the family and community. Finally, it was important that the group be free to steer discussions in directions they themselves determined. For that reason, I planned a session outline only after we as a group had discussed our direction. I felt that if I began each group with the pronouncement that we were going to discuss a 'collective problem' the group had named, it would have been my issue and the group would never have taken ownership of the problem or the discussion.

Personally, I was a bit nervous about my own 'location' as an able-bodied, 'gringa' academic from 'los estados' doing research. What I hoped to represent and embody was a safe person who could help them organize and structure their thoughts, opinions, questions and doubts in a way that could productively facilitate meaningful analysis, discussion, group-building and the desire to become change agents and take action. I wanted to share the tools and skills of gathering information, documenting, organizing and analyzing information that the group had never had the opportunity to gain. Finally, I wanted to help them see that not only could this research process be interesting, but that they were all capable of doing it.

Moving into action

Action took place on a number of different levels. The first tier of action was to find other disabled women outside of San Salvador. The second tier of action was the decision to hold group meetings focusing on skill building so that this group of women could go out and find other disabled women and help them analyze their own social realities about being disabled in El Salvador. Another action happened when many group members, who had never written before, submitted poems, life stories and/or dictated things for the *boletina* (bulletin) that the ACOGIPRI staff published And finally, the group members mentioned wanting a space for women to discuss their problems and concerns in a safe environment.

ACOGIPRI staff and I assumed that if sufficient funding were received, the Women's Program of ACOGIPRI would host a Summer Institute for Women with Disabilities from the entire Central American region. In this way, interested women could act as co-facilitators and play a key role in the organization and implementation of this event. This, in turn, would enable ACOGIPRI staff and me to identify potential facilitators and leaders for the future of the organization. We also identified the need to educate not only other disabled women but to educate the entire able-bodied community about the issues important to disabled women (and men) in El Salvador.

Generative themes

The following generative themes, identified by the ten women I interviewed, are listed in order of frequency as they were named by the women:

- architectural obstacles;
- transportation problems;
- lack of support from family and/or community;
- misconception of disabled women and their abilities;
- lack of educational facilities and/or opportunities;
- lack of acceptance in educational settings by peers and teachers;
- low self-esteem;
- inability to find a love relationship;
- the importance of fulfilling the traditional role of mother and/or wife and/or care giver;
- lack of work opportunities for the disabled.

I will illustrate each of these generative themes with quotes from the women themselves. These quotes are sometimes anonymous and sometimes not, depending on the instructions of the interviewee.

Architectural obstacles

It was too far to walk to school, it was a very hilly place, and of course, there were no buses. So I used a horse, that was my means of transportation. They would put me on in the morning and my sister would carry my notebooks, and my dad, who was a teacher, would lift me off when I got to school. This was fine until the war, then there were barricades and mines in the roads, we couldn't go to school.

There aren't many places to go shopping. At Metro-Centro [a big shopping mall in San Salvador] for example, there are some ramps and things but I can't fit through the doors to the stores (in my wheelchair). They don't really think about us.

Transportation obstacles

Puchika! [expletive in Spanish] Sometimes, I wait in the center (of San Salvador) for hours trying to get back to Soyapango. There is no way to get into a bus, and anyway, what mostly goes are vans anyway. But people don't want to have to deal with helping me up and then dealing with my seat (wheelchair). By now I know who will be willing to help me, but if I need to go anywhere during the rush hours, forget it!

Ay! To get from Santa Tecla to San Salvador, in the morning! Firstly, I can't do it alone, because I change buses at the Hospital Rosales. Someone has to help me get through those awful hordes, and carry anything I need for the day, and there I am trying to stand up with my crutches, worrying that someone will push me.

Lack of acceptance by peers and teachers

The second semester of university I was taking an accounting class. Towards the end of the class, the professor came near me and said, 'Are you taking this class?' and I answered that I was. He then said, 'I don't think you will pass. I don't know why people like you study, you'd be better off staying at home. Because here (in this lecture hall) the student's benches are very high and this class is very hard, I don't think you will pass.' But I ignored him. Then, one time, during the fourth or sixth class, the professor called on me to go do an exercise on the blackboard. And he knew I couldn't (physically). So I stood up and said that I could walk down to the last row of chairs, but since the stage on which he lectures was so high, I couldn't climb up to it. And he said to me that if I was in university, it was expected that I could do the work, and if not, why were you here. And I said, I can do the work, what I can't do is get up the stairs. But if I dictate all the answers to you to write down or to another student to write down for me, and he said, 'No, what I want is for you to come up front' and I said, 'Truthfully, I can't.' And then he said, 'Within two weeks is our first exam, and I don't think you will pass.' In front of the entire lecture hall. And this was the second or third time he had said things like that to me.

During the war, we were displaced and went to Soyapango. My mother put me in high school, but the vice-principal didn't believe I had finished grade school. We waited a month, because of the war, to get my certificates to show [that I had graduated]. And finally one day at eight in the morning, I went to school. And all the students stared at me and said that maybe the woman (my mother) had made a mistake and meant to bring me to a health clinic rather than to high school or perhaps I belonged in fifth grade or first grade or something like that. But certainly not for high school, and they would laugh.

Lack of support from family and community

Because at the beginning I lost the ability to speak and also my memory, I had to begin with the syllables like little children learn the a, b, c. I couldn't understand, for example, if a clown was a clown, because I didn't know the word. So, they left it to my brother to teach me how to speak again. He was a very strict professor and I was so delicate and frail (emotionally) and I just couldn't learn that way. And instead of telling him, I would just start to cry, he couldn't be of much help during that stage of my recovery.

Ruth goes on to explain:

Sometimes I felt rejection from my older sister. Instead of helping me, she would put up obstacles to my ideas when I mentioned studying, working. And she made me angry because she said, 'Ruth, how are you going to go out [of the house] after being so coquettish [before the stroke] in your high heels and nylons?' Because I was very coquettish when I left the house to go to work. But now I had to wear orthopedic shoes. And she would say, 'Ah, no, what are your friends going to say? They will pretend they don't know you.'

Misconception of disabled women and their abilities

In Cecelia's case:

after high school, there was no more talk of school or work. They [family members] told me it was better to stay home. But I always wanted to be an architect. [She proceeded to show me drawings from her sixth grade mechanical drawing class.]

At my workplace, the *licenciada* [a person who holds a university degree] told me that I could no longer do my job and she let me go. I still give injections to people who need them, so it's obvious I can still do it.

Lack of educational facilities and opportunities

They told my sister that it is illegal for anyone with any type of disability to enroll in the faculty of medicine; but you must just have patience and thank God. Right now I am trying to get documents together and present a case for a human rights abuse.

This is the first time anyone has ever talked to me about 'this stuff.' Usually they want us to learn a new skill or try to make us do something we don't need. You are letting us talk about what we think is important.

Low self-esteem

I would really like to learn to use a sewing machine. But, I don't have a sewing machine, and really to go to an academy for sewing and confection, I couldn't do that, because I would have to leave the house. But really, it's my family, they over-protect me and I just couldn't do it anyway.

I didn't want to go to any more meetings. They talk a lot and then it would be my turn to talk, and I didn't want to talk in front of the group because all I wanted was to be like before (my stroke) and I could feel a lump in my throat.

Inability to find a love relationship

I don't think I will marry, never. If I had a boyfriend, yes, perhaps I could marry, but since I don't have a boyfriend. I would like to have children but since I can't. … It's because I am so serious, that's what they tell me. … Since I never go anywhere, then, of course I don't have a boyfriend.

Now as an adult, I often feel like that people don't accept me, that they reject me. I have gone out on dates, maybe because they feel bad for me, they feel like it would be nice, but then I never get a call back. I've been told that I am pretty but no one ever approaches me.

The importance of fulfilling the role of care giver, wife and mother

I can cook, iron, wash, all the things I need to do. I have the right to love and all of that, we all have that right to love and be loved. We, the disabled, have to educate the rest of the population to understand that we can and have the right to love, because now, if I said that I was in love, they would ask, 'Who would want to be with you?'

I talk to some [girl] friends I have, and we all think alike. That we will get married and have children, have a house to take care of, we are all in that age when you begin to do all that.

Lack of work opportunities

FUNTER [a Salvadoran NGO that focuses on rehabilitation] always calls to say that there is a job opening and they want to hire a disabled person. But when I go to these, they then say that we don't have the right skills. If we are never given a chance how are we going to get these skills?

I went for an interview once. What they wanted me to do didn't seem that complicated, but, when I went and they saw me limp, they told me I wouldn't be able to do it.

Regardless of their age, educational and socio-economic background, all of the women I interviewed faced most of the problems named above. The hardest part for these women seemed to be the ability to name the causes of these problems or why the problems they identified exist. When I asked the two questions in the first interview, 'Why do you think these problems you mentioned exist?' and 'What causes these problems?', most of the women said, 'I don't know' or often blamed that common 'they,' meaning society in general. Because so many of the people they know and love fit into this 'they' who really didn't understand them, many women would frequently add, 'It's our culture and traditions, and it's not so-and-sos fault' as causes of their problems. In the ten interviews, only one woman began to extrapolate towards a systemic analysis of the problems and causes, focusing on relationships of problems faced by the collective group of 'disabled women' and their relationship to the bigger structural problems of the society:

the question is our society. Not because we have a disability, for me it isn't that. The problem is to be able to learn more about the problem. It's the same thing with the economic factor, which is really principle. The role I must play is as a helper and a voice, because I have studied and understand the importance of changing the system.

This same woman analyzed her polio which she contracted when she was three. She understood her polio as the problem of the government that resulted in poor health care in the country, and not only as the individual problem of not being vaccinated.

And ... I lived in Morazan, it's more remote there. My mother would always take me to get the vaccine, and they would tell me I was sick and to come back. Let's wait until the next time, and the next time I had something else, and so on. And to me, that was a factor, how can I say, bad health care in our country.

Culture was also to blame for why society marginalized women with disabilities even more than it marginalized women. All ten women agreed that in their society women were *already* marginalized for being women. As women with disabilities, they were doubly marginalized (six women used this term) and things were much more difficult for them than for men with disabilities.

When asked, 'What can be done to change these problems?', most women replied that a place like ACOGIPRI was necessary, but made no mention of the activities that they felt a place like ACOGIPRI should offer to disabled women.

In response to the question, 'What kind of support or lack of it have you received from your family members in order to overcome obstacles presented to you?', there were various opinions:

my family never stopped me from doing anything. The only thing was if I had continued to go to school, I would have returned very late at night.

And, well, I was alone, so ... I never worked outside the house. I've always stayed at home with my mommy and my dad. After high school, I looked for work, but they didn't give it to me. Now, the only time I leave the house is with my family. I'm afraid, I might fall.

Some responses, such as the comment above from Cecelia, had a sort of double message, almost as though she and other women were repeating what they had been hearing from their family members. Other women could easily identify what kinds of support they did or did not receive from their family members and how:

Practically, I had a lot of moral support from my mom most of all and physical support also because wherever I wanted to go she would accompany me. It wasn't the same with my brothers or with my dad. Because inside, my dad felt bad, and sad because he would say, 'Ahh, poor thing. My daughter when are you going to walk like before?' And I would begin to feel very bad for myself. But now I say to him, 'Daddy, it is done and now you just have to get used to how I am. I am happy how I am. And look, for me, walking differently from other people isn't an obstacle. ... And don't look at me with that look of poor thing, my girl.'

Disabled women and the family

All the women I interviewed individually spent the beginning part of the interview talking about their families. Research has continually shown that families act as the first teachers and the first school for most people. This is just as true for the disabled women I interviewed. Not only are family members responsible for educating disabled women, often when the disability occurred later in life, family members are responsible for rehabilitation as well. Moreover, family members are the ones that seem to most often influence the disabled woman's sense of self and her capacity to do things – study, travel, leave the house, go out into the world, work, etc.

Family members decide (directly or indirectly) what is possible for the disabled woman especially when she is a young girl – whether she will choose the path of the abled (attending school, working, having home and civic responsibilities) or the path of a 'dis'abled person (i.e. who understands herself as someone fit only to stay home and learn to perform the more critical and important tasks of the house such as cleaning, washing clothes, cooking, making tortillas, etc.). This second path hopes the disabled woman might have a normal life by making her appear 'marriageable'. Unfortunately for the disabled woman, the messages that accompany these two distinct paths are powerful forces that will either help her become 'literate' about her world and her possibilities, or will keep her illiterate about her world, more in keeping with the common image of a 'dis'abled person. As Angelica explains:

> From my point of view, I don't have any disability. Everyone else says I have a disability, but for me it isn't that. I can study, do everything, I can cook, iron, wash, do my things, but, more slowly than other persons. I need to have help to go here, there and sometimes, I get frustrated, but I never say I can't do it. They say I am disabled because I use crutches, but for me, I'm not. It's not *my* [emphasis Angelica's] disability.

However, Cecelia tells a somewhat different story:

> I wanted to travel. To go somewhere far away, like Santa Ana [two hours from San Salvador] alone, different places. But I can't. Firstly, they don't let me. Because they say it is very dangerous to travel alone. And I might fall. So, I can't.

Cecelia also talked about wanting a college education to be an architect or engineer, or have a small business at home, or even to climb the hill near her sister's house, but she ended every wish with, '*pero entonces, no puedo*' ('however, I can't').

When a disabled women continually hears that she *can't*, is not *capable*, is not *equal*, these words, of course, affect the way she sees herself. As time goes on, these are not only the words she hears, they are the words she herself uses, or if not, they are the words she has internalized to define herself, her abilities and her overwhelming disabilities. As Freire describes in *Pedagogy of the Oppressed*:

> The oppressed, having internalized the image of the oppressor and adopted his guidelines, are fearful of freedom. Freedom would require them to eject this image and replace it with autonomy and responsibility.
>
> (Freire 1972: 31)

Many families are not intentionally discriminating against one of their own. They too hear from their peers and the outside world about what disabled people can and cannot do. They are just trying to do what they believe is best for their disabled family member. Often, they feel that less discrimination will take place if the disabled woman stays at home among family members. At home, the family can protect her from the mean comments, the odd stares and the unfair treatment she will receive from the outside, 'abled' world.

> My mother was more traumatized than I when I left the hospital. As I told you, I really didn't have any hair when I left the hospital. And she gave me a hat to wear when I left the hospital. But when I couldn't stand the heat, I would just take it off. And since there are always people who are jerks, they would say things like, 'Hey, baldy, baldy,' things like that … My mother would get upset and get into fights defending me. As I said, she was more traumatized than I was, to the point where she didn't want me to go out alone, so afraid of what the people would say.

At home, the family members can control to some degree what kind of influence the outside world has on their family member, whereas when venturing out into the world it is harder to protect her. Explains a friend who works at ACOGIPRI,

> We both won a place at the Very Special Arts Festival in Brussels. We were the only two from El Salvador or Central America chosen. I won a prize for a poem I wrote and she won for a painting. I did everything I could think of to get us plane tickets for Brussels. All we needed was the airfare, everything else was covered. When I called up her parents to tell them that I was busy trying to find a way for us to go in June they said to me, 'It doesn't matter if you do find the tickets. Mary won't be going with you. There is no way we can let her go to a far away place just like that. Who knows what could happen?'

On the other hand, it is often a family member who makes it possible for the disabled woman to pursue her dreams.

> My mommy went everywhere with me. She would get on the bus with me, help me into the taxi, take me to school, take me to ACOGIPRI, wait for me, everything. She was my mental and physical support. When I didn't want to go to any more meetings at ACOGIPRI, she would talk me into going.

> My family always helped me. My mommy used to pay little girls to play with me. What she would do was to say to other women who also made tortillas and tamales, 'Lend me your daughter and I will give you a quantity of money so that they will play.' And the girl and I would play, making tortillas, tamales of corn, houses. And later, she would ask to play with me, and I would ask to play with her. Then later when I started school, my mommy said, 'Look, lend me your daughter and I will pay for her studies.' And she would go and study with me. And so my mom would pay for the schooling of her, my studies, and we would study together. And it was like this until high school.

Action + Reflection = Praxis

The next section describes in greater detail Components II and III of the project: analysis and problematization, examining the broader structures of disabled women's lives, information collecting and, finally, action.

Of course, these events did not fall into neat little categories or a sequential order. Because these activities rarely occurred in isolation and were often jumbled together, I will discuss them that way. For each meeting or set of meetings, themes are described, as well as how members of the group participated, the decision-making process, leadership styles and any action that was taken.

By the middle of February, the ten women I had interviewed were eager to meet as a group. Without discussing any themes as a group, most had mentioned that they saw a support group as a place to share and solve problems, and also do community outreach to identify and incorporate other disabled women not only in the capital but also in the countryside of El Salvador.

Getting acquainted

Meeting one: Conociendonos

The first meeting began with excitement on both my part and on that of the women. Not only did the ten women I invited attend, but five women I had not interviewed were also present.

I began the meeting welcoming everyone and outlined our agenda for that day. I also gave a brief review of the purpose of the group, based on the comments from the first meeting. Eileen then spoke to the group, sharing some of her hopes and expectations for the next five months for the group and for ACOGIPRI.

Three-quarters of the meeting was used for introductions and an activity to help group members get to know each other better, followed by an activity for the women to examine their own lives a bit more. The activities were structured so that everyone had to participate to some degree or another. These included introducing a partner to the large group and sharing pieces of their lives from their 'tree of life' with the group. Many women commented that they had never shared their hopes and dreams with other people before, and that no one had ever asked them what they thought in such a manner. Some women participated only in these two activities where speaking was required, while others were quick to ask questions and give opinions throughout the session.

The last part of the meeting was dedicated to administrative matters such as reconfirming the best time to meet, discussing transportation issues which were paramount for most of the women and, finally, talking about the methodology I as a facilitator would be using throughout our sessions together. My role during this part of the meeting was mostly to ask the group questions about meeting structure, schedules, what procedure we could use to tackle issues, and helping them reach consensus. I also helped a few of the less vocal women have their voices heard. The entire group agreed to meet every two weeks on Saturday mornings. It was obvious that a few of the women had experience with being in a group, and were quicker to formulate and express their opinions than others. Other women were more quick to say, 'You decide,' and seemed frustrated when I would not do that. I discussed the general outline of the next meeting, telling the group that at the next meeting they would have to decide on the direction we would take.

Facilitator reflection

Because the group was made up of women with such varying skills and abilities, I decided that alternative kinds of communication and literacies that may not always rely on reading, writing or speaking were particularly important to enable all the women to express themselves. It was evident from our first group meeting that a few of the women had the ability to verbally express themselves very well, while others might be able to draw, sing, write or express themselves with a literacy strategy I had never considered. For the rest of the meetings, I relied heavily on techniques I had developed working as a trainer as well as the skills I developed working in literacy programs. I felt that modeling alternative communication techniques was very important because most of the women who attended the meetings were used to lectures and not accustomed to popular, participatory methods. I looked for ways in which varying communication techniques could be used by the group as material for discussion, dialogue and reflection.

Investigation, momentum and conflict

Meetings two, three, four, and five: Diagnostica personal y de la comunidad *(personal, family and community diagnosis)*

Keeping in mind my personal desire to acknowledge and validate various types of expression and knowledge, I decided to begin exploring the generative themes around self, family and community without complicated writing and reading exercises.

For the second meeting, there were two overlapping agendas: to share training skills in popular education so that this group would be able to work with other disabled women and, at the same time, to introduce research activities that required the use of analytical tools to help them reflect about their own situations.

The second and third meetings, which dealt specifically with the individual and the family, were important because women who had less group experiences and had not said much at the first meeting began to participate and voice their opinions more, especially when we began discussing family. I felt a good momentum take shape as we developed as a group. Also, we were using a less traditional way of documenting, exploring and talking about issues. Instead of writing about these topics, we used drawing, cutting, pasting, painting, singing and other techniques. This seemed to make a big difference for the women who felt inhibited by their ability to express themselves through writing. It also set up a nice dynamic of acknowledgment and praise among the group members for those who had hidden talents. During the second meeting, we looked at the generative themes that I had arranged on flip chart paper, on small pieces of cardboard and that I also read to the group. Small groups discussed and reflected on what these quotes were saying. The analysis was a difficult task for the group because it touched very personal issues, but the group wanted to discuss them, especially when I told them that each small group needed to present their ideas to the large group using anything except writing to express their opinions about what they had been examining.

Themes at the third and fourth meetings were varied. They included family members' ability to help or hinder individual women's desires, opportunities for self-development, loneliness, difficulties at school or finding a job, financial problems, transportation problems and health problems. I used techniques such as family configurations, genealogy charts and community mapping to discuss self, family and the community. The fifth meeting ended with two women disagreeing over an issue relating to disability oppression which left the entire group feeling a little low.

Facilitator reflection

These meetings allowed for a lot of dialogue and discussion among group members and also challenged them to think about how to do that. There were lots of friendly disagreements, and although people were more comfortable telling each other they didn't agree, they still looked to me to provide the leadership and end an argument by saying who was correct and who was mistaken. I felt uncomfortable being seen this way and wondered if my facilitation style was contributing to this perception of me by some group members.

The other reason I thought I was seen as the dispute settler had to do with my credentials and the fact that I was an able-bodied '*gringa*' from the outside. Perhaps this was why they thought I must have the correct answers.

Many disabled women develop low self-esteem after years of being told, 'You can't do it, you can't possibly know.' Judged by the outside world as being disabled both in spirit and body, and therefore incapable of knowing, many disabled women often give up the notion they can achieve things with other parts of their beings, principally because they have been told for so long that they *cannot*. Some of the women in the group would immediately back down if their opinion was challenged by another woman, often saying, 'You must be right.' The few women who felt more comfortable disagreeing were mostly the ones with a higher formal educational level, whereas the quieter ones were often the less educated and had less experience working in groups.

Equally as interesting was one woman who believed that every opinion she had was correct. Using complicated academic vocabulary to intimidate other group members, she would scare them away from a theme, using flowery language about such themes as feminism, women, disability and oppression, economics, development – anything she felt was relevant at the moment. Once during a conversation where she stated that all women with disabilities should be feminists to fight for their human rights, she belittled another woman who said she didn't want to be a feminist. The 'feminist' accused her, 'You say you are not a feminist because you think they don't want to get married and form a home.' The offended women answered, 'No, I just don't want to be associated with feminists if it means I have to talk like you.'

Although I was excited by the increased energy and excitement in the group, I was worried that two particularly vocal women who frequently argued could easily upset the delicate balance the group had achieved. Since the group was beginning to take more initiative in relation to dialogue and decisions about what issues to raise, I decided we would just go for it and use the group structure to mediate any serious conflicts.

Ownership and new motivations

Meetings six and seven

Meeting six ended up being cancelled as only two women had turned up by 10.15, and I wondered if the tone at the end of the last meeting had influenced individual women's decisions about whether or not to come to ACOGIPRI.

Meeting seven: Como ser facilitadora (How to be a facilitator)

At this meeting, we had visitors from Guatemala, who had come to ACOGIPRI to learn about the Women's Program. Three women from a religious-based disabled persons group spent three days with us to learn more about forming a women's group.

Because we had visitors that wanted concrete skills in organizing women, Eileen asked me if I could do a workshop that would touch on basic skills for facilitators. At first, I wasn't sure this session would really fit into what we had been doing as a group, but, after thinking about the failure of the previous meeting to materialize, I wondered if some concrete skills that could be tried in the community would in fact be a good thing. With the help of Maritza, a group member, we called and sent telegrams to the other members, informing them of the meeting as well as the topic.

This meeting was very well attended and some women brought friends as well. Comments from the group included, 'Now we can go out and find other disabled women and know how to talk to them,' and 'I could never talk in front of a group like that.' Other women were eager to hear about Guatemala, and asked the three women to share their experiences where they were in the process of organizing a group of women, and what some of the key issues were for their Guatemalan counterparts. Although I facilitated a formal part of this meeting, a great deal of participation and taking initiative seemed to illustrate increased ownership of the process on the part of the group.

Facilitator reflection

I think that having the women from Guatemala was important to the Women's Program. It made them look at themselves and all the work they had been doing, not only personally, but as a group in order to keep the momentum of a women's group going. Towards the end of the meeting, when the sharing was taking place, many of the women at the table were able to contribute at least one strategy they had used in order to either attend a meeting or involve other women in the group. This meeting gave a much needed boost to the self-esteem of individual group members and the group as a whole. Listening to lunchtime conversation, I heard comments about how far the Women's Program had come: 'Isn't it funny that they want our opinions about how to work with women?'; 'Remember when we were in the initial organizing stages like they are?'

Action and reframing: gathering more information

Meetings: Comunicacion y la mujer discapacitada (Communication and disabled women)

The previous meeting had set the stage for thinking and talking about action. The workshop on facilitator skills had resulted in group members thinking in different directions. The environment was also providing opportunities to think about action. At the end of April the group was invited to give two *charlas* (talks) – one in San Salvador and one in Metapan, in the north-west corner of El Salvador.

This meeting focused on language and its use. The topic came up at the beginning of our meeting when the women began to discuss what they wanted to be called/labeled. In disability circles in the US this is always an issue, and in Latin America it is equally important. Brainstorming about the various terms used in society to describe disability or those who have a disability led to lengthy discussion. Women were very vocal about what they thought society meant by different terms used to describe a disabled person, and how that often led them to see themselves as having ability or dis-ability. There was agreement that terms such as *invalida* (invalid) and *minusvalida* (less than valid) should never be used to describe anyone because these terms made women (and men) see themselves as useless and also conveyed that image to society. Other terms, such as *discapacitada* (disabled) and *con limitaciones* (with limitations) were felt by the group to be more acceptable because the disabled women or the women with limitations could still have abilities. To use these terms means to be seen as more than just a disability or limitation.

When they asked me how disability was labeled in the US, I told them that currently some say 'persons with different abilities.' Everyone at the table said that they didn't like the term because it didn't really say anything, because everyone has different abilities.

The discussion was pushed into another direction by one group member who asked, 'How do people who can't communicate verbally describe themselves?'

Before the group could attempt to answer this, another women asked, 'How can we work with women that don't read, write, see, or hear? How can we help them see themselves differently?'

An enormous list was generated by the group, and I was encouraged to add to it, which I did. Then the idea from the floor was that everyone would develop a communication technique (listed during this brainstorm) with the idea of how to reach women out there.

The meeting ended with much excitement, and as we discussed the upcoming workshops everyone agreed that we should wait to see what was produced by the group to see if it was something we could use.

Facilitator reflection

Although the entire group agreed to create a communication tool, it was obvious that a few of the women had more invested in it than others. It had been an exciting meeting, and a lot of ground had been covered. Group members varied in their willingness to take on responsibility to create something, and I think the ones that were most eager to do something had made the less eager ones feel pressured into saying, 'Oh yes, of course we will do that.'

The next meeting and the outreach workshops that were to follow were definitely the highlight of the project. The other exciting piece of information for the group was that we had received funding for a Summer Institute. This meant that group members could use the skills they were gaining in the field and take on facilitator roles during the two-week summer seminar.

And finally, outreach had begun in earnest. With the impetus of recruitment for the Summer Institute, members of the Women's Program began looking for places to give *charlas* (talks) for interested women to find out more about ACOGIPRI and the possibility of forming a local support group.

Together we brainstormed what an informational *charla* could look like, and also got a planning committee together, not only for recruitment and outreach, but also for other parts of the upcoming seminar. Actions included:

1   choosing teams to go out on outreach visits;
2   developing a short *charla* about the history of ACOGIPRI and the Women's Program;
3   developing a short *charla* about why women need the opportunity to meet without men;
4   working to develop a communication tool for outreach.

Meeting nine was postponed a few times and ended up happening three weeks later than originally scheduled. Although not all members created a tool, the ones that were presented to the group were well thought out, extremely creative and also something that could be reproduced and implemented in community programs. The members who had created tools felt good about them and most talked about why it was important to use them, not only with other disabled women, but also in the able-bodied world so that they could reframe (author's word) society's views of women with disabilities.

The last activity of this meeting was a report given by the group who had given a *charla* in Metapan. They shared with the group what that experience had been like. I had gone along to observe and be there as support. It was interesting for me to hear them tell the others how they felt it had gone, what was positive and negative about their presentation and what could be improved upon for next time.

End of the research/support group

La ultima reunion – evaluacion *(The final meeting)*

As we geared up for the Summer Institute, my own research was coming to an end, and the group was feeling like they were being pulled in too many directions. Our last meeting as a support group was held as an evaluation and also with the understanding that after the Summer Institute, they would begin again in some form or another. The entire group was not present at the final meeting. We discussed what ending the group meant, we shared what our individual experiences had been, and evaluated what we had accomplished. We discussed what impact we had made as a group on both the disabled community and the able-bodied community.

We listed recommendations for future support groups. Those who wanted to write were given that opportunity. There was consensus that this type of support group was important and necessary. Other suggestions included possible topics for future discussion and that more time be spent on self-esteem needs of the group members and less time spent on issues of disabled women outside the group. Some women recommended different meeting times, and the possibility of shifting/rotating meeting locations to accommodate those who had to travel a great deal. Everyone agreed that refreshments were very important. Everyone also said they appreciated the support group and it was an important piece in their lives.

Facilitator reflection

The atmosphere was not quite as upbeat at this meeting as in past meetings. Part of it may have been the extreme heat and also the fact that it was an afternoon meeting as opposed to our normal morning meetings. The women did seem to appreciate the support group, and they all said that they would continue to participate when it started up again.

Reflections and outcomes

Group recommendations

I led the evaluation discussion that took place during our final meeting in the third week of June 1994.

Group members recalled that they had many purposes for wanting to meet as a group:

1   to find other disabled women outside of San Salvador and work with them;
2   to build skills so they would be able to hold meetings and discussions with other disabled women; and
3   to provide a forum where they could meet as women to discuss and share common problems and possible solutions.

Every woman agreed that the support group was beneficial and should continue. The group saw that they could have a greater role in helping other women with disabilities find a space and voice by doing it first themselves:

> I see my role as being to fight for people with disabilities. I can be that voice for those women who can't yell. I can go out and help women find a way to be productive, just like when I first began coming to ACOGIPRI in August of last year. It's a process.]

> All that I have learned. ... I wasn't like this six months after my accident. Now, I think that when someone sees me, they see me for my capacities, and the way I see myself and my value. These are all things that we have to share with other women, and here [ACOGIPRI] is the best place to do it.

Women gave recommendations about format, schedules, purposes and goals. Although they had started with the goal of wanting to do outreach with other disabled women, upon reflection many also felt they wanted more time to devote to their own needs. When asked about recommendations for future discussion topics, almost all of the women mentioned wanting to spend more time on self-esteem and the issue of their own sexuality. A few stated the need for more time for themselves and that they were not ready to think about other disabled women.

Most members agreed that the group fulfilled its purpose of providing a space for collective discussion of problems, concerns and possible solutions, but again, many women wanted more time for this activity and less for the outreach aspect. Because of the feeling of camaraderie, group members began to see that they weren't alone in their problems:

It was important to know that what I have to say is important to other people. I never thought other people wanted to know about my disability and how it felt every day of my life, but you asked.

Evaluation of the process

My broad goal was to use a participatory research framework of investigation, education and action to understand the social reality of disabled women and to help facilitate a participatory research process with these women. There was no guarantee that the 'action' would lead to social transformation on either the personal or collective level, or that group members would see the need for change. Another purpose of my research was to understand the knowledges created by this group of disabled women, and how these kinds of 'literacies' allowed for the possibility of reframing and transforming actions. But, did the group engage in 'research'? Did they formulate an explicit research problem and collectively design, conduct and measure (qualitatively) the participatory research investigation? No, not exactly. So, what did we do? At the beginning, the women produced knowledge about themselves: the documenting, writing, dictating, drawing, pasting, cutting, singing and other communication techniques became the tools of analysis that helped them investigate them-selves, their families, their communities and their worlds. The collection of information, analyzing and summarizing done in these activities helped group members recognize that things they knew about their world were valid and that others felt similarly. What happened next? The women moved from discussing and informally 'researching' their own realities to reaching out collectively to other disabled women. Group members took ownership of these skills we were trying together in the group, and saw them as useful tools for working with other disabled women. Small actions were taking place within the program: some of the women were going out to give talks, others were writing their stories for the bi-monthly *boletina*, some were acting as scribes to document others' stories. Women who did not talk during the first meetings, or if they did, would not look anyone in the face, were now quicker to give an opinion without being asked what they thought. In themselves, these may not seem to be revolutionary activities that contribute to major social transformation, but, on the other hand, we did begin to challenge the oppression of silence, invisibility and isolation felt by most disabled women. The realization of many of the women that the critical problems they face as disabled women were collectively held was also new knowledge.

One important lesson for me as a researcher in this process is that it is imperative to remember that social and personal transformation is not an event but a process that takes time. We all operate on our own very personal time lines and it is important not to examine the validity of our efforts towards emancipatory acts as the end results but rather as a process of struggle that should be celebrated at all points of the process.

As one participant said,

> But, to get to there, how can I do it? Perhaps it is a process. ... We pick a goal. In this case it is to know the world of the disabled woman. I have theoretical knowledge, but now it's the practice. ACOGIPRI opened the doors for me, now I need to show that I can open more spaces, and I will. But I'm not going to achieve it in one day or alone, it's a process.

Acknowledgments

This research project came about as a result of many years of hard work by the founder and members of the Women's Program at ACOGIPRI de R.L. in San Salvador, El Salvador. I owe them all 'muchas gracias' for allowing me to become a part of their extended family and community so quickly. The lessons and inspirations I gained from my seven and a half months with these extraordinary women and men will be carried with me forever.

Special thanks go to Eileen Giron, founder of ACOGIPRI and the Women's Program, whose strength, courage, insight and friendship were an inspiration to me and made this project possible.

Notes

1   In Spanish it reads *charlasa esta problematica de salud.*' See *Politica Nacional de Atencion Integral a las Personas con Discapacidades*, March, 1994, p. 8.
2   The term 'disabled women' (or 'women with disabilities') was discussed both during our training sessions and during the Summer Institute. This was the term chosen by the Salvadoran women with whom I did my research and is the term I use throughout this document.
3   See Sherry Kane (Fall 1993) 'Theoretical foundations of popular education and participatory research', unpublished training design, Center for International Education, School of Education, University of Massachusetts.
4   Here and in other places of my discussion, 'literate' and 'literacy' are used in very broad terms. Torruellas, Benmayor, Goris and Juarbe in their piece 'Affirming cultural citizenship in the Puerto Rican community: critical literacy and El Barrio Popular Education Program' in *Literacy as Praxis: Culture, language and pedagogy* (1991), edited by Catherine E. Walsh, come closest to the way I use literacy here. They advocate:

> A broader conception of literacy as popular education, developed within the Latin American context, [that] offers a viable paradigm for innovative educational practices. ... Within this framework, illiteracy is recognized not as the cause, but the manifestation of the systematic exclusion of minorities and the poor from economic, political and educational opportunities. Hence, learning how to read and write becomes a vehicle for developing collective solutions that address the underlying conditions of inequality. Literacy moves beyond decoding printed symbols to developing critical thinking skills. (p. 184)

5   All of the deaf women in the study could read lips. However, at different points of the study, interpreters were used, particularly during group work.

References

Armstrong, R. and Shenk, J. (1982) *El Salvador: The face of revolution*, Boston: South End Press.

Belenky, M., Clinchy, B.M., Goldberger, N.R., Tarule, J.M. (1986) *Women's Ways of Knowing*, US: Basic Books.

Boylan, E. (1991) *Women And Disability*, London: Zed Press.

Burrel, G. and Morgan, G. (1979) *Sociological Paradigms and Organizational Analysis*, Exeter, NH: Heinemann Educational Books.

Carter, B. (ed.) (1989) *A Voice Compels Us: Voices of Salvadoran women*, Boston: South End Press.

CONAIPD (Consejo Nacional de Atencion Integral a la Persona con Discapacidad) (1994) *Politica Nacional de Atencion Integral a las Personas con Discapacidades*, San Salvador: Publicorp/Multigrafica.

Fals-Borda, O. (1987) 'The application of participatory-action research in Latin America,' *International Sociology* 2 (4): 329–47.

Fine, M. and Asch, A. (eds) (1988) *Women and Disabilities: Essays in psychology, culture and politics*, Philadelphia: Temple University Press.

Foucault, M. (1980) *Power/Knowledge: Selected interviews and other writings, 1972–1977*, (ed. Colin Gordon, trans. Gordon) *et al.*, New York: Pantheon.

Freire, P. (1972) *Pedagogy of the Oppressed*, New York: Continuum.

—— (1973) *Education for Critical Consciousness*, New York: Continuum.

Glade, W. and Reilly, C.A. (1993) *Inquiry at the Grassroots*, Arlington: Inter-American Foundation.

Golden, R. (1991) *The Hour of the Poor, The Hour of Women: Salvadoran women speak*, New York: Crossroad.

Gramsci, A. (1971) *Selections from the Prison Notebooks of Antonio Gramsci* (ed., trans. Q. Hoare and G. Smith), New York: International Publishers.

Heath, S.B. (1983) *Ways with Words*, Cambridge: Cambridge University Press.

Hennessy, R. (1993) *Materialist Feminism and the Politics of Discourse*, New York: Routledge.

Kleymeyer, C.D. (1992) *La Expresion Cultural y el Desarrollo de Base*, Arlington: Inter-American Foundation.

Lather, P. (1991) *Getting Smart: Feminist research and pedagogy with/in the postmodern*, New York: Routledge.

Luke, C. and Gore, J. (eds) (1992) *Feminisms and Critical Pedagogy*, New York: Routledge.

McLaren, P. and Leonard, P. (eds) (1993) *Paulo Freire a Critical Encounter*, New York: Routledge.

Maguire, P. (1987) *Doing Participatory Research: A feminist approach*, Amherst: Center for International Education.

Mohanty, C.T., Russo, A. and Torres, L. (1991) *Third World Women and the Politics of Feminism*, Bloomington: Indiana University Press.

Oakley, A. (1981) 'Interviewing women: a contradiction in terms,' in *Doing Feminist Research* (ed. Helen Roberts), Boston: Routledge and Kegan Paul.

Park, P. (1992) 'The discovery of participatory research as a new scientific paradigm: personal and intellectual accounts,' *The American Sociologist* 23 (4).

Smith, D.E. (1987) *The Everyday World as Problematic: A feminist sociology*, Boston: Northeastern University Press.

Spivak, G. (1989) 'A response to "the difference within: feminism and critical theory",' in *The Difference Within: Feminism and critical theory* (ed. E. Meese and A. Parker), Philadelphia: John Benjamins Publishing Co., pp. 207–20.

Street, B.V. (ed.) (1993) *Cross-cultural Approaches to Literacy*, Cambridge: Cambridge University Press.

Walsh, C.E. (ed.) (1991) *Literacy as Praxis: Culture language and pedagogy*, Norwood: Ablex Publishing Corporation.

Premises and principles of emancipatory research

Part III

Premises and principles of emancipatory research

Chapter 11

From critical thought to emancipatory action

Contradictory research goals?[1]

Beth Humphries

Introduction

This chapter has arisen from my reading of two books: Patti Lather's *Getting Smart* (1991) and Martyn Hammersley's *The Politics of Social Research* (1995). Lather's book discusses feminist postmodernist research and pedagogy and Hammersley's is a critique of Lather and other explicitly political research. In particular, Hammersley is concerned that emancipatory approaches to research represent the abandonment of the obligations of the researcher.

Since this is a serious accusation it is important to reflect on the arguments for emancipatory research and to unpack some of the concerns that are at issue in these different conceptions of research. There are a number of dimensions to this which I have been exploring, four in particular. First, the notion of agency – who can be a knower? Second, legitimacy – what tests do claims to knowledge have to pass? Third, truth – can we speak of certainties which are universally valid, in all places and at all times? And finally, purpose – what are legitimate goals of research?

It is the last of these – purpose – which I want to focus on in this chapter. My aims are to examine claims made by emancipatory approaches, to ask why they are different from those of traditional approaches and to explore how we might generate knowledge that takes us 'beyond ourselves'. In particular, I want to focus on two aspects which they have in common: appeals to a metanarrative of emancipation, and a will to power.

The terms of the contest

Let me first rehearse the debates, which are by now familiar to all. Traditional (positivist-influenced) approaches to research see the proper role of the researcher as committed to the discovery of the truth by means of reliable research instruments and rational discussion, being prepared to offer evidence for claims made, to submit to the scrutiny of the research community, and to be willing to change her/his views on the basis of compelling evidence to the contrary. The concept of 'disinterested knowledge' is central to this approach – it is innocent knowledge, untainted by political agenda. Such knowledge may of course be used in unethical and oppressive ways, or towards a market orientation, or for ideological ends. The researcher may have a concern that the knowledge produced may be abused, but nevertheless these consequences are outside her/his control. The major goal is to achieve an accurate representation of reality.

Hammersley's book contains arguments depressingly similar to those he offered in an article some years ago (Hammersley 1992), sparking a debate in the journal *Sociology* to which a number of feminists contributed (Ramazanoglu 1992; Gelsthorpe 1992; Williams 1993). His concern is that the politicisation of research is founded on 'arguments which are defective and which serve to undermine research as a distinctive form of activity. To the extent that they becomes widely accepted they negate social researchers' attempts to preserve some autonomy from the state and other powerful social interests, thereby destroying the conditions in which research can flourish, perhaps even threatening its survival' (Hammersley 1995: vii). (This of course assumes that research was not political before it was politicised.) He points out that positivism takes a number of forms, and that its influence has faded in recent times. However, its continuing significance is apparent in its role as a norm against which other perspectives can react. In this sense, however it is conceived, it remains a primary signifier and an absent presence in the discussions about alternatives.

Definitions of positivism are many and, for example, Halfpenny (1992) describes twelve different meanings, and Hammersley himself does not subscribe to a crudely positivist view. However, his view of what we can learn from positivism is revealing in his claim that positivism is prepared to address difficulties and to resolve them (Hammersley 1995: 18). The assumption here is compatible with a view that problems in social research are largely methodological, resolvable by more refined and more reliable research instruments. There is no admission of notions of contradiction, tension and contingency implied in this position. He insists that the natural sciences should remain the primary model of research (*ibid*. 18) but he does not make clear why he holds this opinion. Ramazanoglu (1992) suggests an answer to this when she identifies his 'uncritical privileging of reason in some sort of established scientific community' (*ibid*. 207). Hammersley admires 'clarity' of expression in positivism (1995: 19), but this does not sit easily with his statement that feminist critiques have revealed the hidden bias in traditional research (*ibid*. x). His critique of 'emancipatory' research falls into the trap of stereotyping and caricaturing alternative approaches (similar to the caricaturing of positivist philosophies from some elements of the 'emancipatory' camp). As a result he sets up a series of straw people which he proceeds to knock down and makes his point by ignoring the diversity of 'emancipatory' positions and being highly selective in his critique (see also Ramazanoglu's 1992 response). For example, he devotes a chapter to arguments for a specifically feminist methodology, expressing his concern that he is not suggesting he is assessing a single position, yet he presents the issues as though they are uncontroversial. He chooses to discuss the themes of: (i) the omni-relevance of gender; (ii) personal experiences versus scientific method; (iii) rejection of hierarchy in the research relationship; (iv) emancipation as the goal of research. He is rightly critical of any claim that gender alone should be the basis of analysis, and that other phenomena are not also important   incidentally, a claim not made by most feminists – and a lively debate continues about the intersection of different sources of divisions amongst women. His discussion gives only cursory acknowledgement of the developments in feminist theory. The work of bell hooks (1994) and Audre Lorde (1984) on the importance of analysing the interaction of class, race, gender and sexuality, are ignored. Are these women not feminists also? Why has Hammersley chosen not to include them and to present such a static view of feminism?

Hammersley's discussion of 'personal experience versus the scientific method' suffers from a similar exclusionary treatment. The work of Birke (1986), Harding (1986), Haraway (1981, 1991) and Rose (1983) on feminism and science is excluded from his discussion and the result is a reductionism which does not reflect the dynamic debates in process. His discussion of the feminist 'rejection of hierarchy in the research relationship' ignores writings by, for example, Bhavnani (1991), and Mohanty's (1991) critique of imperialist feminist research, thus creating an homogeneous feminism which falls over with the touch of a finger. As to the final theme, 'emancipation as the goal of research', the criticism of political research goals is his main topic for the book. He appears to see no contradiction between this criticism and his apparent approval of the radical and liberatory goals of early positivism (Hammersley 1995: 9). I return to this topic below. Finally, as Williams (1993) pointed out when Hammersley's article was published in 1992, his argument fails to recognise the feature which, despite differences in approach to issues around power, on the whole unites many feminists. That is, they are committed to ways of knowing that avoid subordination, and have questioned the taken-for-granted dichotomies around issues to do with knowledge creation, particularly objective/subjective, reason/emotion, grand theorising/lay theorising and researcher/researched.

In the discussion above I have tried to show that the concerns expressed by Hammersley are based largely on stereotypical, selective debates which do not do justice to the controversies to be found in alternative research approaches. His arguments are structured in simplistic, reductionist and binary terms. This discourse of derision obscures those characteristics which 'traditional' and 'emancipatory' approaches might have in common.

In contrast to the position represented by Hammersley, theorists in the 'emancipatory' camp argue that all research is value-laden and is inevitably political, since it represents the interests of particular (usually powerful, usually

White male) groups. Neutrality is seen as problematic, arising from an objectivism which assumes scientific knowledge is free from social construction. What is required is research which 'brings to voice' excluded and marginalised groups as subjects rather than objects of research, and which attempts to understand the world *in order to change it*. Critical, feminist, participatory and anti-racist approaches to research all have this explicit purpose as a fundamental and legitimate premise. Lather says:

> Rather than the illusory 'value-free' knowledge of the positivists, praxis-oriented inquirers see emancipatory knowledge ... [which] increases awareness of the contradictions distorted or hidden by everyday understandings, and in doing so it directs attention to the possibilities for social transformation.
>
> (Lather 1991: 52)

What Lather attempts to do in her book is to bring together three 'discourses of emancipation' in order to draw out an approach to research which is genuinely liberatory. These perspectives are feminism, neo-marxism and poststructuralism. In engaging with them she argues that the focus needs to shift from a search for formal structures and universal values to how we are constituted as subjects of our own knowledge. This she claims is neither 'for' nor 'against' the Enlightenment, but rather is against that which presents itself as finished and authoritarian and for that which is indispensable for the constitution of ourselves as autonomous subjects – a permanent critique of ourselves 'always in the position of beginning again' (*ibid*. 38). In her view the 'courage to think and act within an uncertain framework emerges as the hallmark of liberatory praxis in a time marked by the dissolution of authoritative foundations of knowledge' (*ibid*. 13).

Out of the crisis of marxism, where claims to totality and certainty have been undercut, the binaries that structure liberatory struggle implode from 'us versus them' and 'liberation' versus 'oppression' to a multi-centred discourse with differential access to power. In the resultant decentring of marxism as the dominant explanatory system of the Left, Lather argues, comes a repositioning of marxism as one among many modes of analysis. She posits feminism as 'the site where the theory/praxis nexus is being most creatively interrogated ... the cultural site most disruptive of the alleged impotence of the subject' (*ibid*. 27).

Lather argues that the Enlightenment project via reason has deteriorated into social engineering and rationalist planning – the technologies of normalisation which domesticates and analytically fixes and mobilises pro and anti positions. She argues for a strategy of displacement, i.e. deconstruction, rather than strategies of confrontation, in order to multiply the levels of knowing and doing upon which resistance can act, and which does not negate a discourse of emancipation. Such deconstruction she argues (following Grosz 1989) can be broken down into three steps: (1) identify the binaries, the oppositions that structure an argument; (2) reverse/displace the dependent term from its negative position to a place that locates it as the very condition of the positive term; and (3) create a more fluid and less coercive conceptual organisation of terms which transcends a binary logic by simultaneously being both and neither of the binary terms (Lather 1991: 13).

Lather of course represents one of a number of feminist positions. Other feminists, whilst agreeing on a goal of social transformation, are reluctant to throw out the baby of science with the bath water. Haraway, for example, asks 'Would a feminist epistemology informing scientific inquiry be a family member to existing theories of representation and philosophical realism? Or should feminists adopt a radical form of epistemology that denies the possibility of access to a real world and an objective standpoint?' (Haraway 1991: 470). And Harding (1986) asks, 'Does our recognition of the fact that science has always been a social product – that its projects and claims to knowledge bear the fingerprints of its human producers – require the exaltation of relativist subjectivity on the part of feminism?' (*ibid.* 137). Hilary Rose envisions a distinctive feminist science and epistemology, fusing subjective and objective knowledge (i.e. the personal, the social and the biological) to make new knowledge (Rose 1983: 88). In a postmodern world where boundaries amongst animal, human and machine are being challenged (Haraway 1991), it may no longer be appropriate to conceive of research paradigms in polarised ways. All claims to truth are historical and cultural constructs and all need to be examined in that light. At the same time, the feminist approaches referred to above rest on an assumption that the distortions of patriarchal science will be corrected through the inclusion of feminist insights, and thus more objective, more true. But this raises other issues. For example, is the Enlightenment vision of progressive and cumulative knowledge an appropriate one? If feminist perspectives enhance knowledge, which feminists and which perspectives?

Some issues

Those briefly are the protagonists. They are presented as at different poles, and employ 'discourses of derision' to vilify each other. But their relationship is more complex. It seems to me appropriate to rethink some of the issues raised, and in particular to remind us of what they have in common, so that we are clear as to the differences.

Appeals to a metanarrative of emancipation

For example, we forget that both appeal to a metanarrative of emancipation. The production and dissemination of scientific knowledge is legitimated on the grounds that it represents the disinterested pursuit of truth, the pursuit of which will contribute to progress and to the ultimate general good of humanity. As Lyotard notes, although there have been wars and disputes over the name of the subject we are to help to become emancipated, 'all the parties concurred that enterprises, discoveries and institutions are legitimate only insofar as they contribute to the emancipation of mankind' (Lyotard 1993: 172). Alternative approaches, on the other hand, embrace more particular emancipatory goals and claim empowerment for specific oppressed groups. And although we need to acknowledge a range of critical positions and feminisms, the knowledge assumptions which underpin them are similar to those of scientific knowledge, rooted in the ideals of the Enlightenment – that is, a view of the subject as powerful and self-consciously political; a belief in reason and rationality; and a belief in social and economic progress through grand schemes of change (Barrett and Phillips 1992: 5). Where they have diverged is in the exposure by feminists, critical theorists and anti-racists of capitalist and male-centred interest at the root of claims to 'neutrality' in the construction of scientific knowledge. Furthermore, feminism developed a critique of critical and participatory perspectives (Maguire 1996) for their failure to take account of gender in any serious way. In its turn, White feminist theory and research has had its universalist and imperialist assumptions challenged by Black and Third-World feminists, by lesbian feminists and by disabled feminists. In these ways, although the *nature* of knowledge is hotly contested (who can be a knower and what kinds of knowledge are legitimate as 'truth'), the debate is premised on a tacitly agreed set of rules within a metanarrative of the liberation of human-kind.

The shift to poststructuralist thinking has had an influence on the development of feminist thinking in particular. Poststructuralism has displaced the subject as conscious, rational and coherent, pointing to a variety of different subjectivities and realities. It has challenged the materialist, determinist and structuralist mode of explanation for social phenomena and emphasised representation, symbols and language. In place of the development of societies as an onward movement of progress, poststructuralism focuses on the specifics of time and space and localised struggle. In the consideration of poststructuralism's contribution to feminism, there has been recognition of its conflict with emancipatory ideals in its concern to emphasise *difference* and the *particular*.

So to summarise, scientific research and alternative research approaches both appeal to a metanarrative of emancipation and have their roots in Enlightenment ideals. Poststructuralism challenges these roots and dismisses a metanarrative of justice as an organising concept. I shall return to this presently.

The will to power

Emancipatory research approaches identify traditional research as deeply implicated in power, and set as their goals the equalising of power between researcher and research subjects and the changing of oppressive relations of power. However, both approaches are implicated in power. The very act of engaging in an activity implicates us in power, so that our efforts to liberate perpetuate the relations of dominance. The concept to 'empower' is a metaphor similar to Derrida's definition of 'to enlighten', which he describes as a light-based metaphor which positions the emancipators as senders of light and receivers as passive. Foucault argues that there may be projects whose aim is to modify some constraints, 'to loosen, or even to break them, but none of these projects can simply by its nature, assure that people will have liberty. ... Liberty is a *practice*' (Foucault 1993: 162). Emancipation cannot be conferred on one group by another. Martin's (1994, 1996) descriptions of experiences of feminist participatory research return again and again to this contradiction. In her attempts to share power as a researcher, she is inevitably implicated in power in the process.

The issue of the will to power has been less overt in traditional approaches to research, largely because where power issues are acknowledged, they are seen as a problem to be solved through greater reliability of the research instruments or through the application of ethical standards. It is in critiques of traditional methods that the relations of power are foregrounded (in, for example, Oakley 1981; Reinharz 1992), and in the debates which are central to alternative discourses. For example, Williams (1993) points out the differences amongst feminists in the debate on power. Oakley (1974, 1981) and McRobbie (1982), for example, both recognise the complex dynamics of researcher–researched relationships, but

> while the former sees close kinship between women researchers and women subjects of research, the latter is concerned that women's willingness to talk to researchers is an index of their powerlessness. Finch (1984) taking yet another view, writes that women as a group are powerless, whether they are researchers or subjects of research, and it is precisely this which underlines kinship.
>
> (Williams 1993: 581)

Other research in the emancipatory tradition, such as critical approaches (Harvey 1990) and participatory approaches (Tandon 1996), are preoccupied with issues of power in traditional research, and in the implications of power in the research process in which they are engaged.

The uncovering of power as intrinsic to all social research demonstrates that instead of a scientific community which is autonomous and free from political interest, we now know that an intimate relationship exists between the projects of science and other intellectual and political interests in the cultures where science is practised.

Going beyond ourselves

The identification of these commonalities between scientific and emancipatory research – appeals to a metanarrative of emancipation and the will to power – leads me to ask a number of questions:

- If both appeal to a metanarrative of emancipation, are we then simply talking about different approaches of equal status which have the same ends in their sights?
- What are we to make of the poststructuralist challenge to emancipatory ideals, and its concern to emphasise *difference* and the *particular*?
- What does emancipatory research mean if researchers are inevitably implicated in power, so that our efforts to liberate perpetuate the very relations of dominance?

In the light of my arguments here, it would not be appropriate to offer a recipe for resolving these tensions. Instead I shall point up a number of areas which emancipatory researchers will need to confront, if their efforts are not to perpetuate relations of dominance. First, we need to remind ourselves that the status of scientific knowledge has been privileged over other forms of knowledge. It has been sanctioned by the state, which spends a lot of money in the production of knowledge to obtain public consent to its decisions. Furthermore, the dominance of such a discourse is predicated upon the authority of a research community concerned about the truth of claims to knowledge. Hammersley depends on such a community and appeals to a set of rules and ideas about the construction of knowledge which have been the orthodoxy in social research. Such authority is invested with the force of exclusion and enforcement. Edwards and Usher say:

> the logic of modern scientific knowledge and its assumptions of its own legitimacy as a discourse of truth about the world results in the exclusion of other ... forms of knowledge and a denial of their legitimacy.
>
> (Edwards and Usher 1994: 158)

Such 'other' knowledge belongs to a different mentality – 'savage, primitive, underdeveloped, backward' (Lyotard 1984: 27). Writers such as Hammersley (1995) exercise that exclusion by declaring feminist, anti-racist, critical and emancipatory 'truths' outside the norms of legitimate research. By a discourse of derision they are dismissed as prejudiced, ignorant and ideological. In doing so the threat to notions of knowledge and to sources of income is diverted. We are not talking about different kinds of knowledge of equal status. Stanley (1990: 5) describes how, within the 'academic mode of production', official and unofficial gatekeepers use myriad ways of controlling academic inputs and outputs. At the centre of these is a notion of scientism, grounded in Cartesian dualisms as to who can be a knower and what can be known, and concerned with producing knowledge through the observation of the real – those objects which exist independently of our beliefs about them. It explicitly excludes knowledge produced through alternative research approaches. It is therefore of crucial importance to claim the legitimacy of low-status knowledge, of subjugated knowledge, of the knowledge of the other which has been silenced and excluded, and to continue the deconstructive process of thinking about 'the danger of what is powerful and useful' (Spivak 1989: 135). Although scientific knowledge appeals to a metanarrative of the liberation of all, the general thrust of the knowledge produced is *ownership by a privileged research community in the interests of dominant groups*. The claim to a metanarrative of emancipation in both scientific and alternative research should not be a source of discomfort to emancipatory researchers. *Both* have to be interrogated as to the basis for such claims, and *both* may be found wanting.

The challenges of poststructuralism lead us to ask: Can we appeal to a metanarrative of emancipation whilst retaining a concern with the particular and the local? McNay, from a feminist perspective, has grappled with this and she concludes

> feminists cannot afford to relinquish either a general theoretical perspective, or an appeal to a metanarrative of justice. I contend that gender issues cannot be fully comprehended without an understanding of general social dynamics, nor can gender oppression be overcome without some appeal to a metanarrative of justice.
>
> (McNay 1992: 7)

Surely it is possible to recognise the particularities of struggle without abandoning metanarratives of emancipation and justice. There can be no universalising in the sense that struggles have to be open and contingent on changing conditions. Both Lather and Harding, from different starting points, argue that the greatest resource for would-be knowers is our 'non-essential, nonnaturalizable, fragmented identities and the refusal of the delusion of a return to "original unity" ' (Harding 1986: 193). Here is a basis for continuing the struggle to throw off the regulating 'regimes of truth', whatever form they take – an acceptance of the permanent partiality of the point of view of those of us seeking to construct emancipatory research.

The issue of power has been treated (by feminists as well as others) in terms of a commodity which can be handed over from one person to another, or wrested from one group by another – possessed rather than exercised. Equally, empowerment has been used in simplistic and reductionist ways which treat it as just a matter of will, either on the part of those who are disempowered, or on the part of those in a position to empower. People who do emancipatory research are as much at risk of depoliticising their activities as others who use the concept of empowerment. Elsewhere I have written about the culture of empowerment (Humphries 1996), identifying themes in the discourse. These include *containment* – where the demands of oppressed groups are incorporated or accommodated without a radical reordering of social structures. Related to this is a theme of *collusion* – where subordinate groups accept unequal terms and in turn obtain resources in competition with other oppressed groups. Moreover, a discourse of empowerment is located largely *within existing socially powerful groups* – it is not the oppositional agency of the poor and disenfranchised, but the enforcement of the concerns of hegemonic groups. Finally, a theme of *empowering nihilism* (Grossberg 1988) leads to the identity of the other being appropriated by marginalised groups to form a clear, strong identity and sense of power. At the same time this identity is disrupted by a confirmation of the characteristics displayed by them of the essence of their alien nature, therefore requiring containment. Is this what is meant by emancipatory action?

Any notion of emancipatory research needs to recognise these contradictions, and must refuse a naive and self-deluding approach. It will acknowledge the *practice* of liberty – it is not something which can be conferred; it is not something gained once and for all, but has a view of power as fluid, a back and forward movement rather than binary; which is available to dominated groups; which is multifaceted and contradictory; which recognises both discursive and material realities; which is historically and culturally specific; and which is grounded in the struggle for survival of the most disadvantaged and the poorest, not in the privileging of the researcher or other groups as the norm or referent (Humphries 1994). As researchers, commitment to self-reflexivity is fundamental, although this can deteriorate into a self-indulgence which places the researcher as the norm. An emancipatory intent is no guarantee of an emancipatory outcome (Acker *et al.* 1983: 431). A self-critical account that situates the researcher at the centre of the text can perpetuate the dominance our emancipatory intentions hope to fight. Our own frameworks need to be interrogated as we look for the tensions and contradictions in our research practice, paradoxically aware of our own complicity in what we critique. Said talks about 'writing turning back on itself to consider, questioningly, its beginning validity and principles' (Said 1975: 335). This, I think, lays the groundwork for praxis-oriented research which can open up new possibilities for emancipatory action.

Note

1   This chapter was first published in Sociological Research Online, vol. 2, no. 1, 1997 (http://www.socresonline.org.uk/socresonline/2/1/3.html).

References

Acker, J., Barry, K. and Essevold, J. (1983) 'Objectivity and truth: problems in doing feminist research', *Women's Studies International Forum* 6: 423–35.
Barrett, M. and Phillips, A. (eds) (1992) *Destabilising Theory: Contemporary feminist debates*, Cambridge: Polity Press.
Bhavnani, K.K. (1991) 'What's power got to do with it? Empowerment and social research', in I. Parker and J. Shotter (eds) *Deconstructing Social Psychology*, London: Routledge.
Birke, L. (1986) *Women, Feminism and Biology: The feminist challenge*, Brighton: Wheatsheaf.

Edwards, R. and Usher, R. (1994) *Postmodernism and Education*, London and New York: Routledge.

Foucault, M. (1993) 'Space, power and knowledge', in S. During (ed.) *The Cultural Studies Reader*, London and New York: Routledge, pp. 161–9.

Gelsthorpe, L. (1992) 'Response to Martyn Hammersley's paper "On feminist methodology" ', *Sociology* 26 (2): 213–18.

Grossberg, L. (1988) 'Putting the Pop back in postmodernism', in A. Ross (ed.) *Universal Abandon*, St Paul: University of Minnesota Press.

Grosz, E. (1989) *Sexual Subversions: Three French feminists*, Sydney: Allen and Unwin.

Halfpenny, P. (1992) *Positivism and Sociology: Exploring social life*, Hampshire: Allen and Unwin.

Hammersley, M. (1992) 'On feminist methodology', *Sociology* 26 (2): 187–206.

—— (1995) *The Politics of Social Research*, London: Sage.

Haraway, D.J. (1981) 'In the beginning was the word: the genesis of biological theory', *Signs: Journal of Women in Culture and Society* 4 (1): 151–89.

—— (1991) *Simians, Cyborgs and Women: The reinvention of nature*, London: Free Association Books.

Harding, S. (1986) *The Science Question in Feminism*, Milton Keynes: Open University Press.

Harvey, L. (1990) *Critical Social Research*, London: Unwin Hyman.

hooks, b. (1994) *Outlaw Culture: Resisting representations*, Boston: Turnaround Books.

Humphries, B. (1994) 'Empowerment and social research: elements for an analytic framework', in B. Humphries and C. Truman (eds) *Rethinking Social Research*, Aldershot and Vermont: Avebury.

—— (1996) 'Contradictions in the culture of empowerment', in B. Humphries (ed.) *Critical Perspectives on Empowerment*, Birmingham: Venture Press.

Lather, P. (1991) *Getting Smart: Feminist research and pedagogy with/in the postmodern*, New York and London: Routledge.

Lorde, A. (1984) *Sister Outsider*, Trumansberg, New York: The Crossing Press Feminist Series.

Lyotard, J.-F. (1984) *The Postmodern Condition: A report on knowledge*, Manchester: Manchester University Press.

—— (1993) 'Defining the postmodern', in S. During (ed.) *The Cultural Studies Reader*, London and New York: Routledge, pp. 161–79.

Maguire, P. (1996) 'Proposing a more feminist participatory research: knowing and being embraced openly', in K. de Koning and M. Martin (eds) *Participatory Research in Health*, London, New Jersey and Johannesburg: Zed Books.

Martin, M. (1994) 'Developing a feminist participative research framework: evaluating the process', in B. Humphries and C. Truman (eds) *Rethinking Social Research*, Aldershot and Vermont: Avebury.

—— (1996) 'Issues of power in the participatory research process', in K. de Koning and M. Martin (eds) *Participatory Research in Health*, London, New Jersey and Johannesburg: Zed Books.

McNay, L. (1992) *Foucault and Feminism*, Cambridge and Oxford: Blackwell.

McRobbie, A. (1982) 'The politics of feminist research: between talk, text and action, *Feminist Review* 12: 46–57.

Mohanty, C.T. (1991) 'Under Western eyes: feminist scholarship and colonial discourses', in C.T. Mohanty, A. Russo and L. Torres (eds) *Third World Women and the Politics of Feminism*, Bloomington and Indianapolis: Indiana University Press

Oakley, A. (1974) *The Sociology of Housework*, London: Martin Robinson.

—— (1981) 'Interviewing women: a contradiction in terms?' in H. Roberts (ed.) *Doing Feminist Research*, London: Routledge and Kegan Paul.

Ramazanoglu, C. (1992) 'On feminist methodology: male reason versus feminist empowerment', *Sociology* 26 (2): 213–18.

Reinharz, S. (1992) *Social Research Methods: Feminist perspectives*, New York: Oxford University Press.

Rose, H. (1983) 'Hand, brain and heart: a feminist epistemology of the natural sciences', *Signs: Journal of Women in Culture and Society* 9: 1.

Said, E. (1975) *Beginnings: Intention and method*, New York: Basic Books.

Spivak, G. (1989) 'In a word: interview by Ellen Rooney', *Differences* 1 (2): 124–56.

Stanley, L. (ed.) (1990) *Feminist Praxis*, London and New York: Routledge.

Tandon, R. (1996) 'The historical roots and contemporary tendencies in participatory research: implications for health care', in K. de Koning and M. Martin (eds) *Participatory Research in Health*, London, New Jersey and Johannesburg: Zed Books.

Williams, A. (1993) 'Diversity and agreement in feminist ethnography', *Sociology* 27 (4): 575–89.

Chapter 12

Critical education for participatory research[1,2]

Marion Martin

Introduction

This chapter aims to address three questions: What constitutes critical education for participatory research (PR)? Why is this approach to learning crucial? What form can it take? These questions are considered in relation to work I am currently engaged in as a lecturer in Education for Primary Health Care (EPHC) on a postgraduate course for development professionals. Following an introduction to the course itself and something of my history in relation to it, significant issues in the development of PR are introduced. This is followed by an examination of the meaning of critical education, as it applies to the course. Finally, ways in which critical learning processes are applied as a means of exploring PR and its relevance to PHC are considered.

The Education for Primary Health Care (EPHC) course

The Masters course in EPHC has a history of twelve years, ten years of which I have shared as co-ordinator and lecturer. The course is designed for development workers, many of whom are health professionals and include nurses, medical assistants, health visitors and medical doctors. Other professionals are among the minority and include teachers from all levels of education who have an interest in community health, community development workers and social workers. On average there are twenty course participants in a year, each bringing considerable experience. This creates a rich and vibrant learning environment, enhanced by the high level of motivation and commitment to learning that participants bring.

On average, approximately fifteen of the course participants come from countries of the South, primarily Africa, with the remainder from countries of the North, with experience working in the South. Participants vary in age from 25 to 55 years old and represent diverse cultures.

The Masters course runs for twelve months full-time. It is divided into eight modules. Six modules are taught with the remaining two forming the dissertation. A module refers to a set of twelve teaching units, each of two and a half hours. Each module is focused on a particular topic; for example, 'Re-thinking research for PHC'. A taught unit examines some aspect of the overall subject. The module is assessed.

The course aims to provide an international learning forum for students and tutors to reflect critically on practice in the light of a range of theoretical perspectives that relate to health, education, research and, broadly, the management of community-based development activities. A major goal is to strengthen the capacity of learners to critically examine development theory in the light of experience and reading. The ideas of the Brazilian educationalist Paulo Freire (Freire 1972) have helped to create the learning methods employed on the course. Critical, international feminist perspectives, as represented in the work of, for example, Maria Mies and Vandana Shiva (1993) and Chandra Mohanty (1991) inform the content, process and thinking, which emphasises a people-centred philosophy of education for development (see also Kirkwood and Kirkwood 1989; Mayo and Thompson 1995). This explicit political bias finds its mandate in the Primary Health Care Report (WHO/UNICEF 1978), and the International Declaration of PHC, emphasising the right of all people to equality and the opportunity to participate in decisions concerning their lives.

I came as a lecturer and tutor to the course at a time when my own critical consciousness was beginning to emerge. I have a long-established link with India which dates back to my birth and early upbringing there until I was 8 years old. My professional career has spanned several disciplines. Following a number of years in nursing, I decided to move into community-based work, and undertook a course in social work. This was followed by five years in social work with a special interest in community health. An opportunity then arose to return to India to work with a rural health and development project. It was the challenge of this experience, perhaps more than any other, that encouraged me to question the widening inequalities and injustice I saw in the world about me.

On my return to the UK three to four years later, I moved into community-based adult education. I was drawn into this field partly through experiences in India, and also by a growing interest in the writings of critical thinkers like Illich and Freire. The next few years were spent working with women's health groups in the north-east of England and completing an MPhil. Throughout this period, a political consciousness was gradually awakening within me and something of this was expressed in political action in personal and public life. Working across several areas of development – health, community work and adult education – has helped me see the need to make connections across these disciplines, and to recognise the need for development professionals to take seriously issues of inequality.

Having offered something of an introduction to the course and my history in relation to it, I move on now to explore some of the more significant trends in the development of participatory research.

Significant trends in the development of participatory research

Participatory research has its origins in the countries of Africa, Asia and Latin America. It emerged almost three decades ago as one of several critiques of the claims of orthodox positivist research to value-free impartial research. A major concern of PR has been to raise questions about the power relationship between researchers and researched. In presenting an historical perspective of PR, Rajesh Tandon (1996) identifies several trends that have contributed to the development of this emancipatory approach to research. The earliest of these has its roots in the debate on the sociology of knowledge, with its implications for epistemology; namely, the recognition that both dominant and alternative forms of knowledge have existed in all societies. A second trend arises from the experiences of adult educators of the South. Concerned with the need to promote dialogical educational processes between educators and students, adult educators created a process that enabled learners to take greater control over their own learning. They discovered, however, a contradiction between the processes they now worked with as critical educators and those with which they carried out research activities, drawing on orthodox, top-down research methodologies (Martin 1994). They needed to find a way of carrying out research which was consistent with the principles of adult education they had developed. In this way PR was born with its roots embedded in the principles of adult education.

One of the most important influences in the development of PR has been the work of Paulo Freire. Freire linked the process of knowing with that of learning, through an ongoing cycle of reflection and action (praxis). This learning process stimulates the growth of critical thinking, which raises in learners critical awareness of the world about them. Alongside Freire's ideas came a parallel development – that of the phenomenologists who held experience as a legitimate source of knowledge. Thus, experience was added to reflection and action as factors that could influence practice. Finally, the late 1970s brought the re-emergence of the debate about the right of people to participate in their own development.

Participatory research: some contemporary issues

Budd Hall (1992), a leading practitioner and theoretician in PR, has identified several components in this research methodology, some of which are high-lighted here: that the research involves professionals working alongside marginalised and oppressed groups; that it recognises the knowledge, power and strengths these groups already possess, and seeks to develop these qualities through the process of research; that research questions emerge from the priorities of these groups who become active subjects rather than passive objects of research; that those taking part in the research become committed participants and learners in the process which leads to a committed involvement rather than the impartial detachment claimed by the positivist paradigm. In researching with marginalised groups, PR sets out to facilitate the empowerment of the participants through the creation of knowledge and the taking of action that leads to change on structural and personal levels (Maguire 1996).

As the term empowerment can now be found in the vocabulary of virtually all political perspectives today, some clarification of the meaning ascribed to it here is necessary. Empowerment refers to peoples' access to resources which increase their capacity as individuals and groups to take greater control of decisions at personal and community levels, so they might challenge relationships and structures of power. Chambers (1994) draws attention to the need to understand that empowerment of, for example, the poor, should not just entail representing their concerns, but should empower them to take action which they themselves identify as important:

> Poor people have many priorities. What matters most to them often differs from what outsiders assume. If poor people's realities are to come first, development professionals have to be sensitive, to decentralise, and to empower, enabling poor people to conduct their own analysis and express their own multiple priorities.
>
> (Chambers 1994: 10, quoted in Novak 1996: 92)

Participatory research: a feminist critique

Patricia Maguire (1987) has been a leading voice in developing feminist critiques of PR. Maguire argues that while PR acknowledges the centrality of power in the social construction of knowledge, it has failed to recognise the centrality of *male power* in that construction. This has been left to feminist researchers:

> While PR builds on the Freirian notion of man's alienation in the world, it still too often minimizes or ignores women's alienation from a man-made world.
>
> (Maguire 1996: 30)

Maguire (1987) draws attention to several aspects of PR which reflect male bias. She argues that the language in which PR is discussed by academics and practitioners is more often than not male-centred; that feminist perspectives are not represented as crucial to PR debates; that women are frequently excluded from decision making, especially in research design; and that the benefits of PR accrued to men (training opportunities, access to information, resources, etc.) may not automatically be attributed to women.

It can be seen from the above that PR seeks to challenge and break down knowledge hierarchies and to create opportunities for development workers, among others, to work alongside marginalised groups. This becomes a greater possibility when both share similar motivations and interests (see, for example, Khanna 1996). This way of working *with* community groups rather than *for* or *over* them requires a fundamental shift in attitude for professionals, and in their perceptions of their role. The majority of professionals, no matter how well intentioned, have been trained to perceive themselves as experts in their field of specialisation. Their often hard-won training has taught them that they should be (or at least appear to be) in control: to diagnose, to prescribe, to treat and to hide uncertainty. This mentality can change, though change is likely to be gradual. The shift in attitude is not easy for most professionals to take. It can be unnerving to discover that the taken-for-granted principles and values that have guided your life need to be questioned. It is this road that critical education can take the learner along, provided she/he is ready to take on board the many uncertainties that are an inevitable part of the journey (*ibid.* 1996).

While some participants of the course come with highly developed critical faculties, this is not the case with the majority. Stimulating a critical thinking process presents a tall order for any education course and there are inevitably varying levels of success, as well as resistance to moving towards this goal. Before discussing ways in which I try to facilitate this learning process in relation to PR, I would like to consider something of the philosophical roots of this approach to learning, and to explore ways in which we seek to integrate it into the course.

Towards a critical learning culture on the EPHC course

Critical education requires a reflective learning culture within which critical intelligence can develop. The ideas of Freire form the theoretical backbone to this educational strategy (Freire 1972). Freire helps us see that (formal) education is one of the major channels through which dominant groups maintain inequalities, but education also has the potential of facilitating the promotion of critical intelligence for social transformation:

> There is no such thing as neutral education ... education either facilitates the integration of generations into the logic of the present system and brings conformity to it, or it becomes the 'practice of freedom', the means by which men and women deal critically and creatively with reality and discover how to participate in the transformation of their world.
>
> (*ibid.* 1972: 38)

Critical education requires both an ontology and an epistemology. The ontology of critical education begins when learners reflect on their experiences and ask themselves what it means to be a human being living within the social relations of present-day society. This enables learners to become aware of how structures constrain and oppress specific groups (Allman and Wallis 1995). This process takes place when course participants begin to address the following type of question: *What* is happening in the world about me in relation to issues of power? This question leads the learner to identify increasing inequalities in wealth and health, increasing unemployment in certain sections of the community, increasing poverty, homelessness, violence, racism, etc.

The next questions learners are asked to address include: *Why* are these things happening? *Who* controls the political, economic and social systems that impact on our lives? For whose benefit do oppressive systems exist and at *whose* costs are benefits derived? Questions such as these help learners see the influences of power in their daily lives and to question purpose in a way in which they may not have done before. In doing so they are encouraged to situate themselves within the political framework. This analytical framework is taken on board throughout the course, though the way it is introduced in terms of educational methods varies.

While ontology and epistemology are essential elements in critical education, so too is methodology. The methodological aim of critical education is to transform learner/educator relationships from conventional hierarchical ones to those which enable learners and educators to become critical co-investigators of knowledge, through the process of dialogue. A more critical understanding of knowledge emerges from dialogue in which all sources of knowledge (formal and informal) are opened to challenge and critique. This helps learners see that critical learning need not be confined to the duration of the course, but can become a life-long process.

In my experience, although the dialogical learning relationship between learner and educator is easily forged, both student and teacher can be resistant to it. The learner may feel confused and insecure as the relationship may not meet with expectations and past experiences of education. The educator in turn may feel threatened when the power base of the relationship is questioned. The process of building the relationship will vary with those involved. In cases where it does develop, this is likely to be gradual, as the relationship is tested out.

Some course participants only gradually integrate a critical perspective, while others remain resistant throughout the course. Most of us will generally accept a particular explanation of the world only when we are ready to do so. Weiler (1991) draws attention to the confusion that questioning issues of power can give rise to, particularly among women learners she has known. Conditioned within patriarchal cultures, they have been led to perceive themselves as passive, not expected to 'question the way things are, to consider how things could be different ... such thinking involves an active not a passive, relationship to the world' (Weiler 1991: 462). Perhaps inevitably, many obstacles stand in the way of pursuing this approach to learning within the context of a formal course in higher education, yet progress can be made, as the remainder of this chapter aims to illustrate.

Towards critical learning for participatory research

In exploring the why, what and how of critical education for PR, it is important to establish what kinds of people participatory researchers need to be. Clearly there can be no blueprint, as what is appropriate in one context may vary in another. Nevertheless, some discussion of the often neglected area of attitude in research is important. Appropriate attitudes and skills to engage with local groups are necessary if shared agendas and issues of immediate relevance are to be discussed. As marginalised groups may well be suspicious of outside professionals, development workers need to recognise, respect and value relevant indigenous practices and knowledge systems that the community may bring to the research, and to believe in the capacity of local people to tackle problems and create change. Novak (1996) argues that the extent to which professionals will be able to do this will depend mostly on *where* they perceive themselves to be in relation to poverty and injustice – as part of the solution or part of the problem:

> Recognising that they can be part of the problem, rather than simply accepting that what they do invariably benefits the poor, is an important first step.
>
> (*ibid.*: 91)

This has implications for critical education for PR. The recognition that we are part of the problem can enable professionals committed to social justice to work towards empowerment of the marginalised, respecting their strengths while also aware of the myriad factors that disempower them. This asks professionals to give time to be with local people, to come to know them, be known by them, to be informed by them. Respect, humility, adaptability, empathy and patience *born out of critical consciousness* are among the important attributes of those working in this field of research. These qualities may not be much valued or fostered in professional training and conventional research contexts.

The research for PHC module

Each course module, as explained earlier, focuses on a particular subject. In this case the subject is 'Research for PHC'. As the module runs in the second part of the year, participants are already familiar with examining issues from critical perspectives. The module aims to continue critical dialogue in relation to a range of research issues. The concern is not to train participants to 'do' participatory research, but to enable them to critically evaluate a range of approaches to research, and to identify the assumptions that inform them.

Research practice in PHC has been dominated by positivism (de Koning and Martin 1996). This is not surprising, given the powerful influence of the biomedical model in the training curriculum of health professionals. A critical analysis of dominant research paradigms can draw the learners' attention to ways in which research designed and conducted from orthodox (particularly positivist) positions is, more often than not, imposed on local groups by researchers who do not belong to the community and who may know very little about it. Such studies can be experienced by communities as aggressive, intrusive and insensitive (Pratt and Loizos 1992). This interventionist or invasive approach (Freire 1972) has been criticised as taking little or no account of the needs, interests or involvement of local groups as subjects of research (Tandon 1996). The module aims to encourage participants to recognise different paradigm positions (positivist, ethnographic, participatory, feminist), and the epistemological and ideological roots within which they are embedded. As learners become critically aware of the belief systems and values that underpin these paradigms, they become more able to identify research approaches appropriate for PHC.

Much of the learning takes place using interactive methods in small groups of two to eight people. Within these groups, learners are encouraged to critically reflect on practice, to give one another space to speak, to express their views, to listen, to question one another's perspectives as constructively as possible. As we are six months into the course, these learning processes are familiar to them, and many are skilled in their use.

It is important at the start of the module to help the group feel relaxed with 'the idea' of research. For many, research is perceived as a highly specialist subject which belongs to the expert alone. Time is spent encouraging participants to share their views and experiences of doing research. This leads to a broad definition of the term. Once basic research terminology has been clarified, the concept of the research paradigm is presented. This is done by introducing a variety of case studies that the group are asked to read and examine from critical perspectives. The case studies represent research studies designed from different paradigm positions: dominant (positivist and ethnographic) and alternative (participatory and feminist). Each group member is given one case study to read individually, then joins others who have read the same study. Once some familiarity with these studies has been reached, participants are asked to consider which questions they might address to the case study in order to examine the power balance in the researcher/researched relationships. A range of suggestions may emerge. These might include questions concerning the social class, gender, race, culture and educational background of researched and researcher. Once these factors have been identified, the group is asked what significance this has for the research design, process, outcome and dissemination of findings. This exercise helps participants move towards recognising different paradigm positions in research and to see how these are informed by different value assumptions influencing design, process and outcome.

While participatory research aims to reduce inequalities, an examination of much of what may be described as PR reveals that it is not in fact rooted in concerns for radical transformation of inequalities. Rather, it involves local people participating in research often initiated by outsiders and carried out *on* local groups rather than with them. Such research may be concerned with benefiting outsider research interests rather than those of local groups (Pratt and Loizos 1992). I have found that a more critical approach to what constitutes participation and what does not can be developed if the *participatory process* is examined using the concept of a continuum. Heron (1981) suggests it is useful to conceive of PR as taking place along a continuum. At one pole is what he describes as 'experiential' or community-controlled processes, and at the other, 'traditional' or researcher-controlled processes. It becomes possible to think critically about power distribution in research by drawing on a similar method to the one described above, addressing a series of questions to a study that uses the term 'participatory' to describe itself. Questions might, for example, include: Who initiated the research? Who funded it? Who is likely to have benefited from it? Who decided which problems or issues the research should focus on and which research methods to use? Who was given access to resources such as information, money, skills, etc., through the research process? These questions encourage the group to raise further questions: Who has decision-making power? Who is denied this? Does the research result in the transformation of local structural inequalities by, for example, the inclusion of marginalised communities such as poor women, disabled people, children, Black communities, etc., in decision-making processes?

In order to carry out this exercise, we use case studies from the participants' experiences whenever possible. These provide diverse examples of research in terms of cultural, political and economic contexts. Once participants, working in small discussion groups, have addressed the questions to the case studies and established at which point(s) on a participatory continuum their case study can be placed, they are asked to use a framework such as that provided by Pretty (1995) (reproduced here as Table 12.1 on p. 200), to consider in which *mode* of participation they would place their case study. Learners who prefer to develop their own participation framework do so, as not all feel able to 'fit in' with conceptual frameworks constructed by others. A danger of drawing on a framework such as Pretty's is that it can reduce participatory processes to simplified and fragmented explanations, thus defeating the original educational purpose. At the same time, a framework offers a useful conceptual model that all learners can relate to and from which critical dialogue may be triggered.

Table 12.1   Participatory methods: means to what end?

Mode of participation	Involvement of local people	Relationship of research and action to local people
co-option	token; representatives are chosen, but no real input or power	on
compliance	tasks are assigned, with incentives; outsiders decide agenda and direct the process	for
consultation	local opinions asked, outsiders analyse and decide on a course of action	for/with
co-operation	local people work together with outsiders to determine priorities, responsibility remains with outsiders for directing the process	with
co-learning	local people and outsiders share their knowledge, to create new understanding, and work together to form action plans, with outsider facilitation	with/by
collective action	local people set their own agenda and mobilise to carry it out, in the absence of outside initiators and facilitators	by

Source: Adapted from Pretty (1995), in Cornwall (1996: 96).

Having discussed, identified and, to some degree, agreed upon *where* on the conceptual framework the research should be placed and, more importantly, *why* it should be placed at that point (for example, at the point of *consultation* on Pretty's framework), the next step is to consider *why* participation is limited and whether or not it would be possible to increase participatory processes in that context. This entails an examination of the obstacles that might prevent participation and a discussion of how these might realistically be tackled, through short- and long-term strategies. This exercise enables learners to identify factors that may be constraining participation and those that appear to promote it. The exercise can be used equally well in the research situation itself, as a form of ongoing praxis.

I have found critical education for participatory research, as outlined here, a valuable means of introducing learners to the critical inquiry of research paradigms and the participatory process. It helps to demystify research so it is less likely to be regarded as solely the realm of the 'expert', and more as an activity that local groups can and have a right to contribute to. Participatory learning processes help engage learners in an active role of inquiry in which they share experiences and reflect critically on practice in a context that many group members find stimulating and relatively safe.

Some concluding points

Evaluation has consistently shown that the majority of participants find the process of critical education, as experienced on the course, challenging and enlightening. To many it affirms their understanding of the world in relation to their own observations and experiences of inequality. The course content speaks to their lives in a way in which former experiences of conventional education have not done. This has been most marked among those who have known themselves, or through the experiences of others, what it is like to be excluded from mainstream society because of gender, race, sexual orientation, disability, etc.

The course has raised the confidence of many learners and has helped them find a language with which to articulate their ideas. However, there is concern expressed about how, on returning to their own countries, they will be able to influence colleagues and employers in putting their ideas into practice. We try to deal with this at various levels while students are still on the course. For example, one of the objectives of dissertation work is to develop small-scale manageable strategies for developing more critical approaches to training, research and management activities on the return home. This, however, may not be possible where, for example, the political situation is sensitive or unstable. But where it is possible, the dissertation provides an opportunity to think through realistic strategies for change. Whenever we can, we (my colleague and I) keep in touch with students to offer encouragement and support. An effort is made to meet them in their work settings when there is an opportunity to visit their countries. Some, however, are posted to remote areas where it is difficult to make contact. The course selects applicants from the same training institutions in some countries where links are long established. This means that, on leaving the course, colleagues can network, offering support to one another in creating change in their institution. To date, this strategy has been most successful in Tanzania, Zambia and the UK, where contacts have now been well established for over a decade.

On returning to their home country, students have been able to rewrite aspects of the training curriculum for PHC in order to include critical perspectives and draw on educational methods that help learners reflect on their practice in the field. Others have developed small-scale participatory research projects linked to local concerns of inequality. These include improving the quality of local health services for disabled people in village communities as part of a wider community health programme in Uganda, increasing access to and control of basic drugs distribution to poor and marginalised groups in a district in Kenya, and identifying and prioritising the needs of carers of people with Acquired Immune Deficiency Syndrome (AIDS), as well as developing local services more appropriate to their needs, in a country in Central America.

Many course participants from the UK choose to return to work in countries in the South. Of those who have taken up work in the UK, several have moved into health promotion at community level. Many maintain links with the course and return to share ideas about ways they have applied their work on the course to their professional and personal lives. Examples of politically active community-based initiatives course participants have taken part in are varied. For example, one person working with a Manchester community group helped to acquire resources, establish and offer ongoing support to a health group for young women from materially poor backgrounds. This followed a participatory needs assessment in which she incorporated ideas she had developed on the course. The young women themselves control and run the group which has now been in existence for over seven years. Following this, the same person went out to Mozambique where she worked with local health workers in the training of indigenous midwives from rural communities. Another went out to a country in West Africa where she was involved in establishing literacy and health groups among women in the poorer marginalised communities. The literacy work here draws on Freire's ideas. Yet another went to a central African country where she is living and working with marginalised groups in urban areas. Storytelling and drama are used as ways to provide opportunities for groups to discuss their health development needs and to see how these might best be met. Other course participants have taken up employment as lecturers on health courses in institutions of further and higher education, and we network closely, both in the UK and overseas. Much of the work mentioned above has involved small pieces of research which might not have been carried out from a critical perspective had the learner not been encouraged to think critically about research issues in PHC.

It should not be assumed that the critical perspectives presented on the course speak to the needs or interests of all participants. There are those who are uncomfortable or threatened by radical, controversial perspectives. The intention here is not to suggest that critical education as developed on the EPHC course is always successful in awakening or raising critical consciousness. There is no doubt, however, that the course can make an important contribution to this process. At a time when formal education in the UK is undergoing rapid change, and increasingly an instrumentalist mentality permeates educational policy and practice, an education strategy that stimulates a critically reflective learning culture of resistance has an important contribution to make.

Notes

1   This chapter was first published in Sociological Research Online, vol. 2, no. 2, 1997. (http://www.socresonline.org.uk/socresonline/2/1/3.html).
2   Keywords: primary health care; inequality; critical education; critical intelligence; participatory research.

References

Allman, P. and Wallis, J. (1995) 'Challenging the postmodern condition: radical adult education for critical intelligence', in M. Mayo and J. Thompson (eds) Adult Learning, Critical Intelligence and Social Change, Leicester: National Institution of Adult Continuing Education, pp. 18–33.

Chambers, R. (1994) 'Poverty and livelihoods: whose reality counts?', paper prepared for the Stockholm Roundtable on Global Change, July, pp. 22–4.

Cornwall, A. (1996) 'Towards participatory practice: participatory rural appraisal (PRA) and the participatory process', in K. de Koning and M. Martin (eds) Participatory Research in Health: Issues and experiences, London and Johannesburg: Zed Books, pp. 94–103.

de Koning, K. and Martin, M. (eds) (1996) Participatory Research in Health: Issues and Experiences, London and Johannesburg: Zed Books.

Freire, P. (1972) Pedagogy of the Oppressed, Penguin: Harmondsworth, UK.

Hall, B. (1992) 'Rich and vibrant colours: 25 years of adult education', Convergence XXV (4): 4–15.

Heron, J. (1981) 'Philosophical basis for a new paradigm', in P. Reason and J. Rowan (eds) Human Inquiry: A sourcebook of new paradigm research, Chichester: Wiley.

Khanna, R. (1996) 'Participatory action research (PAR) in women's health: SARTHI, India', in K. de Koning and M. Martin (eds) Participatory Research in Health: Issues and experiences, London and Johannesburg: Zed Books, pp. 62–9.

Kirkwood, G. and Kirkwood, C. (1989) Living Adult Education: Freire in Scotland, Milton Keynes: Open University Press.

Maguire, P. (1987) Doing Participatory Research: A feminist approach, Amherst, MA: Center for International Education.

—— (1996) 'Proposing a more feminist participatory research: knowing and being embraced openly', in K. de Koning and M. Martin (eds) Participatory Research in Health: Issues and experiences, London and Johannesburg: Zed Books, pp. 27–39.

Martin, M. (1994) 'Developing a feminist participatory framework: evaluating the process', in B. Humphries and C. Truman (eds) Re-thinking Social Research, Aldershot: Avebury.

Mayo, M. and Thompson, J. (1995) Adult Learning, Critical Intelligence and Social Change, Leicester: National Institution of Adult Continuing Education.

Mies, M. and Shiva, V. (1993) Ecofeminism, London: Zed Books.

Mohanty, C. (1991) Third World Women and the Politics of Feminism, Bloomington and Indianapolis: Indiana University Press.

Novak, T. (1996) 'Empowerment and the politics of poverty', in B. Humphries and C. Truman (eds) *Re-thinking Social Research*, Aldershot: Avebury, pp. 85–97.

Pratt, B. and Loizos, P. (1992) *Choosing Research Methods: Data collection for development workers*, Development Guidelines No. 7, London: Oxfam.

Pretty, J. (1995) 'Participatory learning for sustainable agriculture', *World Development* 23: 193–204.

Tandon, R. (1996) 'The historical roots and contemporary tendencies in participatory research: implications for health care', in K. de Koning and M. Martin (eds) *Participatory Research in Health: Issues and experiences*, London and Johannesburg: Zed Books, pp. 19–26.

Weiler, K. (1991) 'A feminist pedagogy of difference', *Harvard Educational Review* 61 (4): 449–74.

WHO/UNICEF (1978) *Primary Health Care*, Geneva: WHO.

Chapter 13

An integrative human rights approach to social research[1]

Stanley L. Witkin

According to Denzin (1994), 'researchers work outward from their own biographies to the worlds of experience that surround them' (p. 512). In my own case, my professional identity as a social worker and my experience as the parent of a child with disabilities influenced my 'work outward'. Social work is a profession whose primary constituencies are powerless and devalued people. It is also a profession whose code-of-ethics calls upon its members to work towards a more just social order. This professional orientation seemed largely uncon-nected with my (conventional) research practice. This estrangement was echoed in my personal life where I found myself devoting numerous hours advocating for my son's basic rights. Traditional research had little to offer me. Its fact–value dichotomy, non-reflexivity and so-called objectivity rendered it superfluous to the 'real life' challenges facing people with disabilities.

In an effort to find more meaningful and 'connected' models of social research I began exploring various philosophical and methodological ap-proaches to knowledge and inquiry. Over the past two decades, this exploration has taken me from empiricism to critical social constructionism. With the latter, I could retain the roles and associated values of social worker and advocate while developing and carrying out research. Critical social construc-tionism incorporates the social constructionist's interest in the historical and social determinants of knowledge, while emphasizing the political, moral, and practice implications of theory and research (Gergen 1986; Sampson 1989; Witkin 1995). By providing an alternative ontological and epistemological understanding of social life, critical social constructionism encourages alternative forms of inquiry and theory development (Gergen 1985; Gergen and Davis 1985). One expression of my constructionist work has been the consideration of human rights within the research process. Thus, this interest is congruent with other chapters in this book.

As will be discussed, human rights are claim rights; that is, to have a right is also to make a claim on others for the exercise of that right. These claims extend not only to individuals, but to communities and governments. In this sense, research that protects and advances human rights can be a form of emancipatory social action providing a rationale for government action aimed at protecting and promoting freedom and well-being (Gewirth 1996). Thus, fundamental human rights are at the root of all emancipatory and anti-discriminatory research, because without such rights emancipation and anti-discrimination become vacuous ideals.

Traditionally, human rights and social research have been viewed as relatively independent. Human rights are derived from beliefs about morality, values, and human nature; research, on the other hand, is concerned with documenting what is – the extant universe. Even when research is directed toward human rights issues as, for example, in a survey of human rights abuses, the distinctiveness of each domain is preserved: the 'objective' lens of research is focused on the 'subjective' terrain of human rights.

Thus, while human rights and research may inform each other, they remain within separate spheres of activity. In contrast, the aims of this chapter are to provide a rationale for the integration of human rights and social research, and to propose some ways in which this integration could occur.

The possibility and desirability of a human rights approach to social research is connected to various social movements over the past three decades that have heightened peoples' awareness of the oppressive forces within their cultures and to changes in our understanding of knowledge development. The latter has had broad implications for foundationalist theories of knowledge and has led to the development of interpretive and ideological forms of social science. These developments have led to the formulation of alternative criteria for the assessment of knowledge claims (e.g. Witkin and Gottschalk 1988); to increased understanding of how social research generates categories of understanding and prescriptions for ways of acting (Gergen 1986; Gottschalk and Witkin 1988, 1991; Witkin 1989); and to the development of new approaches to inquiry that are responsive to social issues.

Foundationalism and the search for meaning

Foundationalism (or justificationism) is the doctrine, at least in its empiricist version, that knowledge rests on the brute facts of experience (Trigg 1985). This foundation provides the ultimate justification for knowledge claims and is assumed 'as the starting point for empirical knowledge' (Weimer 1979: 21). Over the last several decades, the basis for foundationalism has eroded to the point where it is no longer considered tenable as an arbiter of truth claims. In particular, the theses of factual relativity and the theory-ladenness of observations have undermined the belief that experience can provide an absolute foundation for knowledge (Hanson 1958; Weimer 1979). A troubling consequence of this critique has been the specter of relativism in which no reason for warranting a knowledge claim is seen as superior to any other (cf. Feyerabend 1976). This has led to extensive debate about how knowledge claims are and should be assessed (e.g. Kuhn 1970; Morawski 1986; Laudan 1977). The attempt to find a rational (scientific, valid) way of distinguishing knowledge claims has led to consideration of nontraditional criteria such as utility, emancipation, empowerment, dialogue, and social justice (Smith 1990; Witkin and Gottschalk 1988).

The search for nonfoundationalist epistemologies encouraged new ways of looking at theory and research. Philosophers such as Wittgenstein (1963), Dilthey (1976 [1883]), and Gadamer (1975), as well as social scientists like Winch (1958), Berger and Luckmann (1966), and Garfinkel (1967), laid the groundwork for alternatives to conventional inquiry. Although diverse in their style of inquiry, these alternative approaches have led to heightened awareness of the historical, cultural, and political nature of social theories and methods of inquiry. In particular, the recognition that empirical social research was value-laden and socially embedded facilitated the development of approaches to inquiry that could acknowledge and draw upon these connections.

The self-fulfilling nature of social research

All researchers work within multiple, interrelated contexts. From the 'macro' context of history and culture, to the 'mezzo' context of academic institutions and scientific communities, to the 'micro' context of personal beliefs and values, these contexts affect research in various ways. For example, Western ideas about individualism and marriage may provide unquestioned presuppositions from which research questions are generated and results interpreted. Similarly, requirements for academic tenure or the need for grant funding may increase the value of certain types of research methods or encourage questions consistent with the prevailing political philosophy. Finally, an individual's unique life-experiences may provide an incentive to pursue certain areas of inquiry or influence her/his interpretation of existing theory (see Riley 1988 for examples of how such influences affected the work of various sociologists). The interaction of these contexts eventuate in the studies that fill journals and books. From this perspective, social research informs as much about the ideas and beliefs of researchers and the ideology of social institutions as it does about the objects of inquiry.

Context influences not only research implementation, but also observation and description. Trigg (1985) notes that, 'instead of facts being discovered in the world, our descriptions are governed as much by our interests and purposes as by what is there' (p. 9). For example, descriptions of mental health and mental illness are not pure linguistic representations of empirical reality, but reflect ideological beliefs, values, institutional relationships, and cultural mores (cf. Albee 1986). Similarly, when women whose male partners are alcoholics are described as 'co-dependent', this is an evaluation (and implicitly, a prescription), not a description. Thus, social research is as much a statement of what should be than a description of what is (Bellah 1983; Howard 1985).

Truth claims are always pursued within a context of taken-for-granted assumptions; for example, that people are responsible for their own misfortunes, that children 'entice' their abusers, that Blacks are prone to violence, or that people with cognitive disabilities cannot learn. Often, these assumptions reflect societal stereotypes or beliefs that are based on various institutional arrangements. For instance, blaming poor people for their own plight deflects attention away from broader social issues and how these issues might contribute to poverty. Assumptions such as these are not easily discovered by the research process and often remain implicit, unchallenged, and even 'confirmed' by research data. In the Western world, women, people of color, people with disabilities, lesbians, and gays have often been
the 'victims' of such research (e.g. Gould 1981; Kitzinger 1987; Peterson 1987).

Theories and generalizations in the social sciences are not neutral, but favor certain social arrangements, views of human nature, and forms of social life over others. Additionally, the language, concepts, and explanations provided by the social sciences play an important role in how people view themselves and others and in the reproduction of social life. In this sense, social research is a value-based culturally situated process whose knowledge claims are inherently political.

Once the social and dialectical nature of research is realized, its veil of neutrality parts to reveal researchers actively involved in constructing the social reality that they discover. Like practitioners and policy analysts, researchers both reflect and shape the social landscape: 'As language users with a high degree of visibility in the culture, sociobehavioral scientists are positioned to have enormous influence on the dominant theories of society and thus on its social patterns and institutions' (Gergen 1986: 153). From a constructionist perspective, not only is this involvement inevitable, but it is a legitimate, even desirable, aspect of social inquiry.

Normative social research

This conceptualization of social science has led to a redefinition of the role of researchers and to new goals for research. Once researchers can embrace, rather than try to eliminate, the normative aspects of their inquiry and its influence on understanding, they are free to engage openly in the dialogue surrounding the important social issues facing humanity. Researchers can move beyond what is to what should be, from a focus on means to one of ends, and from analyses of knowledge claims limited to traditional epistemological criteria to ones that incorporate alternative moral criteria as well. Value choices become more explicit. Commenting on social work research, Witkin and Gottschalk stated, rather than focusing on poverty and its disabilities, social work researchers might concern themselves with the social destructiveness of inordinate wealth. They might investigate the implicit violence in contemporary concepts of power and the institutional legitimation of selfishness within political and economic theories.

(Witkin and Gottschalk 1988: 219)

Researchers can challenge the status quo and generate liberating alternatives. They can 'work for the transformation of social orders which inhibit the realization of basic human needs and thus obstruct development, toward alternative orders whose institutions, values, and dynamics would be conducive to the full development and self-actualization of every human being' (Gil, nd: 7). Research thus becomes a form of social action and practice. And, like practice, it is not confined to a narrow set of methods, but encompasses a range of approaches to inquiry and analysis. The broad goals of social justice and human betterment are now as accessible to researchers as they are to practitioners.

Given the above interpretation, social research must address two issues: how to warrant knowledge claims and how to generate 'knowledge in the service of action' (Argyris et al. 1987: 78). A starting place for the emancipatory researcher is with fundamental human rights.

Fundamental human rights

Human rights are those rights persons are entitled to simply by virtue of their being human beings. Fundamental human rights are those rights which are primary, that supersede all others. They are required of all persons in order to fulfill their basic humanness and, therefore, 'essential to life worthy of a human being' (Donnelly 1985: 9). Following Gewirth (1978), these rights are the right to freedom and the right to well-being.

The right to freedom entails the right of individuals to act as they wish without interference from others, including the state. The only limitation on such action is that it 'does not threaten or violate other persons' rights to freedom (by coercing them) or to well-being (by harming them)' (Gewirth 1982: 17). Kent (1986) sees the right to freedom as including the protection of freedoms that are guaranteed by the state from the interference of other citizens. For instance, one's freedom to seek employment or attend school should be protected from the interference of others.

The right to well-being consists of the 'various abilities and conditions' necessary for 'successful action' (Gewirth 1982: 139). Although the determination of well-being involves a value judgment, it is a special kind of value judgment that is 'so consistent and so predictable that we can treat it as fixed, as if it were an objective part of nature' (Veatch 1986: 137). Gewirth (1982, 1996) discusses three levels of well-being distinguished by whether one is referring to conditions and abilities that are: (1) essential for successful action (e.g. life); (2) necessary to maintain one's general level of successful action (e.g. not being lied to); and (3) likely to enhance one's well-being (e.g. education). By this definition, the right to basic necessities such as food, shelter, medical care, and education would supersede claims such as the right to eat caviar or own a Mercedes.

Obviously, not all cases will be as clear as the above example and difficult judgments may be required. However, the same is true when applying *any* criteria concerning the justification of claims. Thus, the element of judgment does not, in and of itself, negate the value of this approach.

Rights imply duties; that is, calling something a 'right' means that a person has a legitimate, forceful claim on others to comply with that right (Donnelly 1985). In this way, rights have an instrumental function in social life. The obligations associated with human rights are not limited to individuals, but extend to governments and social institutions. Thus, there exists an interactive relationship among human rights and society. The recognition of basic human rights shapes society, which in turn creates the conditions within which human rights can be realized (*ibid.*). Therefore, human rights can be seen as a social practice that provides the foundation for a just society.

Human rights and social research

Theory and research can influence how human rights are understood and applied to others. Conceptualizations of persons and explanations of behavior may serve to obstruct or foster human rights. For example, psychiatry and psychology have a long history of characterizing marginalized persons in ways that legitimate their social control. These include the confinement of such people in institutions, the construction of various 'diseases' associated with a particular group (ranging from 'drapetomania', manifested in the penchant of slaves to escape from the plantations, to more contemporary diagnoses of hyperkinesis in children), and the support of the status quo through the depoliticization of potential social issues (Kitzinger 1987). Research which assumes the reality of such conceptualizations and then 'documents' their characteristics (e.g. the personality traits of hyperkinetic children) may further legitimate human rights restrictions in the name of science. To the extent that conventional research, such as surveys and outcome studies, isolates (decontextualizes) its subject matter and maintains researchers' hegemony over knowledge, the ability to address such human rights issues is restricted. In contrast, research that treats putative knowledge claims as historical, cultural, and political expressions may be more sensitive and responsive to human rights issues.

The latter approach allows one to go beyond consideration of how research can provide information about human rights, to how human rights can inform and be integrated with research practice. Three possibilities are considered: (1)

human rights as research goals; (2) human rights as evaluative criteria; and (3) human rights as a guide for conducting research. These practices are not independent and may all be found in a single study.

Human rights as research goals

Human rights are transparent when they are freely exercised and protected. Persons make human rights claims when they perceive that such rights are being obstructed, suppressed or not honored. Individuals who are vulnerable or socially disadvantaged and are unable to secure their rights through their own efforts may make claims against others who are better off, particularly governments, to provide the conditions and resources necessary for them to achieve a minimal level of freedom and well-being (Gewirth 1996). Human rights researchers help to articulate, illuminate, and warrant these claims and provide a vehicle for their expression. They also seek to foster conditions that will enhance and safeguard human rights. Thus, human rights research goals are change-oriented and emancipatory. They aim to empower people to claim their rights, to disempower rights violators, and to bolster mechanisms for protecting rights.

Merging human rights and research goals requires a shift from seeing the purpose of research as uncovering existing 'truth' to seeing it as a social practice that generates and legitimates 'truths'. From this perspective, the inescapable value dimension of inquiry is not an impediment to be ignored or controlled, but an opportunity for researchers to participate more fully in the significant social discourses of their culture. Feminist researchers have been particularly successful in articulating and using this approach to develop a body of knowledge that empowers women in the sense of 'analyzing ideas about the causes of powerlessness, recognizing systemic oppressive forces, and acting both individually and collectively to change the conditions of our lives' (Lather 1986: 64).

Although various 'activist' research approaches might be used to address human rights goals (Thomas 1993), two approaches, transformative criticism and generative theorizing, are highlighted. Because of their conceptual rather than method-based nature, these forms of inquiry are not often considered as forms of research. Additionally, they have particular importance for human rights goals because they address and challenge the contexts of assumptions and social conditions within which research is carried out.

Briefly stated, transformative criticism involves the conceptual critique of the underlying assumptions of theory or research. The discourse generated by such critique may lead to a modification of these assumptions (Longino 1990). Generative theory proposes alternative conceptualizations of taken-for-granted assumptions and commonplace understandings and provides guides for action (Gergen 1978). Critiques of the assumptions underlying explanations of spouse abuse, challenges to the assumptions about its persistence (Davis 1987), and the reconceptualization of violence against women (including what is meant by 'violence') as a human rights issue (Bunch 1990; Chapman 1991) illustrates the power of these approaches.

A more extended example is found in a study I conducted with my colleague, Lise Fox, on the concept of 'least restrictive environment' (LRE) as it is applied to the education of children with disabilities (Witkin and Fox 1992). The concept of LRE gained prominence in the US in 1978 with the passage of a law (The Education for All Handicapped Children Act) that attempted to ensure that the rights of students with disabilities to a public education would not be unduly restricted and that, to the maximum extent appropriate, these students would be educated with their non-disabled peers.

Our analysis suggested that within schools LRE was treated more like an educational objective than a human rights protection. For example, in the development of the legally required 'individualized educational plans' (IEP) for students with disabilities, the assessment of whether an environment was 'least restrictive' was typically not done until *after* instructional objectives for the student had been formulated. But since the development of these objectives was based on the existing (physical and organizational) environment of the school, the assessment of the LRE presumed that environment. For instance, segregated (self-contained) classes might be viewed as least restrictive simply because the school provided no other alternatives for students with disabilities. In this situation the LRE became the 'LREE', the least restrictive *existing* environment (*ibid.*: 327).

Based on this analysis, an alternative conceptualization called the 'most enabling environment' (MEE) was proposed. The MEE was based on the notions of fundamental human rights as *minimal* guaranties for all students regardless of disabling conditions or individual learning goals and on the interpretation of social justice as equality of outcomes. The aims of this alternative conceptualization were to sensitize educators to human rights issues regarding students with disabilities, provide new ways of addressing the educational needs of these students, and be a catalyst for school restructuring. The transformational critique made it possible to set aside the implicit assumptions about the LRE. The alternative of the MEE encouraged educators to think in terms of rights protections and to develop new practices based on this reconceptualization. Although other research methods could have been used to supplement our analysis, such data by themselves would not necessarily lead to a critique of the underlying assumptions of the LRE concept or its connection with human rights.

Human rights as evaluative criteria

Viewing knowledge claims as reflecting neither an independent reality nor invariant observational transcriptions, but rather as reflecting social practices, encourages consideration of alternative criteria for assessing research. This broadened perspective elevates the warranting power of social and moral criteria. Thus, research might be assessed according to the extent to which it contextualizes its subject matter, attributes agency to participants, is grounded in their life-worlds, and promotes social justice (Witkin and Gottschalk 1988); for its 'catalytic validity', the extent to which the research process enables participants to understand reality in ways that helps them change it (Lather 1991); or in relation to its ability 'to maintain, to question, and to transform traditions' (Gergen 1994: 55).

Within this expanded valuational framework, fundamental human rights can play an important role. Because these rights are either prerequisite or critical to all other criteria, they occupy a 'foundational' position in the assessment of research quality and findings. Thus, we may ask to what extent do particular research practices or studies protect or advance human rights in contrast to thwarting or subverting them? In answering this question, we need to consider not only methodological rigor, but research goals, the research protocol, the interpretive frames or theories, and the kinds of social practices that are encouraged or discouraged. For instance, explaining poverty as a result of psychological deficits or low moral standards which would justify restrictions on freedom and well-being would be less favored than explanations identifying social and political inequalities that could lead to more social support and a more balanced distribution of resources.

The criteria used to assess research will influence the way research is organized. For instance, if controlling for researcher bias is a major concern (e.g. influencing participants to respond in ways that confirm the hypothesis), then studies will be organized in such a way as to eliminate or control the kinds of factors that are considered biasing (e.g. following a strict protocol). Similarly, if human rights are a primary criterion, then research will be organized to address or account for this. Although there is no one way to do this, it most likely would require that researchers attend to the presuppositions implicit in their theories and methodology, the contextual dimensions of the study, the function and treatment of study participants (discussed in more detail below), and the representation and use of findings.

Human rights as both a goal and necessary criterion of research opens the door to a variety of methods that can include these as desiderata. Thus, practices that are reflexive, that equalize power between researchers and participants, that locate themselves in cultural and historical space, and that afford participants and others opportunities for changing their lives, gain increased legitimacy. For example, co-operative inquiry (Heron 1996), fourth-generation evaluation (Guba and Lincoln 1989), critical ethnography (Thomas 1993), and qualitative activist research (Fine and Vanderslice 1992) are among the many approaches that fare well under the human rights criterion.

Human rights and the research process

An integrative research approach to human rights must also extend to those who participate in our research studies and to the conduct of the studies themselves. It would be highly contradictory to tout human rights as goals and valuative criteria while carrying out research in a way not consistent with these rights. Thus, issues of power, participation, voice, disclosure, and relevance become relevant to the discourse on methodology.

Traditionally, research ethics have been concerned with potential harm to participants as the result of certain practices; for instance, the use of deception or lack of confidentiality (Gilchrist and Schinke 1988). Less often identified are the human rights issues involved in treating people as objects – receptacles for 'data' which are 'extracted' by research instruments – or in representing participants in ways that distort their experience (e.g. through discounting their language), or in excluding participants from any input into the research process. This broadened ethical position engenders serious questions about the maintenance of a researcher–subject dichotomy and the role of researcher as expert. Instead, it invites the use of participatory and co-operative forms of inquiry in which participants are encouraged to enter into a dialogue that co-constructs the meaning of the research. Such research strives to reduce socially-conferred status differences and to create a reciprocal inquiry process. Researchers become 'real' people whose interest in the research topic is related to their experiences and values. (In a similar fashion, I attempted to decrease my invisibility and increase my humanness by describing, in the beginning of this chapter, how my interest in human rights developed from certain personal experiences.)

According to Heron (1981), '[T]he moral principle of respect for persons is most fully honored when power is shared not only in the application ... but also in the generation of knowledge' (cited in Lather 1991: 55–6). Researchers who work with people for whom human rights is a critical matter (i.e. those who are marginalized within a particular society) must avoid imposing their own understandings and sensibilities on the participants. Opportunities to participate meaningfully in all aspects of the research process, including the representation of the results, models a human rights-based social process, combines the legitimation of knowledge associated with research with the richness of language and meaning of the participants, and is beneficial in itself to the participants.

A graduate student project that I supervised (Palmer 1992) illustrates some of the above points. This project grew out of a request by a local mental health agency to develop an evaluation of their services to people with severe and persistent mental illness. In responding to this request, we focused on how to meaningfully include the intended service recipients in the evaluation process. Our aim was to find out from the clients themselves what it was important to know about the agency. Rather than assume that we knew the best way to go about this task, we decided to ask them directly. Thus, the project started with the following statement and question to the clients: 'The [mental health] agency wants me to help them develop a way of evaluating services. How should I go about doing this?' This request precipitated a dialogue that took place over a series of meetings and was both revealing and valuable. In fact, the process of exploring *how* to conduct an evaluation itself became an important source of evaluative information. For example, clients' fears about the possible repercussions of providing negative information and their lack of awareness of agency services and policies were important data about the quality of services. Participation in this process seemed empowering to the clients: they were more aware of agency options, how they were being treated relative to the agency mission, and how they might go about changing their situation. Treating them as collaborators from the very beginning of the project, listening to their views, and respecting their suggestions, was rights-confirming.

Issues and tensions

Research on the margins

The human rights approach presented here stands in contrast to conventional research thinking. Rather than a focus on methods (means), the emphasis has been on research goals. Rather than a value-neutral process that discovers ahistorical, acultural truth about the world, research has been portrayed as value-driven and 'openly ideological' (Lather 1986), and research knowledge as historical and cultural expressions. And rather than a highly structured process in which knowledge and power resides with the researcher, we have advocated for research in which expertise and power are more evenly distributed across all participants.

Thus, practitioners of this approach may find themselves somewhat on the margins of mainstream research. This can have implications for research support as government agencies (the primary supporter of research in the US) tend to favor more conventional views of research. Evaluation researchers may also face challenges. It is unusual for funding agencies or the stakeholder groups that support them to have human rights goals in mind when they seek to evaluate their programs. For example, Rodwell and Woody (1994) reported how their proposed 'constructivist' evaluation of a child guidance clinic was rejected by agency administrators due to its departure from conventional research methods and its potential threat to the status quo at the agency. On a more optimistic note, there is a growing acceptance across the social sciences of 'alternative' forms of inquiry and a increasing demand from research participants to participate more fully in the generation of knowledge about them.

Human rights in a cultural context

Throughout this chapter, I have argued for a greater awareness of the cultural in research. Therefore, it is reasonable to ask whether culture extends also to human rights. And, if human rights is a cultural construct, can its centrality in research be justified, or does it reduce to whatever persons within a particular culture deem as human rights?

My response to the first question is that conceptions of human rights are as cultural-bound as other concepts. No matter how strongly we may feel about the superiority of our own position, contemporary views on rights (including this view) are products of our history and culturally-shaped notions about individuals, society, human needs, morality, and so on. This concession, however, does not dislodge human rights from its proposed place in the research process. Human rights need not be foundational or transcultural in order to be important. We cannot avoid using *some* organizing concepts for our inquiry and the argument here is that human rights offers a useful alternative to the more typical practices – useful in that it appears to have potential to help us build the kind of world we might want for our great-grandchildren (Rorty 1993).

That the concept of human rights might have different meanings across cultures should not, in and of itself, prevent its use. There are many concepts (e.g. dignity, happiness, god) whose meaning (or existence) varies across cultures, yet we do not eliminate them from our discourse. What we can do is to try and understand these differences within various cultural contexts and to explore how the contexts themselves give rise to these differences. This approach also encourages us to examine the cultural trappings of our own human rights ideals. For example, the idea of human rights as applied to children is of relatively recent origin. For centuries, children were considered property rather than persons (Hart 1991) and issues of rights were not considered relevant. Examining the social conditions that accompanied this movement from property to personhood can help us to understand both our own and other cultures' conception of rights.

If there is anything approaching a constant within human rights research, it is, in my opinion, the mandate to amplify the voices of the powerless. This can be as uncomfortable and difficult in our own culture as in those which hold different views of human rights. Regardless of the identifying label – mentally ill, prisoner, child, homosexual, guest worker, handicapped, or dissident – working with disenfranchised people in a way that respects their human dignity is always risky, yet crucial to the human rights agenda.

The power of social research lies in its ability to create and control conceptual categories and generate new forms of understanding. As Hess (1990) asks, 'who would deny that the power to name is the power to differentiate, to decide what is to be included and excluded from our discourse, and hence our imaginations' (p. 83). Constructionists, feminists, critical theorists, and others sensitive to the social dimensions and political ramifications of science and research have attempted to integrate this power into their approach to inquiry. When this power is guided by a vision of human rights it can be a potent force for the betterment of all people.

Note

1   An earlier version of this chapter appeared in the *Journal of Teaching in Social Work*, vol. 8, no. 1/2, 1993, pp. 239–53, and in Joan Laird (ed.) *Revisioning Social Work Education: A social constructionist approach*, The Haworth Press, 1993, pp. 239–53.

References

Albee, G.S. (1986) 'Toward a just society', *American Psychologist* 41: 891–8.

Argyris, C., Putnam, R. and Smith, D.M. (1987) *Action Science*, San Francisco: Jossey-Bass.

Bellah, R.N. (1983) 'The ethical aims of inquiry', in R. Hann, R.N. Bellah, P. Rabinow, and W. Sullivan (eds) *Social Sciences as Moral Inquiry*, New York: Columbia University Press.

Berger, P.L. and Luckmann, T. (1966) *The Social Construction of Reality*, Garden City, NY: Doubleday.

Bunch, C. (1990) 'Women's rights as human rights: towards a revision of human rights', *Human Rights Quarterly* 12: 486–98.

Chapman, J.R. (1991) 'Violence against women as a violation of human rights', *Social Justice* 17: 54–70.

Davis, L.V. (1987) 'Views of wife abuse: Does the research method make the difference?' *Affilia* 2: 53–66.

Denzin, N.K. (1994) 'The art and politics of interpretation', in N.K. Denzin and Y.S. Lincoln (eds) *Handbook of Qualitative Research*, Thousand Oaks: Sage, pp. 500–15.

Dilthey, W. (1976 [1883]) *Selected Writings*, trans. and ed. H.P. Rickman, Cambridge, UK: Cambridge University Press.

Donnelly, J. (1985) *The Concept of Human Rights*, New York: St. Martin's Press.

Feyerabend, P.K. (1976) *Against Method*, New York: Humanities Press.

Fine, M. and Vanderslice, V. (1992) 'Qualitative activist research', in F.B. Bryant *et al.* (eds) *Methodological Issues in Applied Psychology*, New York: Plenum Press, pp. 199–218.

Gadamer, H.G. (1975) *Truth and Method*, New York: Seabury Press.

Garfinkel, H. (1967) *Studies in Ethnomethodology*, Englewood Cliffs, NJ: Prentice Hall.

Gergen, K.J. (1978) 'Toward generative theory', *Journal of Personality and Social Psychology* 36: 1344–60.

—— (1985) 'Social psychology and the phoenix of unreality', in S. Koch and D.E. Leary (eds) *A Century of Psychology as Science*, New York: McGraw-Hill, pp. 528–57.

—— (1986) 'Correspondence versus autonomy in the language of understanding human action', in D.W. Fiske and R.A. Shweder (eds) *Metatheory in Social Science*, Chicago: University of Chicago Press, pp. 136–62.

—— (1994) *Realities and Relationships: Soundings in social construction*, Cambridge, MA: Harvard University Press.

Gergen, K.J. and Davis, K.E. (eds) (1985) *The Social Construction of the Person*, New York: Springer Verlag.

Gewirth, A. (1978) *Reason and Morality*, Chicago: University of Chicago Press.

—— (1982) *Human Rights: Essays on justification and applications*, Chicago: University of Chicago Press.

—— (1996) *The Community of Rights*, Chicago: University of Chicago Press.

Gil, D.G. (nd) *Social Sciences, Human Survival, Development and Liberation*, Waltham, MA: Brandeis University, Center for Social Change Practice and Theory.

Gilchrist, L.D. and Schinke, S.P. (1988) 'Research ethics', in R.M. Grinnell, Jr. (ed.) *Social Work Research and Evaluation*, 3rd edn, Itasca, IL: F.E. Peacock Publishers, pp. 65–79.

Gottschalk, S. and Witkin, S.L. (1988) 'Ideology, social justice, and social work research', *Journal of International and Comparative Social Welfare* 4 (1): 1–11.

—— (1991) 'Rationality in social work: a critical reexamination', *Journal of Sociology and Social Welfare* 18: 121–36.

Gould, S.J. (1981) *The Mismeasure of Man*, New York: W.W. Norton.

Guba, E.G. and Lincoln, Y.S. (1989) *Fourth Generation Evaluation*, Newbury Park, CA: Sage.

Hanson, N. (1958) *Patterns of Discovery: An inquiry into the conceptual foundations of science*, Cambridge, UK: Cambridge University Press.

Hart, S.N. (1991) 'From property to person status: historical perspective on children's rights', *American Psychologist* 46: 53–9.

Heron, J. (1981) 'Philosophical basis for a new paradigm', in P. Reason and J. Rowan (eds) *Human Inquiry: A sourcebook of new paraidgm research*, Chichester: John Wiiley and Sons.

Heron, J. (1996) *Co-operative Inquiry: Research into the human condition*, London: Sage.

Hess, B.B. (1990) 'Beyond dichotomy: drawing distinctions and embracing differences', *Sociological Forum* 5: 75–93.

Howard, G.S. (1985) 'The role of values in the science of psychology', *American Psychologist* 40: 255–65.

Kent, E.A. (1986) 'Taking human rights seriously', in M. Tamny and K.D. Irani (eds) *Rationality in Thought and Action*, New York: Greenwood Press, pp. 31–47.

Kitzinger, C. (1987) *The Social Construction of Lesbianism*, Newbury Park, CA: Sage.

Kuhn, T.S. (1970) *The Structure of Scientific Revolutions*, 2nd rev. edn, Chicago: University of Chicago Press.

Lather, P. (1986) 'Issues of validity in openly ideological research: between a rock and a soft place', *Interchange* 17: 63–84.

—— (1991) *Getting Smart: Feminist research and pedagogy with/in the postmodern*, New York: Routledge.

Laudan, L. (1977) *Progress and its Problems: Toward a theory of scientific growth*, Berkeley, CA: University of California Press.

Longino, H.E. (1990) *Science as Social Knowledge*, Princeton, NJ: Princeton University Press.

Morawski, J.G. (1986) 'Contextual discipline: the unmaking and remaking of sociality', in R.L. Rosnow and M. Georgoudi (eds) *Contextualism and Understanding in Behavioral Science*, New York: Praeger, p. 51–64.

Palmer, H., III (1992) 'The inclusion of mental health clients in program evaluation activities: a case study', unpublished paper, Department of Social Work, University of Vermont.

Peterson, V.S. (1987) 'Re-constructing the "individual" in human rights', paper presentation at the National Women's Studies Association Conference, Atlanta, GA.

Riley, M.W. (1988) *Sociological Lives*, Newbury Park, CA: Sage.

Rodwell, M.K. and Woody, D., III (1994) 'Constructivist evaluation: the policy/practice context', in E. Sherman and W.J. Reid (eds) *Qualitative Research in Social Work*, New York: Columbia University Press, pp. 315–27.

Rorty, R. (1993) 'Human rights, rationality and sentimentality', in S. Shute and S. Hurley (eds) *On Human Rights*, New York: Basic Books, pp. 111–34.

Sampson, E.E. (1989) 'The deconstruction of the self', in J. Shotter and K.J. Gergen (eds) *Texts of Identity*, Newbury Park, CA: Sage, pp. 1–19.

Smith, J.K. (1990) 'Alternative research paradigms and the problem of criteria', in E.G. Guba (ed.) *The Paradigm Dialog*, Newbury Park, CA: Sage, pp. 167–97.

Thomas, J. (1993) *Doing Critical Ethnography*, Newbury Park, CA: Sage.

Trigg, R. (1985) *Understanding Social Science*, Oxford, UK: Basil Blackwell.

Vaughter, R. (1976) 'Psychology: review essay', *Signs: Journal of Women in Culture and Society* 2: 120–46.

Veatch, R.M. (1986) *The Foundations of Justice*, New York: Oxford University Press.

Weimer, W. (1979) *Notes on the Methodology of Scientific Research*, Hillsdale, NJ: Lawrence Erlbaum Associates.

Winch, P. (1958) *The Idea of a Social Science and its Relation to Philosophy*, New York: Humanities Press.

Witkin, S.L. (1989) 'Scientific ideology and women: implications for marital research and therapy', *Journal of Family Psychology* 2: 430–46.

—— (1995) 'Family social work: a critical constructionist perspective', *Journal of Family Social Work* 1: 33–45.

Witkin, S.L. and Fox, L. (1992) 'Beyond the least restrictive environment', in R. Villa, J. Thousand, W. Stainback and S. Stainback (eds) *Restructuring for Caring and Effective Education: An administrative guide to creating heterogeneous schools*, Baltimore: Paul H. Brooks Publishing Co., pp. 325–38.

Witkin, S.L. and Gottschalk, S. (1988) 'Alternative criteria for theory evaluation', *Social Service Review* 62: 211–24.

Wittgenstein, L. (1963) *Philosophical Investigations*, trans. G. Anscombe, New York: Macmillan.

Chapter 14

Colonial methodology?

Methodological challenges to cross-cultural projects collecting data by structured interviews

Anne Ryen

> 'Is this the way to Arusha?' the Norwegian asked, pointing towards the left at the crossroads. 'Yes', the young Tanzanian answered, smilingly confirming the Norwegian's anticipated direction indicated by him waving his left hand out of the window of the landrover. The guest drove on happily until he reached a large sign on the road saying 'Welcome to Dodoma'. 'Blast him!' the Norwegian sighed, turning round and eventually heading for Arusha.

To the Norwegian, the question is why the young Tanzanian man sent him in the wrong direction.[1] Or is it possible to see this story differently? Who is the honourable man in the story? Could it be that both of them are, simply because there were different cultural 'spectacles' filtering out what they see? Would it be possible that they eventually perceive the situation in the same way spontaneously? If so, how? This points to the main question to be discussed in this chapter: in what ways does culture enter methodology?[2]

The chapter deals with ways to prevent ethnocentric methodology discussed within a micro-sociological perspective. A main objective in projects crossing cultural borders, and familiar to anthropologists, is to work out a design adhering to the data as conceived within a specific cultural context. It is based on experiences from a specific Tanzanian–Norwegian collaboration. Projects within this collaboration depart from traditional anthropological field studies by consisting of a sequence of independent research projects. All projects are time-limited, and data are collected by structured interviews. The topic of this chapter is to discuss methodological challenges in cross-cultural research when data is collected by structured interviews in short-term projects.

The projects referred to later can be characterised as applied to research. They are initiated because of their contribution to the process of rapid and profound qualitative change in a specific culture. Results from research that will function as a basis for political decisions make methodology crucial. If the cross-cultural dimension is underestimated or ignored, the researcher runs the risk of ending up with methodological explanations. If so, the population may become a victim of methodological discrimination.[3] By discussing potential remedies to this problem, the chapter may also be seen as a contribution to anti-discriminatory research.

Background

The year 1990 represented the start of formal institutional co-operation between the Institute of Development Management, Tanzania, and Agder College, Norway. The collaboration was funded by the Norwegian Agency for Development Cooperation (NORAD) for a four-year period.[4] During the first period, fourteen research projects were initiated. All projects are based on data collected in Tanzania which were specific to each project. Most data was collected by structured interviews, and only a few by triangulation (observations, records and documents, panel meetings, etc.). Included in the phases of each joint research project is a pilot study in Tanzania, lasting 2–4 weeks. The data collection itself was often carried out by a Tanzanian researcher assisted by a research assistant (most frequently a junior researcher). In other cases the Norwegian researcher also participated in this part of the process. In some cases data was collected by students (Ryen and Habi 1994), or the team was assisted by field officers (Shio *et al.* 1994).

The impact of cultural knowledge on social perception

The concept of 'culture' is defined in a number of different ways. For this purpose I see culture as 'the knowledge people use to generate and interpret social behaviour' (Spradley and McCurdy 1972: 8).[5] We are taught to attach meaning to social objects and events that we encounter in our environment, enabling us to participate in communication. Cultural knowledge is coded in a very complex system of symbols, and the culture becomes a filter functioning as a frame of reference to the decoding process. These frames of reference guide and influence the perceptions we have in an intercultural setting.

Ethnomethodologists like Garfunkel and Sachs have shown a particular interest in people's ability to develop a common understanding of each other and of social situations in general (Silverman 1993). Crossing cultural borders, interpretation becomes more complicated. A smooth communication process is no guarantee that those involved have perceived symbols in the same way. Words as symbols may be interpreted or conceived in different ways. The criticism directed towards quantitative research includes treating data as 'truth' or as the ultimate account of reality, whereas qualitative researchers are more concerned with the status of the accounts or the data they get. In cross-cultural projects this problem comes to the forefront. The lack of flexibility in structured interviews increases the possibility that the researcher fails to notice cultural differences associated with, for example, words. Awareness should be directed to the problems especially posed by cultural differences in perception and interpretations of symbols, including words. Examples will be given in a later section.

One of the difficulties visitors in foreign cultures experience is the fact that they often enter specialised contexts, like the health sector etc., without having the knowledge required to handle these contexts (Hylland-Eriksen and Sørheim 1994).[6] However, the outcome may depend on the actor's ascribed status, e.g. colour. Individuals belonging to the White, wealthy, Western cultures may in spite of cultural unawareness have a higher probability of success due to the resources attributed to them as part of that culture. One view within exchange theory proposes that norms of justice support and legitimate behavioural inequalities that favour the powerful (Molm et al. 1994). A structured interview is another specialised context, but the definition of success is not necessarily concurrent in daily life and in data collection.

Communication during the interview may be influenced by the structure of the interview, by characteristics of the participants and by the interview process itself. Interviews are frequently performed by researchers who are given a higher rank than others based on their acquired status through education. This may be accentuated by race or colour of the skin. In most projects, the majority of the interviewees are quite ordinary people. The interview is, then, a meeting between actors of different formal and informal statuses accentuated by the structure of the interview itself. In structured interviews the roles of the participants are less flexible compared to unstructured interviews, where control may shift more easily between the interviewer and the interviewee. The interview itself is but one stage in the total research process, leaving the researcher with the final control. The researcher has taken the initiative in arranging the meeting, and she/he controls the main instrument, which is the questionnaire in a survey (or the researcher is involved in a qualitative project involving turn-taking, follow-up questions, time), the interpretation of the data, and also writes the report.

The mechanisms involved in conducting the communication process itself consist of certain elements to be found in all types of interaction at micro-level. In the next section, I will comment briefly on some of these elements. The specific challenge represented by the cross-cultural aspect is demonstrated by illustrations from Tanzania. The researcher who crosses cultural borders is the one who will potentially be accused of ethnocentrism (Hylland-Eriksen 1996). Consequently, the stories illustrate the relationship between the two cultures by showing the contrast as defined by the researcher's frame of reference. The responsibility to gain access to local definitions and meaning of communicative symbols rests with the researcher.

The challenge of social order in cross-cultural meetings

Some main ways in which all interaction is patterned and micro-order is produced will be reviewed here. These include defining the situation, environmental impact, ranking and deference, and co-operation and reciprocity (Broom and Selznick 1977). Each element is followed by stories to illustrate the challenge when communicating across cultures. The stories are not Tanzanian as such, but experiences of Norwegians in Tanzania. My intention is to raise the level of awareness in cross-cultural communication in this particular culture by reproducing episodes that are unfamiliar to the frame of reference associated with the visiting researcher, in this case a Norwegian researcher. The stories will illustrate that in everyday life the elements structuring social order are not separated as shown here, but are interwoven.

Defining the situation

To define a situation, or to give it a specific meaning, implies making it part of the social order. Within micro-sociology, social order is seen as locally produced. Social order at a micro-level consists of a complex mixture of social expectations, spontaneous responses, personal adaptation and calculated strategies. They are all elements in the 'negotiation' between the members involved in defining the specific definition of this specific situation.[7] Our responses refer to the specific definition of each individual. This is summed up in the classical phrase coined by W.I. Thomas: 'If men define situations as real, they become real in their consequences' (Cuff and Payne 1979). The interaction between involved parties is thereby a result of the interpretations or definitions made by each party. Sometimes strategies are deliberately employed in trying to attach a definition of the situation favourable to oneself. For this reason, definitions are not always predictable.

In general, Norwegians are often perceived as being very serious people, planning activities a long time ahead (Dahl and Habert 1986), showing a great respect for the agenda, which can only be changed according to specific norms, respecting the rules of the game, differentiating between the case and the person, and differentiating between job and private life, thereby not necessarily inviting colleagues from work to their homes. In Tanzania, however, one is always invited into the homes of colleagues, and great effort is put into the well-being of the guests – including their leisure activities.

The meanings of actions and symbols are gender specific. In Tanzania, known to be a patriarchal society, sometimes it is difficult to differentiate between general politeness and the extra attention of men. After interviewing African men, more attention was paid to me than my Norwegian male colleagues at the end of the interview. Several male interviewees followed me all the way from their office (often several floors up) to my car. Also, it was never possible to sit alone outside at a cafe to enjoy a cup of coffee and a newspaper. This makes cultural codes and the definition of situations especially difficult for women. Recommendations intended to be helpful are very often gender specific: 'social mingling and participation is rewarding in itself, but it also has a positive feedback effect on formal and informal relationships on the job' (Baklien 1979: 24) and one is advised to invite Tanzanian friends for a beer in the local bar. Going to a bar with another man can be strategic for a man. For a woman, other peoples' definition of the situation would be quite different. This deprives women of public and informal arenas giving access to informal job information. Crossing cultural borders, it thereby becomes even more difficult to manage other people's impressions. Again, we are reminded that the researcher is defined as part of the situation.

Environmental impact

The physical objects and materials of our environment all carry social meanings. Through the socialisation process we adopt symbolic meaning in our culture. Some symbols are more universal than others; for example, uniforms reveal authority. Female shoulders or knees are more controversial, and demand a knowledge of dress codes.[8] Very often, norms are different for men and women, for different occasions and for different sub-groups; for example, the use of make-up and hairstyle.[9]

This is more problematic in foreign cultures. Our behaviour may run counter to its intention. In Tanzania, women are not supposed to show their knees and shoulders, wear long hair hanging down, and must wear an underskirt under the summer dress and always wear a bra.[10] In Norway, not wearing an underskirt is quite usual on a hot summer day, but this is considered to be quite improper in Tanzania.

Lack of cultural knowledge deprives us of the possibility of deliberately creating the impression we want to give. Instead, we as researchers contribute to different definitions of the same situation, thereby complicating interaction. All elements in the communication process become an integral part of the interpretation process carried out by those involved.

Two examples relating to the environment in a wider sense will be described. When calling someone over, Norwegians may signal with one of their hands with the inside of the hand turning upwards waving from the other person towards oneself. In Tanzania, one waves by holding the inside of one's hand held downwards. The former is regarded as being rude.

Conception of time is a well-known difference between Africa and Scandinavia, where in the latter, efficiency and good timekeeping are very important. For example, an African colleague was supposed to come to my office at 9.00a.m. He arrived at 11.00a.m., simply to tell me that he had to go to town for another meeting. He would come back at 3.00p.m. He arrived to tell me that he had to come back at 4.00p.m., which he did. Actually, I had another appointment at 4.00p.m., but in the event, it all worked out, since the other person didn't turn up until 5.00p.m. Confirming an appointment is no guarantee that the appointment will be kept – or at least not at the time agreed upon. Norwegians refer to military time when making appointments. It has been said that work schedules and adherence to military time in Africa is considered to be 'colonial'.

Ranking and deference

Ranking and inequality of power and privilege are vital aspects of the social order in all societies. Moreover, every person is searching for self-respect and respect from others.

Lower status in one setting may be acceptable to the individual, since this may provide him or her with higher status in another group, given that the first group is ranked higher in social prestige compared to the other. The low position of a servant at the local manor may, nevertheless, give her prestige among local friends. However, deference may also be degrading. How to handle ranking and respect is a particular challenge in cross-cultural communication.

One mechanism is to maintain a social distance. Norms often vary according to the position in the relationship. However, existing norms may not necessarily be accepted by the lower-ranked person or by the person towards whom the manipulation is being directed. For example, using first names, jokes and physical contact may be a way of placing the person – a female employee, say – in a subordinate position or may reinforce that position. Social distance can also be maintained by the manner employed; for example, distinguishing between formal and informal approaches.

The historical relationship between Europe and Africa, combined with the present difference in living standards, may affect interaction. Whereas Simmel developed a theory of the influence of absolute group size on interaction, form and process, Moss Kanter concentrates on relative numbers or proportional representation (Moss Kanter 1977; Ryen 1987). The relationship between the kinds of people in a group (based on, for example, gender, skin colour or religion) is influenced by the historical relationship between the larger groups they represent. How this relates to our theme is unclear at a more detailed level, but presumably in general it favours the European.

The relationship between ranking and norms of politeness may be confusing to a foreigner. Politeness may be seen as a sign of subordination. However, what may appear to be resignation to authority may very well simply be an adherence to situational norms.[11] A visitor can be easily led astray.

How to meet persons of high rank in Tanzania is puzzling to Norwegians, who have a limited contextual language. While visiting a public office to pick up a paper, a well-educated person was once observed stopping in the middle of the floor and addressing the female official seated at the table in a very low voice. The woman, still looking at her newspaper and appearing to be annoyed about the interruption, gave him a short answer in a rather offhand way. When asked a second question, the woman, still reading her paper, repeated that she had no knowledge of the application in question, and lazily searched in the drawer. The man thanked her, bowed and left the room without turning his back on her (a public bureaucrat). In other similar situations, people have been observed almost whispering, and with heads bowed throughout the whole consultation.

Tanzanian leadership behaviour is known to be authoritarian. The relationship of Tanzanians to public bureaucrats was once explained to me by a Tanzanian as being a leftover from colonialism. Obviously, codes of rank and politeness are foreign to Norwegians and these codes of behaviour also seem to be applied to researchers when interviewing interviewees of very high rank. Even notes for a meeting are at times handed out in the group according to the anticipated rank in the group (age before formal status) – a unique experience for a Norwegian.

An East-African student in Norway once told me about being sampled for a survey in Africa: 'Me! A doctor from Cambridge coming to my village to interview me! Me, being that important! The day she was to arrive, I dressed in my best clothes, and redressed again. I just couldn't decide what to wear. I am sure I changed clothes ten times. When she arrived, I was so excited I just smiled and answered, 'Yes! Yes! Yes!' (He is now himself working in the health sector. His sister is a medical doctor.)

Not surprisingly, rank and deference are mirrored in a more differentiated way when greeting people. Shaking hands is common. A particular handshake is used to greet a person to be respected and a 'double-hand-grasp' is used among close friends. Verbal greetings are also said to be more complicated than those in Norway. For example, a Tanzanian colleague visiting Norway asked me every single morning how my little daughter was doing.

At the same time, it is said that in Tanzania

> too much verbal argumentation and other forms of verbal dynamism by expatriates is likely to be interpreted as if the local colleague is inferior. ... Tanzanians like relatively relaxed and quiet expert people from abroad who are emotional and openminded, but who are not too dynamic verbally. Giving the host colleague plenty of time to expose and express herself/ himself is part and parcel of a good interpersonal relationship. A high listening capacity and a non-judgement attitude are assets in most work situations, at least initially.
>
> (Baklien 1979: 23)

When speaking, Tanzanians leave longer pauses between each statement than do Norwegians. Not being aware of this, one might easily interrupt someone in the middle of a sentence or a story; for example, during an interview.

Co-operation and reciprocity

There is a clear relationship between this section and the preceding one. Schools of exchange theory deal with norms of different kinds of interaction (Ekeh 1974). The relationship between the actors may be symmetrical or asymmetrical as is the case with co-operation. Dependency, or the distribution of relevant resources, and reciprocity influence the amount of co-operation and its form. Evidence reviewed suggests that reciprocity is a universal norm (Triandis 1978). Co-operation is frequently based upon unequal power and dependency. What contributes to privilege and to power in a society may be specific to that society or culture as may be the case for the symbols of wealth. To compare or to range persons from different cultures is complicated because resources, items, etc., have to be converted into comparable units. 'The process of negotiation' about positions in the interaction may therefore be more complicated and time-consuming than anticipated.

In addition, research usually depends on co-operation, either between researchers, or between interviewer and interviewee. Data collection implies that the respondent possesses information of vital interest to the interviewer, who in most cases is ranked above the interviewee by this formal position. Supporters of quantitative and qualitative research designs offer different solutions to this problem. A major contradiction has been identified between positivistic research and feminist-based interviewing (Oakley 1981). Independent of research strategy, the success of cross-cultural co-operation is closely associated with cultural knowledge, since data collection, especially by means of inflexible structured interviews, to a very large extent is a result of co-operation.

The elements that structure social order already mentioned can only partly explain how social order exists in meetings across cultures where participants operate with different definitions of that same situation. The challenge to the above-mentioned collaboration is the absence of a common standard for interaction in short-term research activity. In spite of a common unawareness of cultural codes, social order still arises, for example, in data collection. Alternatively, social order only appears to exist. Explicit disorder may be effectively suppressed by norms of politeness. In a more rational perspective, the costs of making the interviewer aware of the disorder may surpass the alternative, since the interaction most probably is a one-time event lasting for maybe a maximum of an hour. Yet another possibility is conceivable: social order stems from 'the interviewee's skills in deploying shared knowledge about this shared social world' (Silverman 1993: 104).

These stories tell us about cultural variations between two specific cultures. Research is also social interaction and cannot be isolated from the wider context of the society as claimed by positivists. According to interactionists, 'a clear-cut distinction between research interviews and other forms of social interaction … is unobtainable' (ibid.: 94). This is also relevant to interaction and co-operation within research teams.

The story at the very beginning of the chapter described a Tanzanian man 'misdirecting' a European on his way to Arusha. The story illustrates the importance of understanding the cultural codes. The European man perceived the Tanzanian man as being unreliable. However, the answer to his question was in accordance with local norms. The Tanzanian man was showing politeness towards the European by avoiding opposing the guest. The way the question was worded left the Tanzanian man with no options. The European, by pointing in a certain direction, left the man no choice of directions. It would have been impolite to disagree and choose a different one, even though it was the right direction. A more open question like 'Which way is Arusha?' would have provided the Norwegian with an answer that gave directions and was also polite.

Colonial methodology?

An African student in England once described anthropological field studies as being 'colonial'. Africans have a long history of being regarded as 'objects to fill note books and publications of western anthropologists' who invaded these cultures looking for rationality, organisation and structure. The exotic cultures favoured by anthropologists were often indigenous groups of people from Third-World countries or former colonial states that were far away from the White, Western affluent world of academic and political institutions. The unbalanced colonial relationship between the representatives of the two cultures was encompassed in the research. Researchers frequently came from the colonial states, and local people were often studied from the researcher's point of view. Africans became 'objects' (Enerstvedt 1989; Spradley and McCurdy 1972).

Research ignoring the challenges inherent in the cross-cultural aspect itself may once again become colonial. The term is defined as research across cultural borders, where data, through observations, interviews or documents obtained are seen through the researcher's 'cultural eyes'. Study objects are not solely objects, but also become the victims of cultural mortification. Colonial methodology is thereby also discriminatory research.[12]

Colonial methodology as defined here is associated with former field studies in developing countries performed by Western researchers. However, replacing observations and participatory research with research using structured interviews also runs the risk of being trapped in the inherent difficulty of shared definitions (Converse and Presser 1986). A low level of cultural awareness combined with the objectification of the respondent represents no major change to former traps. Rather, it may be an extra factor in the prolongation of the problems claimed to be inherent in quantitative research.

Interviews imply a relationship between the two (or more) people involved. The ranking of interviewer and interviewee was described as balanced in favour of the interviewer, both due to acquired status and to the structure of the interview situation itself. The fact that the interviewee controls the information of interest to the researcher does not in itself seem to be a resource strong enough to alter the basic hierarchical relationship. Respondents of lower socio-economic status are traditionally regarded as grateful respondents that are happy to be interviewed or are at least not opposing it. This is not always so with respondents placed at the opposite end of the scale. In North–South projects, the imbalance from acquired status and from the structure of the interview situation itself is accentuated by the historical relationship between the cultures often visualised by ascribed status. This is captured by the standardisation of the representative of the culture to which the respondent belongs. It is in this way that the subject is made an object. This limits the interviewer's awareness of both verbal and non-verbal communication. Standard handbooks in quantitative methodology often refer to projects within the same national culture as the author, or to those resembling that culture. No recommendations are given to researchers working on cross-cultural projects.

Methodology across borders[13]

In this section, a set of concrete methodological dilemmas relating to projects across cultural borders will be presented. They all relate to challenges in cross-cultural meetings as illustrated above.

It is a well-known fact that being under scrutiny may affect one's behaviour (e.g. the Hawthorne studies, Schein 1985: 181). During the data collection the respondent may show enthusiasm, or she/he may hesitate to open up to a stranger in spite of a promise of secrecy. The respondent may relate the credibility of the promise to former experiences from other formal situations; for example, treatment by public bureaucrats or others. In the worst case, an invitation to participate in an interview may be perceived almost as a command and the promise of secrecy as a form of words only. Employees may believe that the information given will be checked by comparing it with company documents etc.[14]

Furthermore, words or concepts are often perceived differently in different cultures. The word itself may be the same across cultures. However, our perception or definition of the context of the concept may vary; for example, the meaning of the words 'state' and 'family'.

The use of certain words may also be problematic when referring to moral or private matters. Examples would be terms such as cohabitation, sexual relations, medicine, gender, etc. Other concepts are simply culturally irrelevant or non-existent; for example, 'cold lunch' in Tanzania.[15]

Another problem encountered when crossing cultures is that the same words or concepts may exist in both cultures, but responses are systematically different. The most frequent example of this is our attitude towards health. Within the same population we find that respondents react differently, depending on their socio-economic status. Thus, there is a different attitude towards reporting on health matters (Johnson *et al.* 1996; Mangione *et al.* 1992).

This tendency is complicated by prior knowledge of interviewee response and also the experience and attitudes of the interviewer (Elstad 1981; Svalastoga 1969; Brinkmann 1996).

The significance of categories varies from culture to culture. To go 'across' cultures may lead to ignoring or overlooking categories which are significant to respondents, but which are insignificant to the researcher. This may especially be the case if the phenomena are not communicated explicitly in verbal communication. Examples of such phenomena found in Norwegian research in Tanzania might include such things as 'parastatal sector' which has no equivalent in Scandanavian countries; or 'witchcraft' which falls outside the domain of Western rationality.

Sometimes meanings of words are situational. This may be difficult to capture if the researcher is only familiar with low-contextual languages. In certain cultures 'yes' simply signals that 'I am listening to what you are saying', rather than signalling agreement; see for example, the story above about the young man being interviewed by a British doctor (p. 226).

In some cultures, politeness is given preference over the actual content of verbal communication. Answers that oppose the direction indicated by the visitor's questions are considered to be improper. The response will be to the way in which the question has been posed rather than a response to the content of the question, as illustrated by the story at the beginning of the chapter. The Norwegian listened to the answer and accepted it at face value. The Tanzanian showed him respect by not insulting the visitor who pointed in the wrong direction and by avoiding telling him that he was wrong. Some knowledge about norms in this specific culture would have allowed the visitor to reach his target faster.

This also illustrates another point. Controlling the content of verbal communication may be impossible, depending on the available data on private households or farming. Checking the data with public information at, for example, local or regional level may substantiate findings, but as any interviewee knows, although some data can be checked easily, this is no insurance that it corresponds with the reality of the situation. The following example comes from the behaviour of Norwegian farmers under the German occupation during the Second World War. Some farmers had two account books, an official one for the occupying regime and an unofficial one. To give family and friends some extra potatoes, vegetables or eggs, not all of the produce was recorded in the official accounts. This example illustrates that although the honesty of interviewees is not brought into question, room must be given to individual and rational adjustment to the context.

Furthermore, how life is perceived by members of the culture being researched is a guide to the data analysis. The researcher should ask her/himself what categories are relevant; for example, sex, education, age, or others that may be unfamiliar to the visitor. 'As social scientists, we cannot describe and classify without attending to how members describe and classify' (Silverman on Sacks, in Silverman 1993).

These are some of the dilemmas that will often arise when collecting data across cultures. The responsibility to minimise them is in the hands of the researcher. When collecting data by means of structured interviews, much effort must be directed towards the initial stages in the project. To generate definitive findings, we are dependent on high validity (e.g. Bryman 1989). When the first interview has started, there is no way back.

Can cross-cultural research still be recommended?

My answer is 'yes', but it is not an unconditional 'yes'. A discussion of the problematic aspects of data collection across cultural borders is not an attempt to disqualify cross-cultural research as such. On the contrary, even anthropologists accept quantitative project designs.[16] Projects across cultural borders generate valuable data for theoretical development, and as a basis for political decisions intended to benefit the population of the projects.

However, special attention should be given to the cross-cultural aspect. This is crucial for all cross-cultural research, but especially for short-term projects characterised by inflexible designs. Structured interviews run the risk of collecting data reflecting the processes of producing micro-order and reflecting lack of cultural knowledge rather than data perceived by the interviewer. Efforts to try to understand true meaning as defined by the culture in question should be integrated in the first part of the research process.

To prelude most difficulties when entering a new culture, anthropological textbooks recommend looking for 'informants'.[17] Informants can easily extend the human capital of cultural knowledge that will simplify research work. This refers to an introduction to formal and informal aspects of everyday life, business or whatever is relevant. This gives valuable information to the construction of questionnaires (for example, when deciding on concepts or phrasing, relevance, order, and so on). The difficulties resemble problems associated with the use of an interpreter. One is easily categorised by others according to the characteristics of the informant (or the interpreter) and his or her position in the community.

Formal collaboration is another advantage, as a 'cultural insider' can fill the role of an informant. This is vital to the questionnaire itself, both in terms of phrasing used, questions (variables) and composition. However, in short-term projects, time is scarce. When people from very different cultures meet, time is needed to develop the process of seeing the other first as a representative of her/his culture to the point when her/his personality as an individual becomes visible to the other (see Moss Kanter 1977). This process is important in order to reach a situation of confidence and openness to dilemmas. This problem may depend on the distance between the cultures represented by the researchers, and the way in which the group of researchers has been composed.[18] According to Johnson *et al.* (1995: 52), 'a multicultural research team will clearly have advantages ... when a theoretical or analytical goal of a study being implemented requires data comparisons across racial and ethnic groups'.[19]

The challenge of cross-cultural communication is more problematic for projects of limited duration. A collection of books only on the society to be studied is a very passive and individualised solution.

For research structured as a sequence of different projects, like those initially described, the construction of a 'bank of culture' could represent a more dynamic approach to the project. Diaries of cultural aspects written by each researcher could be a valuable contribution to professional work. The work would also be cumulative if some effort was put into organising these data. If combined with a more systematic dialogue about the culture between researchers representing the co-operating parties (if the research is a collaboration), the problem of the short-term aspect could be diminished.

However, the unequal relationship inherent in the interview itself, and of Northern countries compared to Southern countries, will have to be acknowledged. Power resides largely in Northern or European countries. This aspect is accentuated when the researcher is European doing research in countries of the South. In spite of this, the suggestions above may contribute to reducing problems that, after all, are possible to reduce.

Conclusions

My intention in this chapter has been to raise the awareness of dilemmas in cross-cultural projects based on experiences from a Tanzanian–Norwegian research collaboration. Emphasis has been placed on projects in which data is collected by structured interviews, and organised as a sequence of short-term projects.

Quantitative research has been accused of relating to the 'face value' of data when crossing cultural borders – it becomes a challenge to get access to local definitions and meanings of communicative symbols. This challenge is accentuated in projects where the communication between the interviewer and interviewee is structured beforehand, as in quantitative research projects. In one of the sections of this chapter, elements to be found in all interactions at micro-level were described. The elements were illustrated by stories from Tanzania to give examples of challenges to researchers and traps into which they might fall when conducting projects in this specific culture – in this case, Norwegians. Anthropology in the era of colonialism has later been accused of ignoring theories on power and change. The imbalance in research and in cross-cultural research remains, and the imbalance is in favour of the researcher and Western countries. However, this does not imply that projects cannot be improved, or that colonial methodology should remain a characteristic of research across borders. Several examples are given of how words, local phenomena and situations may complicate data collection due to differences in local and cultural definitions. In spite of this, cross-cultural research is still recommended, though not unconditionally. Suggestions in this chapter show that it is possible to reduce the occurrence of certain problems.

Awareness of the specific challenges inherent in cross-cultural research increases the possibility of getting access to definitions and meanings of symbols in a specific culture. For applied research, this is a vital and necessary step if the results of the projects are intended to benefit those studied.

Quantitative research is accused of accepting data as 'truth', and qualitative research is accused of ending up in a wilderness of different versions of reality. This chapter represents a middle strategy: to accept a satisfying version or the middle way.[20] In cross-cultural structured projects, the researcher is urged to put an extra effort into the planning stage of the data collection. This is one way that interviewees in quantitative research can be better treated as subjects or be given a voice. It is in this way that projects as described in this chapter can be anti-discriminatory.

Notes

1 Scandinavian languages are described as being low-contextual. The message is to be found in the words literally, as opposed to high-contextual languages like Spanish and Italian, where non-linguistic matters contribute to the definition of the content of what is said. This is one of the reasons why the Norwegians find communication in the Latin countries exotic, but complicated (Ryen 1994).
2 The clue to the introductory story will be revealed later in the chapter.
3 To be differentiated from statistical discrimination.
4 On the basis of an application to NORAD, co-operation has been extended to include a new four-year period, 1996–9 (Habi et al. 1995).
5 See also Brinkmann (1996).
6 Research on access to welfare benefits clearly illustrates the importance of managing specific contexts even within one's own culture (Lipsky 1980).
7 See Goffman (1961) on 'impression management'.
8 It has been said that some years ago it was commented on in Tanzania that the Norwegian minister of Foreign Aid wore a mini-skirt when officially visiting the country. Her photograph was printed in one of the newspapers showing almost all of her legs. Her formal position was overshadowed by her legs.
9 To Goffman, these elements become important in 'impression management' (Goffman 1961).
10 Maybe this is related to the questions of tribe, class or nationality.
11 Once, a South-American woman told me how local farmers in a Norwegian valley appreciated the large posters she had given them of people dancing the samba. One of these farmers later told me that when she had left, he had thrown the poster in the dustbin.
12 For a discussion of the relationship between anthropology and colonialism, see Talal Asad (1973), and Finn Sivert Nielsen (1996) briefly on the lack of theories on power and change in classical anthropological studies.
13 The concept of 'border' does not here necessarily refer to national and geographical borders. There are many examples of more than one culture living within the borders of the same state.

14 We experienced the latter in an interview with an employee who was receiving fringe benefits when the respondent said: 'I might as well tell you because you will probably ask my employer' (Ryen and Habi 1994).
15 Preparing the questionnaire for the project on fringe benefits, I was reminded of the difference between the two countries. I wanted to put in a question about access to hot or cold lunch. My colleague told me with a smile that in Tanzania, 'cold lunch is something you serve only to your enemy!'
16 For an anthropologist's guide to surveys on cultural differences see Brinkmann (1996).
17 The concept of an 'informant' has been criticised, and is preferably associated with formal interview techniques (Nielsen 1996). Smedal (1994, in Nielsen 1996) introduces the concept of a 'consultant'.
18 When a research project with the specific collaboration mentioned has been suggested in one country, a project team in the other country has the responsibility to look for people in their own institution to co-operate with. Most researchers have little knowledge of the researchers at the collaborating institution. The research topic will decide whether someone is interested or not.
19 Reference is explicitly made to multicultural societies such as the United States.
20 Looking for the *satisfying* alternative in planning was introduced as part of the criticism of rational planning aiming at the best solution, whereas Aristotle, many centuries earlier, used the term 'the golden middle way'.

References

Asad, T. (1973) *Anthropology and the Colonial Encounter*, London: Ithaca Press.
Baklien, B. (1979) 'Crosscultural communication training for work in East Africa', paper, Michigan State University.
Brinkmann, J. (1996) 'Spørreundersøkelser om kulturforskjeller', in J. Brinkmann and T. Hylland-Eriksen (eds) *Verden som møteplass: Essays om tverrkulturell kommunikasjon*, Bergen: Fagbokforlaget, Chapter 14, pp. 174–220.
Broom, L. and Selznick, P. (1977) *Sociology. A text with adapted readings*, New York: Harper and Row.
Bryman, A. (1989) *Research Methods and Organizational Studies*, Contemporary Social Research, 20, London: Unwin Hyman.
Converse, J.M. and Presser, S. (1986) *Survey Questions*, Series: Quantitative Applications in the Social Sciences, a Sage University Paper, 63.
Cuff, E.C., and Payne, G.C.F. (1979) *Perspectives in Sociology*, London: Unwin Hyman.
Dahl, Ø. and Habert, K. (1986) *Møte mellom kulturer: Tverrkulturell kommunikasjon*, Stavanger: Universitetsforlaget.
Ekeh, P. (1974) *Social Exchange Theory*, London: Heinemann.
Elstad, J.I. (1981) *Kroniske lidelser og sosial klasse. En undersøkelse med data fra helseunder-søkelsen 1975*, Universitetet i Oslo: Institutt for sosiologi.
Enerstvedt, R. (1989) 'The problem of validity in social science', in S. Kvale (ed.) *Issues of Validity in Qualitative Research*, Sweden: Studentlitteratur.
Fontana, A. and Frey, J.H. (1994) 'Interviewing: the art of science', in N.K. Denzin and Y.S. Lincoln (eds) *Handbook of Qualitative Research*, Thousand Oaks, Calif.: Sage, Chapter 22
Goffman, E. (1961) *Asylum*, New York: Doubleday.

Habi, R., Milanzi, M., Ryen, A. and Wiketye, J. (1995) *Report from the Pre-study of a Prolonged Institutional Cooperation between Institute of Development Management, Tanzania and Agder College, Norway,* Mzumbe, and Kristiansand, Norway.

Hylland-Eriksen, T. (1996) 'Det mangfoldige ordet kultur', in J. Brinkman and T. Hylland-Eriksen (eds) *Verden som møteplass. Essays om tverrkulturell kommunikasjon,* Bergen: Fagbokforlaget, Chapter 1, pp. 9–28.

Hylland-Eriksen, T. and Arntsen Sørheim, T. (1994) *Kulturforskjeller i Praksis,* Gyldendal: Ad Notam.

Johnson, T.P. *et al.* (1995) 'Cultural similarities and differences in social cognition when answering survey questions', *American Statistical Association* 47–52.

—— (1996) 'Assessing question comprehension across cultures: evidence from the United States', presentation at ESSEX '96, Essex, UK, July.

Lipsky, M. (1980) *Street-level Bureaucracy: Dilemmas of the individual,* New York: Russel Sage Foundation.

Mangione, T.W., Fowler, F.J. and Louis, T.A. (1992) 'Question characteristics and interviewer effects', *Journal of Official Statistics* 8: 293–307.

Molm, L., Quist, T.M. and Wiseley, P.A. (1994) 'Imbalanced structures, unfair strategies: power and justice in social exchange', *American Sociological Review* 59 (1).

Moss Kanter, R. (1977) *Men and Women of the Corporation,* New York: Basic Books.

Nielsen, F.S. (1996) *Nærmere kommer du ikke. Håndbok i antropologisk feltarbeid,* Bergen: Fagbokforlaget.

Oakley, A. (1981) 'Interviewing women: a contradiction in terms?' in H. Roberts (ed.) *Doing Feminist Research,* London: Routledge, pp. 30–61.

Ryen, A. (1987) 'Kvinnelig datainnsamler i mannsmiljø belyst ved teorien om tokenism', *Agder Distriktshøgskoles skrifter* no. 4.

—— (1994) 'Italienske menn i norske kvinners øyne. En sosiologisk vandring', speech at Dante Alighieri (an Italian–Norwegian organisation), Kristiansand, Norway.

Ryen, A. and Habi, R. (1994) *Fringe Benefits in Tanzania – Access and Distribution: Three case studies,* research report no. 2, ADH/IDM.

Schein, E. (1985) *Organizational Culture and Leadership,* San Fransisco: Jossey-Bass Publishers.

Shio, L., Smukkestad, O. and Mrina, B. (1994) *Rural Development Strategies in Tanzania: The case of RUDEP,* research report no. 3, ADH/IDM.

Silverman, D. (1993) *Interpreting Qualitative Data,* London: Sage.

Spradley, J.P. and McCurdy, D.W. (1972) *The Cultural Experience. Ethnography in complex societies,* USA: Science Research Associates.

Svalastoga, K. (1969) *Sociologisk Metodik,* Bind 1, København: Jørgen Paludans Forlag.

Triandis, H.C. (1978) 'Some universals of social behavior', *Personality and Social Psychology Bulletin* 4 (1).

Chapter 15

Defining without discriminating? Ethnicity and social problems

The case of street youth in Canada

Jacques Rhéaume and Shirley Roy

Introduction

We present here the results of the first, and crucial, part of a complete research program. Our study examines street youth from diverse cultural groups of recent immigrants to Canada, and who are currently residents of community-supported housing. In our field, the terms employed – youth, street, ethnocultural identity, and community-supported housing – may often connote specific meanings. Each constitutes an issue area in itself, and each gives rise to a great deal of scientific research. But these particular four terms have rarely, if ever, been studied in combination. This research gap constituted the first problem encountered, since from the start there were few hints in the literature. The second problem, however, is more directly related to the discussion at hand: it resides in the observation that there are as many basic methodological problems as there are meanings that one may attach to the different terms.

First, it is important to describe the concrete context of our research. North America, Canada, and Quebec serve as the geographical entities for our socio-political analysis of the street youth phenomenon. The framework of our study involves close collaboration between university researchers and community practitioners. This brings us to the main theoretical issue, which we will now discuss: the social construction of the research categories and its methodological implications.

Homelessness: the social phenomenon

Even though homelessness is increasing in every big city in North America, it is, ironically, difficult to obtain precise data for cases where there is consensus regarding the quantitative importance of a particular social group. Thus, it has proved very difficult to comprehend such cases, since they are largely invisible. The terms themselves are quite vague, and frequently quite different from categories that are used in the national census. Yet many studies concur that there is an increasing number of people regarded as homeless, that they present diverse profiles and that they are increasingly subject to declining living conditions (Laberge *et al.* 1995). Let us review some of the basic data.

In the United States, Shlay and Rossi (1992) estimate that the number of homeless individuals lies somewhere between 250,000 and 3 million. In Montreal, the largest city in the province of Quebec, there are approximately 10,000 to 15,000, of which 8,000 to 9,000 have stayed for at least one night in a homeless shelter.

With regard to homelessness among youth, many authors confirm not only an increase in the number of young adults (Wright 1990; Wolch and Rowe 1992), but also an increase in school-age youth on the street (Stronge 1993; Colby 1990). It is worth noting the difficulty of establishing a clear picture of this situation, given that such studies rarely use the same age categories. Thus, some studies define youth as persons under 30 years of age, employing criteria similar to those found in Quebec's social policies. Others define youth as persons between the ages of 12 and 24. In the province of Quebec, there are 3,000 to 4,000 homeless youth under 30, but we do not have a precise figure for minors (persons under 18). In the latter instance, the only figures we have are related to runaway, or throwaway, cases reported by the police. Two thousand such cases were identified in 1991, but most of these were not street youth, and in any case involved only short-term runaways (Bernier *et al.* 1992).

A second characteristic of the homeless is their ethnic background. Most American studies show a predominance of Blacks in this population (Belcher 1992). Even where Blacks form a minority of the homeless population, their corresponding share of this population is always greater than the proportion of the Blacks in the community at large (Kurks 1991).

In Quebec, and this contrasts with data for the United States, the majority of homeless people derive from the French-Canadian majority (Fournier and Mercier 1996a, 1996b). However, practitioners in the field are now reporting that youth from diverse ethnic backgrounds form an increasing proportion of the homeless population. There are also indigenous people among the homeless (Laberge *et al.* 1995).

A final characteristic of the homeless is the growing numbers of families among them. McChesney (1992) and Stretch and Kreuger (1992) state that these are generally single-parent families. On the surface, there seem to be no homeless families in Quebec. We may nevertheless offer two explanations for this phenomenon. First, in Quebec it is influenced by legislation dealing with youth. For there is direct intervention as soon as potential harm to a child's life or security is at stake. If a mother is a streetwalker, begs or sleeps in a park, the social services will react immediately. Her children will be taken away from her and afforded safety elsewhere. Second, in Quebec, as elsewhere, shelters for battered women sometimes host homeless women and their children for an indefinite period of time. However, in the United States, these also count formally as shelters for the homeless, and are defined as such, whereas in

Quebec they do not. For these reasons, homelessness amongst Montreal families is not only somewhat hidden, but also it is not reflected in statistics.

The research partnership and its methodological consequences

Our research originated with a request made by practitioners providing community-based housing for homeless youth. Increasingly confronted with growing numbers of homeless youth belonging to diverse ethnic communities, they wanted to know more about the effectiveness of their methods and sought new approaches. As researchers, we wanted to know if the homeless should be encouraged to identify with a distinct social entity or to develop a sense of belonging to mainstream culture, so as to integrate. In order to respond adequately to the practitioners' request, we felt that it was incumbent on us to ask young people themselves to describe their social experience. Do the social trajectories of young French-speaking Quebeckers differ from those of young people of other ethnic groups ? Were they satisfied with the services available to them? Should these services be adapted to their cultural specificity?

In order to address these issues, we collaborated with practitioners working in autonomous, community-based centers that provide housing for homeless youth. These centers rely for their financing on a variety of sources – depending on the mandate of the center in question. These sources include private funding, state support through regional or local institutions, grants from community-based institutions, financing campaigns, and other sources. Eight housing centers – located in the Greater Montreal area – were selected for our study. One has a special mandate to provide services to young refugees and immigrants from diverse cultural communities. This clientele constitutes the majority of their residents, but the center accepts young people from other backgrounds, too.

We collaborated with the practitioners in defining the objectives, methodological approach, and ethical dimensions of the research. Together, we then submitted a written proposal that was ultimately granted funding by a governmental agency whose selection procedures included peer review. It should be noted that this agency, the Quebec Social Research Council, supports precisely the kind of research exemplified by our project, in which researchers work in close collaboration with community organizations involved in field work. In short, the Council requires that projects involve, in addition to university researchers, at least one community organization. Combining theory with practice is an exciting departure from the classical approach, which has typically maintained an external and distant relationship with social practice, and in which the researcher defines all aspects of the research design. Putting this approach into practice, however, is quite another matter, as we quickly discovered.

Institutions define their users

We found that many dimensions of the methodology were already in place. For example, our point of departure for defining the target population was found in institutional files. Thus, the target population consisted of young people with no criminal record (not bound by law), who were under age (under 18), and had family problems. This constitutes, as we shall see, a rather narrow frame of reference.

In Quebec, there are two types of residential housing available for young people in difficulty. One is community based, non-commercial and not state affiliated. They host young people who have applied to them voluntarily, either directly, or indirectly through legal referral, such as through state services, under the Youth Protection Act (Quebec 1992). The referral may also originate with parents.

There is a second, more formal type of residence. It is state supported and more closely resembles the older boarding-house institution. Residences of this kind host young people with criminal records, those who are subject to court judgments following some illegal act under the Youth Offenders Act (Quebec 1985), those with drug problems, and runaways who are subject to actual or potential family violence.

Working with the first type of resource led us to exclude gangs and those with criminal records considered to be juvenile delinquents. While some users of community-based housing may in the past have contravened the legal system, this no longer constitutes the reason for admitting them to the center.

Choosing to work with underage homeless youth, who formed the majority of residents, constituted another constraint. Legislation in this area sets Quebec apart. Being under 18, these youths are formally protected by law and require special care and supervision, sometimes involving parents and social services. Though regulations are numerous and complex, there are still many young homeless people deprived of regular support and services.

One positive result of having a narrowly defined target group was that it gave rise to a more homogeneous research population. It also had other, less favorable, methodological implications, as we shall see later.

What is meant exactly by homeless youth (Wallot 1992)? They are identified in various ways. For example, homeless youth are sometimes called street kids (Webber 1991), runaways (underage youth leaving their families without parental consent), or throwaways (or push-outs; that is, leaving the family against their will) (Levine et al. 1986). This diversity of meanings stems from the diverse causes for being cut off from a family. Running away may simply be the upshot of a crisis frequently experienced by teenagers, no more, no less. Being a throwaway, however, implies rejection. But living on the street is the most serious situation of all; it refers to a non-integrated state experienced by youth, and can be related to the kind of society we live in, which offers little hope for many young people.

When we decided to study these residences, or housing centers, we already knew that the young people living there were not juvenile delinquents, nor were they street or homeless people, in the strict senses of the words. They were, however, experiencing a serious breakdown in their family, school or housing situations. In some cases, this might involve situations of rejection or exclusion, but usually they seemed to have maintained at least some ties with their parents, since they came to the center voluntarily, which, in the socio-legal context of Quebec, implied some minimal agreement among the parents, children and social services. The key experience shared by these young people involved their difficult relationships with family and parents, relationships which differ from society's norms. The solution to these difficulties frequently involved moving from one house to another in the public and community networks of the housing service. Circulating among family, friends, and housing services created a new way of life for many. They did not have a stable home, but at least they were not sleeping in the street. Nevertheless, for a small minority these services simply constituted a temporary step, since they ended up on the street.

To conclude this section, the interplay of the various situations noted above reflects the progressive steps of a unique and complex social process, one which may lead to social exclusion for the youth involved.

Cultural identity and ethnic origin

In order to establish a qualitative sample of youth from diverse cultural communities, we required three things: first, an overall picture of the entire population of underage youth under study, including their number and socio-demographic characteristics; second, the exact proportion of youth from cultural communities; and third, an overview of the degree of cultural diversity reflected in our sample. This data would enable us to focus on more pertinent cultural cases.

Interviews with the various practitioners revealed a wide range of percep-tions regarding the multicultural nature of the population under study, its quantitative importance, and variety. Did the centers house some ethnic groups more than others, and if so, why? What were the trends in this regard? The responses, which were accompanied by explanations of underlying factors, varied greatly.

The centers, however, had no standard way of recording data of this kind. Since they usually reviewed their activities in their annual reports, we had originally hoped that these reports would provide adequate data on trends over the past five years or so. They did in fact provide data on the number of residents per year, their age, gender, school status, and other information. But the categories used to define the cultural or ethnic identity of residents differed from one organization to another. Some even avoided mentioning it.

Two interesting results emerged. There was no basic agreement on definitions of cultural or ethnic social identity. For some, this relates to being born abroad, while coming to Canada later with their immigrant parents. For others, cultural identity goes back at least two or three generations. In this view, for example, Italians could maintain their Italian identity for fifty years, even though they were full Canadian citizens. Is it admissible to single out people by their color, mother tongue, usual language or refugee status?

There was a second, and related, problem. In many cases, the annual reports reflected the political or ideological viewpoints of the community workers themselves. First of all, should practitioners view the age of their young clients as reflecting youth-related problems? Second, should they make reference to ethnic or cultural identity in understanding the clients' problems? Should both factors be taken into account? Such choices have important consequences for social work. When dealing with young people from diverse ethnic groups, is it better to integrate them by ignoring their cultural identity, thereby treating them like any other teenager, or, on the contrary, take into account their specific cultural frame of reference?

The result was that in their reports some organizations would insist on referring to cultural or ethnic differences, but without defining what they meant. In consulting their files we discovered the groups to which they were referring, be they Haitians, Latino-Americans, Somalis, Quebeckers, and so on, as well as the number of clients in each group. Other organizations would classify their residents according to linguistic differences. Three languages were used in these classifications: French, English, and Spanish.

Further investigation

We could not use the data – in the form it was presented to us – for cultural or ethnic identification. We were unable to estimate the number of young people originating in cultural communities, nor could we identify the largest communities. We needed more information.

The only complete source of data to which we could refer were the personal records of residents. These records, however, are protected by law and may not be viewed by outsiders. They include the youth's life story, as well as that of his or her family, a list of persons involved in the case, and practitioners' comments and evaluations. As professional tools used in casework, these records reflect the continuity of services provided for the youth, and as such constitute a very helpful tool for practitioners trying to better understand their clients. They are not, for evident ethical reasons, available to researchers.

By law, these files could not be consulted, except by special permission of the courts and, of course, that of the practitioner. Obtaining such permission appeared to be a long and tricky process. We decided to use another tactic. Since our partnership was based on close collaboration with the community workers, we constructed a brief questionnaire that could be completed by a worker while a research assistant provided some assistance. Thus, while protecting all data whose confidentiality was of any significance, we were nevertheless able to get access to other basic and reliable data, including immigration status, length of residency in Canada, and the ethnic identity of parents. As a consequence, the data was treated only by practitioners and remained anonymous.

The portrait of the cultural communities: an outline

We are presenting here the most important figures, without going into details. We examined 347 files on youths residing in the eight community residences under study, during the period beginning 1 March 1995, and ending 1 March 1996. We found that 268 files, or 77.2 per cent of these youths, were French-speaking Quebeckers, while the other 79 files, that is 22.8 per cent, came from other cultural communities. Of those in the latter group, 42 were born outside of Quebec, and 22 had refugee status and were not accompanied by parents. Fifteen others were born in Quebec and from a family in which at least one parent was born outside of Quebec.

The 79 youths came from 32 different cultural communities, principally African (N = 17), South American (N = 15), and Haitian (N = 15).

These youths were on average 16 years old. There were slightly more boys than girls – 54 per cent versus 46 per cent. The gap was wider – 66 per cent boys versus 33 per cent girls – in the case of youths who were recent immigrants. Compared to French-speaking Quebeckers, a greater percentage of these recent immigrants – 60 per cent compared to 40 per cent – attended school.

By and large, these young people had family problems. While they sometimes applied for residency voluntarily, it was usually associated with a referral by social workers. In general, this voluntarism was perceived, both by the community workers and by parents, as a positive step, setting the stage for their social reintegration and their return to a normal life.

Lessons in methodology

What are the most important theoretical or methodological lessons to be retained? First, from the start, we never ceased to question our methodological choices, anticipate the consequences of these choices, or attempt to answer a very paradoxical question: is it possible to give something a name without discriminating, to distinguish without excluding (Jodelet 1996)? Let us stress four basic features in this process.

First, the choice of a particular research field always implies social configuration of the phenomenon under study (Tajfel 1981). We have to circumscribe the population and its characteristics. At the same time, this forces us to be clearer about taking names and notions for granted. To be sure, in our case, we changed our focus in mid-stream. It is not so much street kids that we are studying, but, rather, youth in serious trouble, perhaps suffering from family problems. Some may have been on the street for a time. But they are not juvenile delinquents or abandoned children. They are troubled youth who have sought community support voluntarily.

Second, this social construction of the categories (Hopper 1991) used to define youth has influenced the research design in many other respects. For example, dealing with underage children is significantly different from dealing with young adults, given the laws on protection of underage youth. It also creates a framework that has an impact on the way we address certain situations. For example, we do not view a 15-year-old runaway boy in the same way we view an 18-year-old. In the first instance, there could be legal intervention to place the young boy, and social services will attempt reintegration with the family. In the second instance, no such intervention is possible, given social conventions.

Third, the more precise data thereby obtained confirmed the adequacy of the questions posed in the beginning. Let us give some examples. First, the data confirms the impression held by practitioners: there has been an increase in the multicultural population found among their residents, of which 22.8 per cent now originate in 32 different countries. Second, some nuance was expected by many practitioners, as well as researchers, that this increase is dominated by some groups. We had to include the group of Africans to the ones of Haitians and Latin-Americans. Third, and significantly, a previous hypothesis was proven false. Practitioners had held the impression that youth from cultural communities were under-represented in the residencies, compared to their proportion of the population in the province of Quebec. The data now showing a 16.4 per cent rate of residency (excluding refugees) is fairly close to the 12 per cent of the population at large represented by cultural communities.

Fourth, we also found that our more precise categories reflected broader socio-political issues, including those found in the history and culture of the province of Quebec, and Canada generally. For this country, multiculturalism, or biculturalism, are serious matters. 'Unity' and 'distinctiveness' are debated intensely (Labelle *et al.* 1995; Bourque and Duchastel 1995). These issues and opinions surfaced in our discussions with practitioners. Four major opinions were revealed.

The republican stand: integration means assimilation, the French way (Schnapper 1991; Wierviorka 1993)

The stand expressed here is one in which cultural diversity and ethnic membership are considered to be more or less secondary, 'private' matters that should recede before one dominant set of rights: the right to citizenship and the strict equality of rights for all citizens.

Unity in diversity: the model of the American melting pot (Bach 1986)

This second stand gives more space to the diversity of cultures and inequalities that can be related to historical and environmental differences. The main idea is to fight to abolish 'systemic' differences, applying corrective measures that will result in a more 'republican' reality. This implies progressively sharing common rules and putting aside distinctions related to ethnic differences, which constitute a secondary issue.

Multiculturalism: the radical, pluralistic, and federalist viewpoint in Canada (Canada 1987; Taylor et al. 1994; Martucelli 1996)

The third stand is highly visible in Canadian discourse. It was first revealed through the issue of bilinguism and biculturalism involving French Canadians and English Canadians, and rejected the concept of a single culture. To avoid exclusionary tendencies, this approach was enlarged via a Canadian policy paper written in 1971, giving all significant cultural groups equal rights. This was a policy on multiculturalism, in which common institutions and rights (the republican stand) accompanied full recognition of cultural diversity. In later, more radical versions, it held that no single ethnic or cultural community should impose its viewpoint on others. An inspiring utopia.

Cultural integration without assimilation: the policy of the province of Quebec (Quebec 1978, 1990; Harvey 1991; Juteau and McAndrew 1992)

A fourth stand reflects twenty-five years of debate in the province of Quebec: instituting French-Canadian culture, but respecting the diversity of cultures. This is official policy, and was developed in the late 1980s. This particular stand would partially adopt the stands of the three others, giving each equal weight: establishing basic common rights (republican); attaining equality by imposing a dominant cultural reference (melting pot); and, finally, implementing a degree of multiculturalism.

Conclusion

Our research highlights the importance of establishing clear and precise definitions during the early phases of a research project. In the case at hand, the definitions focus on youth who are in difficulty, live in community residences and come from a wide variety of ethnic and cultural communities.

The research also raises a number of social and ethical issues. We also showed that such issues are frequently hidden by various methodological techniques. Researchers may nevertheless reveal these hidden issues when identifying and defining a population, describing basic socio-demographic characteristics, managing information or diagnosing problems.

Indeed, the terms chosen to define and describe the population under study impart meanings referring to the concrete practices of community work. But they also, and above all, impart a sense of the wider social, political, and cultural institutions of a society, in our case those of Quebec, and of Canada generally. Social policy and ideology give structure to identity. Identifying, or avoiding identification of ethnic differences is constantly cutting across community worker practices, with regard to hospitality, problem identification, establishing a relationship of trust, and so on. There is a greater risk of discrimination or stigmatization when too much emphasis is placed on differences, above all when these differences are highlighted in an unequal relationship between majority and minority groups. Conversely, the negation of all differences may lead to the weakening of a youth's identity structure, or worse, to the denial of his own cultural and ethnic roots.

In participative research, these risks affect the relationship between the researchers and practitioners involved. The choices retained by the researchers, the manner in which they, too, assign names to phenomena or account for ethnic differences in their analyses, are inseparable from the choices they make in practicing their profession. It is for this reason that setting aside a time and place for debate and discussion among the various actors involved in the research is so important to the sharing of social analysis. From the start, all will have an opportunity to comprehend the risks of discriminatory bias involved

One might say that the nature of this participative research in a sense over-determines analyses of the ethnic question. Yet, as noted in the first section, it is not simply a question here of ethnic difference, but also of perceptions of homelessness, status of youth, gender, and family. In effect, these too constitute dimensions which are crucial to identity formation and democratic practice. The origin of the crisis faced by youths who find themselves in residences is linked precisely to the manner in which the frontiers of normality are defined, touching on these various frames of reference. The manner in which social workers react to these dimensions, and, indirectly, to researchers, may likewise reduce or accentuate this crisis.

Our interviews with both practitioners and youths allowed us to see the range of positions taken, from an explicit and deep recognition of the cultural (meaning ethnic, but also including gender, age, and economic status) differences that influence problems as well as solutions, to a much more selective and neutral recognition of difference (questions of age and family, but not gender or ethnic differences). In all instances, we have seen at work conceptions of society, of explicit and implicit sociological knowledge, and of the types of practices through which the components of social and personal identity are formed, for the social worker, the youths, and the researchers themselves. Indeed, we are all involved, simultaneously making ourselves aware of the constraints imposed by the social policies and cultural roots of the society to which we belong, and by the required commitments and hopes of building the alternative society, which remains to be built.

Researchers face a recurring question: how does one more effectively name and explain a phenomenon without turning it into a vehicle for discrimination or indifference?

References

Bach, R. (1986) 'Immigration: issues of ethnicity, class, and public policy in the United States', *The Annals of the American Academy* 485.

Belcher, J. (1992) 'Poverty, homelessness and racial exclusion', *Journal of Sociology and Social Welfare* 19 (4): 41–54.

Bernier, L., Morissette, A. and Roy, G. (1992) 'La fugue chez les Adolescent: fuitr d'un milieu ou réappropriation d'un destin', in L. Bisson (ed.) *Les couleurs de la jeunesse: noir sur blanc*, Quebec: Ministère du conseil exécutif.

Bourque, G. and Duchastel, J. (1995) 'Pour une identité canadienne post-nationale, la souveraineté partagée et la pluralité des cultures politiques', *Cahiers de recherche sociologique* 25: 17–58.

Canada (1987) *Le multiculturalisme*, Etre canadien, Ottawa: Secrétariat d'Etat.

Colby, I.C. (1990) 'The throw-away teen', *The Journal of Applied Social Sciences* 14 (2): 277–94.

Fournier, L. and Mercier, C. (1996a) *L'itinérance selon la documentation scientifique*, Montréal: Centre de recherche Philippe Pinel.

—— (eds) (1996b) *Sans domicile fixe. Au-delà du stéréotype*, Montréal: Editions du Méridien.

Harvey, J. (1991) 'Le pour et le contre d'un multiculturalisme montréalais', in F. Ouellet and M. Pagé (eds) *Pluriethnicité, éducation et société. Construire un espace commun*, Québec: Institut québécois de recherche sur la culture, pp. 77–92.

Hopper, K. (1991) 'Homelessness old and new: the matter of definitions', *Housing Policy Debate* 2: 757–813.

Jodelet, D. (1996) 'Les processus psycho-sociaux de l'exclusion', in S. Paugam (ed.) *L'exclusion, l'état des savoirs*, Paris: Editions La Découverte, pp. 66–76.

Juteau, D. and McAndrew, M. (1992) 'Projet national, immigration et intégration dans un Québec souverain', *Sociologie et sociétés* XXIV (2): 161–80.

Kurks, G. (1991) 'Gay and lesbian homeless/street youth: special issues and concerns,' *Journal of Adolescent Health* 12: 515–18.

Labelle, M., Rocher, F. and Rocher, G. (1995) 'Pluriethnicité, citoyenneté et intégration: de la souveraineté pour lever les obstacles et les ambiguités', *Cahiers de recherche sociologique* 25: 213–46.

Laberge, D., Cousineau, M.M., Morin, D. and Roy, S. (1995) 'De l'expérience individuelle au phénomène global: configurations et réponses sociales', *Les cahiers de recherche du CRI* 1: Montréal, juin.

Levine, R.S., Metzendorf, D. and VanBoskirk, K.A. (1986) 'Runaway and throwaway youth: a case for early intervention with truants', *Social Work in Education* 8 (2): 93–106.

Martucelli, D. (1996) 'Les contradictions politiques du multiculturalisme', in M. Wieviorka (ed.) *Une société fragmentée? Le multiculturalisme en débat*, Paris: Éditions La Découverte, pp. 61–84.

McChesney, K.Y. (1992) 'Absence of a family safety net for homeless families', *Journal of Sociology and Social Welfare* 19 (4): 55–72.

Québec (1978) *La politique québécoise du développement culturel*, Québec: Editeur officiel.

—— (1985) *Loi sur les jeunes contrevenants*, Québec: Editeur officiel.

—— (1990) *Au Québec pour bâtir ensemble. Enoncé de politique en matière d'immigration et d'intégration*, Montréal: Ministère des Communautés culturelles et de l'Immigration.

—— (1992) *Loi sur la protection de la jeunesse*, Québec: Editeur officiel.

Schnapper, D. (1991) *La France de l'intégration, sociologie de la onation en 1990*, Paris: Gallimard, coll. Bibliothèque des sciences humaines.

—— (1994) *La communauté des citoyens*, Paris: Gallimard.

Shlay, A.B. and Rossi, P.H. (1992) 'Social science research and contemporary studies of homelessness', *Annual Review of Sociology* 18: 129–60.

Stretch, J. and Kreuger, L. (1992) 'Five-year cohort study of homeless families: a joint policy research venture', *Journal of Sociology and Social Welfare* 19 (4): 73–88.

Stronge, J.H. (1993) 'Educating homeless students in urban settings: an introduction to the issues', *Education and Urban Society* 25 (4): 315–22.

Tajfel, H. (1981) *Human Groups and Social Categories*, Cambridge: Cambridge University Press.

Taylor, C., Appiah, K.A., Habermas, J., Rockefeller, S.C., Walzer, M. and Wolf, S. (ed. and Introduction by A. Guttman) (1994) *Multiculturalism: Examining politics of recognition*, Princeton: Princeton University Press.

Wallot, C. (1992) 'Les jeunes sans abri. Recherche entreprise dans le cadre du projet: La promotion active des droits de la personne comme voie de solution au problème des jeunes sans abri', unpublished report, Consortium de formation sur la défense des droits humains de l'Université McGill, Montréal.

Webber, M. (1991) *Street Kids: The tragedy of Canada's runaways*, Toronto: University of Toronto Press.

Wieviorka, M. (1993) 'Nationalisme et racisme', *Cahiers de recherches sociologiques* 20: 169–81.

Wolch, J.R. and Rowe, S. (1992) 'On the streets: mobility paths of the urban homeless', *City and Society* 6 (2): 115–40.

Wright, D.J. (1990) 'Poor people, poor health: the health status of the homeless', *Journal of Social Issues* 46 (4): 49–64.

Name Index

Subject Index